NOT MANY DEAD

Journal of a year in Fleet Street

NICHOLAS GARLAND

HUTCHINSON

LONDON   SYDNEY   AUCKLAND   JOHANNESBURG

The right of Nicholas Garland to be identified as Author of this work
has been asserted by Nicholas Garland in accordance with the
Copyright, Designs and Patent Act, 1988

This edition first published in 1990 by
Hutchinson

Century Hutchinson Ltd
20 Vauxhall Bridge Road, London SW1V 2SA

Century Hutchinson Australia (Pty) Ltd
20 Alfred Street, Milson's Point, Sydney NSW 2061, Australia

Century Hutchinson New Zealand Ltd
PO Box 40–086, Glenfield, Auckland 10, New Zealand

Century Hutchinson South Africa (Pty) Ltd
PO Box 337, Bergvlei, 2012 South Africa

British Library Cataloguing in Publication Data
Garland, Nicholas, *1935–*
  Not many dead: journal of a year in Fleet Street.
  1. London (city). Fleet Street. National newspapers
  I. Title
  072.12

ISBN 0–09–174449–0

Phototypeset in Baskerville by Input Typesetting Ltd, London
Printed and bound in Great Britain by Richard Clay Ltd, Bungay, Suffolk

Contents

For further entertainment in the long evenings, someone had invented a game – a competition with a small prize for the winner – to see who could write the dullest headline. It had to be a genuine headline, that is to say one which was actually printed in the next morning's newspaper. I won it only once with a headline which announced: 'Small Earthquake in Chile. Not many dead.'

From *The Autobiography of Claud Cockburn* (Penguin, 1967)

List of illustrations

List of principal characters

Don Berry is features editor on the *Daily Telegraph*.

Conrad Black has been chairman of Argus Corporation since 1979 and chief executive since 1985. He owns the controlling share in the *Daily Telegraph*.

Alexander Chancellor was editor of the *Spectator* (1975–84), of *Time and Tide* (1984–86), and deputy editor of the *Sunday Telegraph* from 1986. Later he became Washington correspondent for the *Independent* and is now editor of the *Independent* magazine.

Michael Crosier is ex-editor for Design Office and Pictures at the *Independent*. He is the author of *Designing the Independent*.

Sue Davy was Lord Deedes's secretary at the *Daily Telegraph*.

W. F. (Bill) Deedes, the original inspiration for Evelyn Waugh's *Scoop*, went on to become the Member of Parliament for Ashford, Kent (1950–74) and was a member of the Cabinet for ten years from 1954. He was editor of the *Daily Telegraph* from 1974 until 1986.

James Fenton worked on the *New Statesman* (1976–78) and was German correspondent for the *Guardian* (1978–79), before becoming theatre critic for the *Sunday Times* (1979–84) and chief book reviewer for *The Times* from 1984 to 1986. He has been the Far East correspondent for the *Independent* since then.

Bernard Foyster is picture editor of the *Daily Telegraph*.

Stephen Glover was a leader writer on the *Daily Telegraph*. He was co-founder, with Andreas Whittam Smith, of the *Independent* in 1986, and its first foreign editor. He is now editor of the *Independent on Sunday*.

Morrison Halcrow was features editor and, with Peter Utley, deputy editor of the *Daily Telegraph*.

Lord Hartwell was chairman and editor-in-chief of the *Daily Telegraph* (1954–87), and of the *Sunday Telegraph* (1961–87).

Max Hastings has been a reporter for the *Evening Standard*, columnist for the *Daily Express*, and contributor to the *Sunday Times*. He has also been a reporter for the BBC and has made many TV documentaries. He became editor of the *Daily Telegraph* in 1986.

Anthony Howard has worked on the *New Statesman*, the *Sunday Times* and the *Listener*. He is also the presenter of 'Face the Press' on Channel Four and has been deputy editor of the *Observer* since 1981.

Martin Ivens worked as a journalist on the *Daily Telegraph* and was later foreign correspondent (Washington and New York).

Andrew Knight was appointed chief executive of the *Daily Telegraph* by Conrad Black in 1986. Editor-in-chief since 1987, he resigned his position in the summer of 1989.

Charles Moore joined the editorial staff of the *Daily Telegraph* in 1979 and was its leader writer from 1981. He then became assistant editor of the *Spectator* in 1983, and has been the editor since 1984.

Matthew Symonds was a leader writer on the *Daily Telegraph*. He was a co-founder of the *Independent* and has been its deputy editor since 1986 and features editor since 1988.

Nick Thirkell is a partner in the firm of designers Carol, Dempsey and Thirkell. He was commissioned by the *Independent* as consultant designer.

Peter Utley, who died in 1988, was, with Morrison Halcrow, deputy editor of the *Daily Telegraph*, as well as a leader writer and general contributor.

Andreas Whittam Smith worked on the *Stock Exchange Gazette*, the *Financial Times* and *The Times* before becoming deputy city editor of the *Daily Telegraph* in 1966 and then city editor of the *Guardian* in 1969. From 1970 until 1977 he was editor of the *Investors Chronicle and Stock Exchange Gazette*, and director of Throgmorton Publications. He was city editor of the *Daily Telegraph* (1977–85) and has been director of Newspaper Publishing PLC since 1986. He has also been editor of the *Independent* since 1986, and its chief executive since 1987.

Peregrine Worsthorne joined the editorial staff of *The Times* in 1948 and went on to the *Daily Telegraph* in 1953. He became deputy editor of the *Sunday Telegraph* in 1961, and associate editor from 1976. He has been editor of the *Sunday Telegraph* since 1986.

Introduction

I have been writing journals since I was a teenager. Usually only
fragments get written because as often as not they are started to combat
boredom or loneliness, and as life becomes interesting again there is no
time or need to keep them up. This one was different. As soon as I
began it I felt I was writing a story. I took notes of what people said to
me and wrote the journal in my head during the day, so that I could
record it as accurately as possible later. I used to carry it with me
everywhere, but the actual detailed accounts of the day were mostly
written first thing in the morning or quite late at night. Of course I
didn't know how the story would end, but I knew an end would come
and that I'd recognise it when it did. As a matter of fact I kept the
journal for several months after the *Independent* was launched, but in a
desultory and disjointed way. The story was over; what followed was
quite different. I missed writing it when it was finished. Among other
things a journal becomes a sort of companion. I enjoyed confiding in it
my unguarded reactions to each day's events. They appear here as I
wrote them, except cuts have been made to avoid repetition or to tone
down entries which when spoken or scrawled in a notebook sound one
way but have a different effect when printed. I have also removed
passages that were pointlessly hurtful or which involved significant
contradictions. But I have not tried to alter the sense of anything I
wrote, however much hindsight has altered my view.

When I began this journal I was working for the *Daily Telegraph*,
which I had joined twenty years earlier. The old *Telegraph* had a very
special atmosphere which is remembered with great affection by most
of us who worked there. It was like a small Ruritanian court. Somewhere
above us was the remote benign figure of Lord Hartwell watching over
everything. Lower down, the editor was surrounded by his leader
writers, who met in conference at 3.45 each day. This conference would
be attended by four or five writers, the deputy and features editors; and

three or four times a week by me, although as I took almost no part in the talk I was really an honorary member. The discussion ranged over feature articles, letters and the presentation of news as well as editorials. These sessions might last an hour and were often very serious, even passionate, and at other times were light-hearted. It was very funny to watch leader writers skilfully getting out of, or getting landed with awkward subjects. Colin Welch, then deputy editor, used to salute a specially fine bit of evasion by slowly miming a batsman sweeping a ball for six.

After the conference we would sometimes have a cup of tea in Peter Utley's room to continue with, or hash over, the conversation. There was all the usual office banter and rivalry but (at least so it seems now) even the most serious disagreements were contained in an oddly good-humoured and tolerant atmosphere. The fact that we suspected these days could not last for ever meant there was a nostalgia about the enterprise even while we were engaged in it. Almost none of my friends outside journalism ever reads the *Telegraph* and they could not begin to understand what a peculiar and lovable institution it was.

Towards the end as control slipped out of Lord Hartwell's hands it all became rather sad; and eventually cold winds from outside made the *Telegraph* an uncomfortable place to be. But those happier years were the background to everything that followed and explain some of the turmoil we all experienced as the old order began to pass away. It was particularly difficult for me to leave the *Telegraph* because I had never worked on any other national paper, and consequently I felt I owed it so much. When the *Telegraph* first employed me in 1966, I had never even drawn a political cartoon, let alone had one published. Maurice Green was the editor at that time and he showed quite extraordinary patience and kindness as I struggled to learn the new job. Not only was it extremely difficult to draw political cartoons, but it was also the first time in my life that I had thought really hard about politics at all. It was quite a shock for me to find that colleagues whom I considered the most extreme right-wingers I'd ever met could be the the most agreeable companions and absolutely impossible to beat in argument – though I would sometimes hold them to a draw. My political views were shaped and qualified and my drawing style was formed at the *Daily Telegraph* and it was also there that I first published any written work.

I had attended this workplace-cum-school-cum-club for twenty years, all but a few months, when I first heard that a new newspaper was being planned. The *Telegraph* was already in very serious financial difficulties and the whole of Fleet Street was about to change as the Murdoch empire moved to Wapping and the new technology began to destroy the power of the print unions.

It is difficult to recall quite why I started this journal. The idea of a new newspaper was so wild and so daring that whatever happened I wanted to record it. I also wanted to write about the *Telegraph* and record the great changes that were inevitable there. More personally it was also a time of change. I was fifty years old, my children were growing up, and if I was ever going to do anything other than live out the rest of my working life at the *Telegraph* it would have to be soon. Perhaps I wanted to write about that process too.

NICHOLAS GARLAND
London
November 1989

JANUARY

" It is a far, far better thing that I do, than I have ever done . . . "
— A Tale of Two Cities.

10 January 1986, *Daily Telegraph*

Sometime in 1985 – about June I think it was – Stephen Glover came into my room at the *Telegraph* and told me that he, Andreas Whittam Smith and Matthew Symonds were planning a new newspaper.

He said that though it was early days yet, rather to his amazement interest and even money seemed to be coming their way. Stephen's attitude was wary. The stakes were high and the whole project had a dream-like unreality. Matthew, on the other hand, was tremendously excited, so excited that in a moment of madness he'd told Ed Pearce the secret – but luckily Ed seemed to have not taken it too seriously and forgotten all about it.

I too, that afternoon, thought it unlikely I'd hear any more about it. We discussed Andreas's ambition to be editor of the *Telegraph* and the difficult position he would be in if the new newspaper plot became known. Stephen replied that all three of them would probably be scuppered if it got out, although he thought he and Matthew might be able to survive the row.

In October or November I asked Stephen again about the proposed newspaper. He again began by making me understand how vital secrecy was. Progress had been made. An initial prospectus had been produced and reaction to it was very positive. Money was coming in, and unlikely though it had always seemed he now believed the paper was going to come out.

In the next few days I learnt more about the newspaper, now provisionally called *The Nation*. Stephen described the research that had been done and the type of readership and circulation they were chasing. He told me about the merchant banks and City barons who were interested, and that Saatchi and Saatchi were closely involved. It was about this time that he said he hoped I'd join the paper and that he knew the others were keen that I should.

I was pleased, flattered and excited by the idea, and a bit nervous. I have always dreamt of belonging to a small new newspaper, run by people I liked and knew well, but I have also learnt to value the freedom and security that the *Telegraph* has given me. Here was a dilemma, but luckily I did not have to come to a decision at that time. Stephen explained that he and the others would have to resign their jobs on the *Telegraph* very soon, probably before Christmas. Journalists would not be recruited until May or June 1986. He was worried by the fear that everyone would laugh at *The Nation* and that the organisers would be accused of deceit and disloyalty to the *Telegraph*.

At the same time all this was developing the *Telegraph* was falling on very hard times indeed. For months rumours of take-overs and bankruptcy had been whistling round the building and the name Conrad Black, once a joke, became unfunny and menacing.

The worse things became for the *Telegraph* the more Stephen feared the scorn and disapproval of Fleet Street pundits. He was afraid he and the others would be called treacherous rats who were deserting the sinking ship.

One afternoon we discussed how they would tell Bill Deedes.

'I'm dreading it,' said Stephen.

I urged him to come clean as soon as possible. 'Let him hear it from you, not read it in the paper.'

I didn't think Bill would be all that upset, actually, and I guessed he'd even be attracted by the plotting and adventurous side of it. Obviously they couldn't ask him to keep it secret but as soon as it was inevitable that the story must break they should tell him. It might get him a bit on their side.

I also said to Stephen that because *The Nation* had been planned before the *Telegraph* started collapsing they shouldn't feel too awful about the accusations of being rats. There was a strong element of coincidence about it.

Time went by. Stephen was increasingly agitated about the break with the *Telegraph* but more and more certain that it must come soon. One day Bill was late at the leader writers' conference. This was held every day in the editor's office at 3.45 and was where the policy of the newspaper was discussed and shaped. It was at these often comical, sometimes passionate meetings that I learnt most of what I knew about British politics. It was also where internal office politics are fought out, giving the meetings an added flavour of family wrangling and gossipy indiscretion which was very attractive. On this particular day we were told that Bill, with other department heads, was putting final touches to a statement the management were issuing to the staff. Bill felt every emphasis should be given to the cause of the crisis that was engulfing the paper. What was happening should not be seen as a pure management balls-up but a bold leap into new technology that would result in a new super-clean *Daily Telegraph* that would be the envy of Fleet Street.

He arrived at last accompanied by Andreas Whittam Smith. I couldn't help being aware of the drama of all of us gathered to hear what proved to be a very downbeat and depressing statement while three of the company were about to push off in their own lifeboat. Andreas didn't stay in the room but merely picked up his coat and left before Bill read out the statement. He looked serious and preoccupied. While he read to us I glanced first at Stephen, looking embarrassed and rather unhappy, sitting with one arm on the back of his chair and staring at the floor. Matthew was grinning all over his face. The more gloomy Bill's message became the more merry Matthew seemed to feel.

In early December I had lunch with Tony Howard and he asked me about morale at the *Telegraph*. I told him I could not give him a complete

3

picture without breaking a confidence, which I would do so long as he understood how delicate the matter was. I then told him everything I knew about *The Nation*.

His reaction was not what I expected. Instead of the wet blanket I thought he'd throw over the whole thing, he was very interested. He was guarded in his confidence that they'd make it, but not ready to write them off as foolish dreamers. He said I should think very hard before risking everything to join them, but added that if Black got the *Telegraph* it would change things. He meant the *Telegraph* might not be so agreeable to work for in these circumstances. He asked closely about Andreas and Matthew; he knows Stephen slightly already.

A few days later Black got the *Telegraph* and I found my old loyalty to the paper draining away. I felt I might stay with them if it suited me, but I knew I could leave now without the wrench parting would once have given me.

Matthew Symonds asked me to lunch and told me the whole story of *The Nation* in much more detail than Stephen had done. He came with the prospectus in his briefcase. He spoke with enormous confidence about the future and expressed the hope that I would join them early next summer, 1986. In the meantime he asked if I would come and meet Andreas and also talk to the designer they had working on the look of the paper.

Outside on the pavement I said to Matthew, 'I'm very impressed with all you have achieved. Whatever happens I wish you the best of luck. And I am very interested in your offer.'

He smiled and said 'Good', and we shook hands as if sealing, if not a deal, at least the formal opening of negotiations.

Tony Howard had a profile of Lord Hartwell going in the *Observer* and was keen to use the story of the new paper at the same time, if Andreas and co. were going to break it anyway. I told him that if I heard they were going to make an announcement I'd let him know.

A week or so before Christmas the *Sunday Times* carried a little story of an unidentified group in the City who were planning an as yet unnamed paper. Matthew rang to say he thought he knew the source of the leak but he felt no damage had been done. They were planning an official launch on 8 January. If the story were going to break before that I wanted Tony to break it as a sort of reward for his discretion, but Matthew and Stephen believed they could keep their secret a little longer, so Tony had to keep quiet.

One of the extraordinary things about this business is how it is being kept secret for so long. At least two other *Telegraph* people have known about it for months. Several of Stephen's friends must have been told. I told Tony and Lennie Hoffman who is a judge and whose opinion I valued very highly, and lots of City people had been approached.

4

It all became public on 27 December 1985 on the front page of the *Financial Times*. Tony rang me in the morning and read me the story while I lay in bed nursing an abscess on a tooth. The story was so well told and generally sympathetic that we figured it must have come direct from *The Nation* itself, but Matthew explained to me later that in fact it burst on them out of the blue. Their phones started ringing at about 10.30 the night before as various journalists began to follow up the *Financial Times* scoop. Matthew's mood was like that of a soldier when a long-awaited battle has begun: relieved and excited in equal parts. He said that Andreas had had a reassuring interview with Lord Hartwell whose attitude throughout was sympathetic; he'd asked with interest about the new paper's break-even point and construction, and at the end wished Andreas well. Matthew and Stephen had experienced a much cooler reaction from Bill. He had been neither disagreeable nor friendly, just reserved.

Stephen said to me later that Bill probably did not know how Andreas's interview with Lord Hartwell had gone and therefore did not know quite how to behave. 'With his subaltern's mind, Bill played it as safe as he could. Nothing that was said ruled out our being welcomed back as favoured sons in three months' time – but it was distinctly chilly.'

Both were relieved when Bill made it plain they must clear their desks at once.

The attitude of their colleagues interested and amused them. On the whole they felt that people wished them well and they did not run into the mockery and contempt that Stephen had feared when he first talked to me. Matthew said that most of the journalists from other newspapers to whom he'd spoken had sooner or later said, 'Any chance of a job?'

The difference between Matthew's account of this day and Stephen's was marked, the latter as usual far more thoughtful and reserved than the mercurial Matthew. Stephen's ironic and cool version sounded much the more realistic and confident.

Between Christmas and New Year Caroline and I had a holiday in North Somerset. While we walked in the snow on Exmoor and along the windy beach at Minehead we discussed, among other things, the name of the new paper. 'The Nation' is OK as a name, but for me it has a certain association with the *New Statesman and Nation* that doesn't feel quite right. There is also something too proper and dull about it. Caroline suggested 'The Independent' and I began to think that was better. Once the word shed its ordinary meaning and became the name of something, it had a kind of ring to it. It sounded like an American newspaper of the early 1900s. A slight smack of *Citizen Kane*.

When we returned to London I rang Stephen and he asked me to come and chat with Andreas. The three of us met in their temporary office in London Wall. Stephen and I got there first. It was 4.30 in the afternoon of New Year's Day. We made a cup of tea while we waited. Andreas was clearing his desk at the *Telegraph*. After a few minutes he arrived carrying a framed photograph and a small box of papers and a couple of books.

'I suddenly felt very unsentimental,' he said, 'and decided to chuck everything else away.' I don't know Andreas very well. I always associate him with the Royal Shakespeare Company's production of *Nicholas Nickleby* because I saw him at the theatre with his young family when I was at the play. He has a prominent nose, always a good sign in men, women and children. His face, which is rather red, looks mournful in repose and his smile lights it up quite surprisingly.

We talked about the look of the paper and the arts section of it. He said he'd be glad of any ideas I had for people to edit and write for it. He said he wanted a book review in the paper every day and saw no reason why it shouldn't go on the front page if it were good and interesting enough. He asked me about layout and design, and I said although I'd be pleased to talk to his designer my interest in the arts did not mean I knew the first thing about newspaper design.

Andreas's manner was different from Stephen's and Matthew's. He seemed quietly confident and very ready to listen to ideas. Everything he said was sensible but nothing in the least bit inspiring. He may have felt the sheer excitement and tension the others reveal, but did not show it.

My main feeling, apart from enjoying the chat, was surprise that he should think it worth while spending so much time talking like this to a cartoonist. We hardly mentioned the possibility of my joining the paper but I agreed to ask around for suggestions for possible arts editors, books editors and artists who might join. I told him Caroline's suggestion for a name and he immediately said, 'That's funny, "The Independent" was one of my first choices and for some reason I'd completely forgotten it.' He agreed that it was a good name and that it should go forward to Saatchi and Saatchi for research. They look for negative feedback or something.

By the time I left I felt I'd more or less joined the bloody thing.

The meeting petered out in a slightly unsatisfactory way, and the next day I rang Stephen to ask how he thought it had gone.

'I think Andreas more or less fell in love with you,' he drawled. 'It went fine.'

I laughed. 'It felt ever so slightly awkward as I left,' I said.

'That's because the only thing left to say was "Will you join us?" and Andreas felt the time was wrong for that.'

A couple of days later I asked around at the *Telegraph* about reactions to Andreas's paper.

Peter Birkett said spitefully that it was a bloody good thing Andreas had left.

'Why?' I demanded, bristling.

'Because he's nothing but a bloody trouble maker. He's a bully.'

I was genuinely surprised. 'I've worked for his City pages for a year or so and always found him exceptionally friendly.'

'Oh, he wouldn't quarrel with you.'

'Why not?'

'Because he knows where strength lies. He wouldn't take you on.'

'What on earth are you talking about?'

'He's difficult,' said Peter.

John Miller said, 'Well, some talk of rats leaving the sinking ship.'

'Do you?' I asked.

'Well – no – not really, only a bit,' he said with his famed and characteristic firmness.

Bill laughed when I said to him that half my friends had left while I was on holiday. 'A third – not a half,' he said and went on, chortling, 'They went on their own accord, they weren't pushed.' He has a way of pretending to be a sort of P. G. Wodehouse nitwit when he isn't certain how to behave or when he wants to conceal something. You never quite know where you are with him. To confuse his companions it is his habit to make use of peculiarly fractured clichés. He once said of a leader article he supported, 'We should nail our matchbox to the mast over this one.' On another occasion he remarked that the only time he'd met Edward Kennedy he'd found him to be an agreeable man and added, 'But one impression doesn't make a swallow.' I think he contrives this farcical style to hide his real obsession, which is looking out for himself. He considers it unsafe to make a clear and decisive statement about anything. If he ever does, by now no one believes him. When he told his leader writers that there was a move to cut their expenses he tried to rally their spirits by declaring, 'Don't worry – I see it as my role to stand four-square between my colleagues and any silly nonsense from the management.' Someone muttered, 'Christ, is it that bad?'

Alexander Chancellor's view was the most straightforwardly sceptical about the whole thing. He never appears to be motivated by malice, but with good-natured and self-deprecating smiles he is a master of the disguised put-down. The impression he gave me was that the proposed paper would almost certainly fail and that, while he did not wish it ill, he didn't wish it well either. I said someone must be confident that it would succeed; after all, money was coming in, and lots of people had been saying for years that this sort of newspaper was bound to come. As soon as I spoke he began to agree and laughed his unique hissing laugh and shrugged and blew out clouds of cigarette smoke.

There is no getting away from the fact that I feel protective towards *The Nation* or the *Independent*, whatever it's called, and irritated by a worldly Fleet Street attitude that it must fail. In exact proportion to this feeling of unity with the new paper, I feel my commitment and loyalty to the *Telegraph* dissolving.

Nigel Dudley's opinion was as careful and sensible and middle of the road as could be. He managed to wrap up mild disapproval for Andreas, Matthew and Stephen and steadfast loyalty to the *Telegraph* with friendly good wishes to his ex-colleagues and reasonable confidence that they would succeed. Inside his bluff, roly-poly frame there is a bluff, roly-poly fellow who speaks in deft statements that give no hint of an independent mind.

Ed Pearce spoke of 'Matthew's lot' as if they'd not only succeed but do very well indeed. Whether this was a view arrived at after calm consideration or merely instinctive support flung towards anything that embarrassed and might damage the *Telegraph*, I couldn't say. He and Godfrey Barker were having tea in the café when I talked to them. They both wear appalling clothes. Godfrey's ties and shirts are always carefully chosen and remind me of lampshades and curtains in a newly refurbished hotel: you can see why they've been put together, but they clash. He is a dandy with no taste. Ed's clothes look like what's been left over after an Oxfam sale. His trousers and his thin stretchy socks are too short. His favourite colour is a pale yellowy beige. His ties are hideous. Matthew once said, 'There's not one item of clothing that Ed is wearing that I'd be seen dead in. And I mean that literally.' Ed and Godfrey were sitting close together like a pair of Chinese spies trying to pass as Englishmen, but neither hid their admiration for Matthew and 'his lot'.

No new paper, however magnificent its technology, wide its circulation or unlimited its resources, will ever be able to put together such an army of eccentrics and weirdos as the *Telegraph* has done.

One of the few really sane and straightforward people there is Sue Davy, the editor's secretary. When I asked her what she thought of it all, she said it had all been a bit of a surprise and that she'd miss Stephen. She liked him and having him around. Matthew, she said, might not be such an obviously charming man but she'd miss him too. I can't remember her exact words but she said that underneath he was very nice too.

I asked her about Andreas and told her what Birkett had said. She felt that Andreas could be quite sharp and touchy. She'd never suffered from it but that was his reputation. She managed to imply that anyone would get a bit touchy working in the *Telegraph* nuthouse.

The only other person I've spoken to about the new paper is James

Fenton. As with Tony, I had feared he might be uninterested and scornful about it. But, like Tony, he was immediately both interested and curious. He is not really happy on *The Times*, where he is chief book-reviewer, and he is uncertain about how his career should develop.

I always think his problem is that he is a poet who in order to write must live a stimulating and personally rewarding life. He is the absolute opposite of the navel-watching, hypersensitive poet dwelling in an ivory tower. His work springs from his experiences such as his spells in Germany, Cambodia and Vietnam as a foreign correspondent, and from his love-affairs. In fact his regular journalism could be said to suffer because he jealously saves up his raw material for his poems.

The mother of a teenager once said to me and James that she was exasperated when her son who had spent his entire school-days studying science suddenly declared he wanted to go to university because he wanted to write. James passionately defended the boy. 'He is absolutely right. He, almost alone among his fellow students, will have something to write *about*. Of course he should study English. Of course he has not wasted time on science or made a preposterous change of direction.'

To James, English and writing are not separated from anything, indeed cannot exist if they are isolated from life and the world. This presents problems for James. The more he hurls himself into the world, the less time there is for poetry. He must spend some of his precious experience writing journalism in order to support himself. Now and then he must make a break from desk jobs or long-term commitments to deadlines in order to find time to write poetry, and this gives his career a jerky, apparently unsettled look. In fact it's deliberate and, under the circumstances, sensible.

I could see two things happening as we talked now. First, he began to think this could be an opportunity. Perhaps some sort of loose association could be developed from which he would get a retainer of some sort and perhaps an outlet for the lengthy pieces of writing he would like to undertake. These would be on a variety of subjects, some no doubt requiring study and travel, and they could eventually be collected into book form.

Second, he began thinking, with my deliberate encouragement, how he could so effect the development and staffing of the paper as to give his first ambition a chance.

He said he'd talk with certain friends and give the matter more thought; then perhaps we could have lunch with Andreas and Stephen and take it a step further. I was tremendously pleased by his response and resolved to try to ask around myself in a similar sort of way.

9

Wednesday 8 January

This afternoon I was in Matthew and Stephen's old office at the *Telegraph*. I asked their sometime secretary whether she'd known about their plans before they became public.

'Yes,' she said. 'I picked it up from phone calls, and conversations. Stephen was so careful,' she laughed, 'even destroying carbons of letters, that sort of thing.'

Nigel Dudley, who now uses the office, came in. I was sitting at his desk and said, 'Sorry, sport, your place has been taken over.' He advanced into the room without smiling. I got up. He didn't acknowledge my playful mood. Not that he was in the least bit unfriendly or rude; far from it, but he is not one of those people who likes mucking about.

I asked him whether Matthew and Stephen were being replaced as leader writers. He thought there was one replacement being sought, an economics writer probably. This would still leave a gap because Matthew was good on defence, politics and many general subjects and Stephen knew more about the EEC and Africa than any of the others.

Friday 10 January

This evening we went to dinner with Hilary Spurling and her husband John. Hilary asked me how things were at the *Telegraph* and I replied we wouldn't know until later in the year after Conrad Black had announced any changes he's got in mind. I said I preferred to talk about the newspaper three of my ex-colleagues are starting. Benedict Nightingale, the theatre critic, joined in the game of staffing the arts page. They agreed that there should be an arts editor *and* a literary editor and that both should be prepared to fight like anything for space and the general coverage of the arts. Not, incidentally, that I think that is likely to be opposed by Andreas; on the contrary. Hilary thought it should be someone young because of the enormous amount of work involved and commitment it would require. Martin Amis would be a superb books editor but he's moved on to other things. 'What about you?' I asked. Hilary laughed and said she too had other ambitions now. I'd first met her in about 1946 when she was arts editor on the *Spectator*. She was so keen she used to turn up to work every day at 10.00 as soon as the doors were open. After a bit John Thompson, who was more or less running the place, said to her, 'Look you don't *have* to get here so early every day. Perhaps on printing day and the day before – but otherwise you can take your time, you know.' She said the two editors during her time, Iain Macleod and Nigel Lawson, were both 'absent editors' who, although they had flashes of brilliance, depended entirely on the sensible and responsible John Thompson to actually get the magazine out each week.

I had asked John earlier in the day what he thought about the new paper. He said he wished it well, and that he thought they'd get their money to launch the thing. His one doubt was whether or not Andreas, Matthew and Stephen had the experience to do the very difficult task of bringing out a newspaper.

'It's not just a question of saying to someone, OK, let's have an article on, say, Aids, and then just sitting back. You've got to know how long an article you want, how it should be illustrated, where it should be placed and how to present it.' He made this sound like a real difficulty, not like an old veteran patronising some young upstarts. He also said, 'But they might make it. In a few years' time they could all be millionaires.' He smiled, 'And they'll be looking for a cartoonist soon.'

I tried to keep Hilary and Benedict playing the recruiting game. 'What about Tom Sutcliffe?' He is editor of the radio arts programme *Kaleidoscope* and had been James Fenton's idea.

Both immediately praised him and said he was a very good suggestion. Hilary asked what I thought of Blake Morrison as a literary editor. She thinks highly of him but guessed that he's pretty tied up by the *Observer*. James had also mentioned him but I don't know the guy at all.

Hilary also spoke warmly about Claire Tomalin and John Gross but neither seemed quite right to me. In the end I asked her to think about it more and to play this game with some of her friends, and that when she thought of some names to let me know and I'd pass them on.

Saturday 11 January
James Fenton telephoned this evening, just for a chat. Because he now lives in Oxford we don't meet often but usually talk once or twice a week on the phone. He's been thinking about the new paper and at the same time is growing increasingly fed up with *The Times*.

ME: Do you see Martin Amis these days? Could you ring him and talk to him about possible names for the paper?

J: Yes, I could.

ME: Well, ring him and ask him, particularly about books and literary people. He has blind spots about some areas. (*I was thinking about Martin once saying to James and me that anyone who went to the theatre to see a play was either crackers or a phoney.*)

J: (*laughing*) Yes, he does – most areas, actually.

ME: I want to be able to go to Andreas with lots of good names and several good ideas.

J: You can give people advice too soon. If it's too early for anything to be done it all gets forgotten and lost.

ME: Yes, that's a problem. But I want you and me to be established in

11

their minds as people to turn to for ideas and suggestions, so that things don't happen without us being consulted. I want to keep in touch with them. In fact I'll ring Stephen tonight. And I want you to ring Martin.

J: I will.

ME: Then we should go and meet Andreas. Can I tell them you're interested?

J: Yes, certainly.

ME: And not just in reviewing.

J: Reviewing is useful because you can do it at home and it will keep me here. I should stay in England for at least a year – with the occasional trip, of course. (*When he said this I wondered quite what it meant. Is he thinking of leaving England again for a while? But I let it pass.*) I'm interested in doing the longish pieces I told you about the other day, too.

ME: Can I tell them that?

J: Yes, sure. Mind you, I'm not saying I will join them.

ME: That's OK. We'll try to get dug in there first and decide that later. The more we are useful to them, the more influence we will have, and I suppose the more likely we are to join in the end.

Caroline, who was listening, added 'And the less likely you are to be able to negotiate huge salaries.' She meant we will have shown them how keen we are to join and they won't have to tempt us with cash.

I rang Stephen but he was not in, so I rang Matthew. I wanted to keep in touch but was slightly nervous about ringing in case he sensed my keenness and would use it. As soon as he answered the telephone I felt stupid to have thought that because he was so friendly and chatty.

I began to say that I was not ringing with anything special in mind, just to say 'hello' because I was bereft of friends at the *Telegraph* now. Matthew laughed. He felt that after an initial fairly kindly and sympathetic reaction to their project the knives were coming out. Charlie Wilson, editor of *The Times*, has been going around saying they'll never make it.

ME: Does that matter?

MATTHEW: Well, the object is to scare off investors. Andrew Knight's been saying the same sort of thing, and that our paper is aimed at the *Telegraph* – that's to scare the *Telegraph* minions into being cooperative.

ME: But it's not really true, is it, that you are particularly aimed at the *Telegraph*? You want a young AB1 reader and that's what the *Telegraph* hasn't got. Though I suppose you are aimed at the *Telegraph* in the sense they've also got to attract those readers if they are going to survive in the long run.

12

MATTHEW: That's right.

ME: As you probably are going to get your money, I think the more Wilson and Knight suggest that you won't the better.

MATTHEW: Because when we do they look silly?

ME: That's right. I was talking to John Thompson about you on Friday.

MATTHEW: Ah ha! What did he say?

ME: He wished you well and he was sure you'd get the money.

MATTHEW: Good.

ME: He also had one doubt or anxiety about your chances. He said he wondered about your combined experience and whether it was enough to produce the expertise and know-how to edit a big national daily. (*I phrased this as carefully as I could so as not to make it sound offensive. Matthew at once reacted with modest and frank common sense.*)

MATTHEW: Yes, he's quite right, that's a real anxiety. All I can say is that we are aware of it. To a certain extent, by good recruiting – and we're having masses of applications from excellent people already – we can minimise this difficulty. We are all going to have to study and learn a completely new technology as well. However, once that is mastered, in many ways it simplifies our problems.

He began a typically Matthew-like monologue on the advantages of new technology. What happens during these spasms of his is that you listen because you can't get a word in edgeways, but all you hear is a meaningless jumble of obscure jargon and initials. He goes in for term-dropping when he's not letting you know who he lunched with. What you have to do is cut right across it – don't even pretend to comprehend, let alone be interested.

ME: Andreas said I might come and meet your designer sometime.

MATTHEW: (*Instantly dropping high-tech*) Yes, I hope you can. We're meeting him on Monday at 12.00 actually to have a long session.

I said I'd call on Monday morning if I was free. Matthew suddenly said that although he is sure they'll get the money from the City and that all their calculations are sound, he is overwhelmed from time to time by a sense of being extremely exposed and vulnerable. Coming directly after a display of drawling arrogance, this admission of nervousness is oddly touching and intimate, and I find myself continually swinging from wanting to bring him down a peg or two to attempting to bolster him up.

I meant to tell him that on the day Heseltine flounced out of the Cabinet I had missed him and Stephen at the leader writers' conference at the *Telegraph*. Without Matthew the conversation between Jock Bruce Gardyne, Ed Pearce and Godfrey Barker, the leader writers, was

13

14 January, *Daily Telegraph*

shapeless and diffused. Morrison Halcrow had been editing and had not joined in much. I didn't mention it during our phone conversation because Matthew was in full spate and I forgot; but it made me think that if the absence of Stephen and Matthew can make such a difference their presence somewhere else could be very useful in spite of John T's reasonable enough doubts.

Sunday 12 January

The *Observer* carried a long and flattering profile of Andreas today. It built up my confidence which, like Matthew's, fluctuates all the time.

James Fenton telephoned because he wanted to have a laugh about Heseltine. He takes a curiously venomous pleasure in anything that goes badly for the Tories. It is greater than a straightforwardly pleased reaction to a moment of triumph over a political opponent. He seems moved by a personal and vindictive delight, and he becomes uncharacteristically malicious. Sometimes I think his malice is directed at me because he thinks I am too right wing and therefore a crypto-Tory myself. Maybe I am, but that is not a satisfactory explanation of his bitterness. I believe that what you see in James at these moments are the twitchings of the vestigial reflexes of an ex-revolutionary socialist. For all the jokes and banter, he expresses a hatred for the Conservative Party and for Mrs Thatcher which I think is undeserved, even absurd.

He added a trio of names to our list of possible recruits for Andreas:

Suzannah Clapp from the *London Review of Books* as a possible literary or arts editor, and Christopher Hitchens and Willie Shawcross as roving special writers.

Suzannah is an excellent idea and so is Willie. I had already thought of him although I've no idea what sort of a job he'd want. Something like James's, I should imagine: a massive retainer and the occasional long free trip abroad somewhere he wants to go anyway, with the gradual accumulation of enough long pieces to make a book.

Hitch is a different matter. There have been times when I have intensely disliked Hitch. Years ago I argued with him about a bomb that the IRA let off in Aldershot. It killed a couple of gardeners, a cleaning woman and a priest, or perhaps it wounded them, I can't remember. Hitch's view at the time was that it had been a brave and good thing to do. He supported the bombers because he believed they were merely exercising their right to defend themselves against the British soldiers who were occupying their country. He agreed that innocent people had been killed and wounded, but added, 'If the bomb had gone off twenty minutes later [when some soldiers would have been passing] it would have been a victory.' This tortured point of view has always affected my feelings about Hitch. Of course he wouldn't say the same thing about the bomb now, but I'm not sure why or how or when he changed his mind. I'd guess whatever his current attitude is it has been arrived at by an equally bizarre route. The vexing thing about Christopher is that he writes very well. I always want to read on although I never remember a word. He's like Paul Johnson in that way. He is also very funny and although I always say that you cannot dislike someone who can make you laugh, in Christopher's case it may be possible.

Monday 13 January

Before ringing Matthew this morning to arrange whether or not to turn up at the meeting with the designer, I called Tony Howard, who said at once that the more he'd thought and talked about Andreas's paper the more he'd felt he must tell me to be careful.

He is more or less convinced that the newspaper cannot make it. The reason is that he just doesn't believe that a new product will expand the market. *The Times* and the *Guardian* have loyal readers who won't change, and the *Telegraph* simply will not shed the necessary 300,000. By the autumn, when Andreas would go into production, the *Telegraph* will have switched to the new technology and will be vastly improved in look and presentation, and whatever changes Andrew Knight and Conrad Black will have brought about on the journalism side will in all probability mean that they will attract new readers rather than lose the ones they've got. Furthermore he said my position could become

15

awkward. For a start, the more I go along with Andreas the more difficult it will be for me to get out, and if the *Telegraph*, and particularly Lord Hartwell, know that I'm talking to Andreas I will be told either to clear off or bloody well cut it out.

I said I thought both these last points were true but that I was being quite open about chatting to my friends Matthew and Stephen. If I was told to stop it, well, a decision of some sort would be forced upon me, but couldn't I just go on until that happened? Tony said in a guarded sort of way that he supposed I could, but . . .

I felt a bit uncomfortable. I told him Caroline had said exactly the same thing. We talked back and forth and the upshot was that he felt I could go to the meeting this morning and perhaps even a follow-up one, but that I must realise what I was playing with. He complicated the matter by saying that he thought I probably should leave the *Telegraph* anyway because a change would do me good, new challenge, fresh air and so on, and that the obvious place for me to go was *The Times*. He said that he or someone else could put out feelers to the *Times* editor on my behalf. I said that maybe that would be a good idea, but not yet. I want to see what effect Black's take-over is going to have before I do anything.

As for possibly dropping away from Andreas at some point, I had told Stephen early on that I couldn't take too big a risk at this point of my career. To jeopardise my livelihood by joining a paper that might fold in nine months would threaten my children's education, my house and everything, and I didn't see how I could do that. If I joined the paper I'd have to have some sort of promise of two to three years' pay guaranteed should disaster strike, to give me time to recover.

Tony complicated things still further by saying that should I join Andreas, if I could at the same time get permission to work on Sundays, the *Observer* might find a place for me. I said I couldn't possibly do anything to move against Wally Fawkes who is the *Observer*'s cartoonist, and Tony agreed that was a problem but there might be a way round it. He is a great plotter and felt more and more that I was being drawn into something without having a clear enough idea of what was going on.

I am trying to be honest with everyone in the hope that my talent, whatever that's worth, my luck and my frankness will mean that I'm OK in the end. The trouble is I'm not a holy fool. I'm wheeler-dealing and I'm not very good at it. Apart from anything else, I don't even know what I want.

My disloyalty to the *Telegraph* in playing footsie with a potential rival is complicated by my feelings of great disappointment in the cack-handed way the *Telegraph* has landed itself in its present predicament. I have no loyalty to Black, nor he to me. I do feel some sort of loyalty to Bill Deedes and my close colleagues, but where will they be a year or so from now? I feel loyal and supportive towards Lord Hartwell to whom I owe a lot, but he too has moved from the centre of things.

Generally disturbed and somewhat confused after this conversation, I rang Matthew and arranged to go to London Wall to meet the designer.

The office is a small suite of rooms with a kitchenette and hall in a modern or modernised building set back from the road. When I got there Andreas had his coat on and was clearly about to leave. Both Matthew and Stephen shook hands and Stephen vaguely indicated that he was pushing off to lunch any second. The shaking hands is interesting. As well as being a friendly, albeit somewhat unusual greeting between us, it is for them a reaching out for support and a grasping at a recruit. In my case, as well as friendliness it is shaking hands on an unspoken pact and therefore doing symbolically exactly what Tony and Caroline are telling me not to do.

'Chaotic' is far too strong a word to describe the scene, but the aimless wandering in and out of offices, muttered apologies, quick phone calls and unfinished remarks amused me very much.

Two secretaries were at work. One called Linda used to be at the *Telegraph* with Andreas. 'Hello,' I said. 'Nice to see you. Do you still have a sketch book of mine with drawings of the city? I left it in Andreas's office ages ago.'

'No,' she said anxiously, 'I gave it back to you. I'm sure I did.'

'Oh,' I said. 'I've probably lost it.'

'Perhaps she means those pictures she just had framed for her sitting-room,' said Andreas.

'Oh, shut up. I didn't. I'm sure I gave it back,' said Linda, half flustered, half laughing. She asked about sandwiches.

'I'll have pastrami,' I said.

A man of perhaps 40 came out of one of the offices, and introduced himself. He was neat, as designers usually are. His trousers were pressed and his brown shoes very shiny. That wouldn't have mattered but he was wearing a dark blue blazer and had an enormous brown moustache like Bismark's. It jutted out from below his nose and fell in a great curving wave over his mouth. It dominated everything. It needed an explanation, but like all surrealist objects its *raison d'être* lay in its mystery.

Andreas left and Stephen, Matthew, the Moustache and I sat down in one of the offices. Stephen began the meeting. Or rather, he stood up and said, 'Look, I must be off. I wish I could stay. Boring lunch. Sorry. See you soon, I hope. Really sorry. Love to have, er, um . . . Well, bye then,' and he went out.

Matthew, Bismark and I talked in a desultory sort of way for half an

17

hour or so. I got off on to the wrong foot with the designer, who said that he wanted to revive the more or less lost art of drawing for newspapers by the generous use of illustrations. I said it wasn't a lost art, that most newspapers used several artists in a regular way. I knew he was flattering me in a way, or at least my profession, so I tried to be as polite as possible.

'Take the *Guardian*,' I blundered on. 'They have McAllister on the front page, Gibbard two or three times a week, big four- or five-column drawings across the special pull-out supplements, drawings in the letters column and women's pages as well as Posy Simmonds, just for a start.'

'Mmm,' he said.

'There's me, Colin Wheeler, Michael ffolkes and several freelance cartoonists in "Peterborough" on the *Telegraph*. And Maddocks on the City pages.'

'Mm.'

He was a nice enough guy but I didn't think he was up to the job. I must reserve final judgement until I see something he's done, but nothing he said was encouraging. He had believed he was coming to this meeting to be given copy with which to start making mock-ups. Matthew and the others were under the impression that he was arriving with some mockups for them to discuss. So in a way there was not much to do.

Linda brought in the sandwiches. I drank coffee, Matthew had lager. Sometimes I listened to myself talking away about layout and the presentation of news, and thinking, 'If I was that designer I'd be feeling really fed up at having to listen to this jerk.' But he listened politely and once or twice Matthew even appeared to be taking notes.

At about 2.00 the designer left and Matthew apologised to him for the wasted time.

We then had a more interesting conversation. I told Matthew what Tony had said about new products not expanding the market. Matthew said, 'He's wrong.'

'It doesn't matter whether he's right or wrong. What's interesting is that's what people are saying. So if you get the chance when speaking to journalists or TV people your point is worth hammering at.'

'Yes, OK.'

We then talked about people who might join the paper. I gave him the names of Tom Sutcliffe, Suzannah Clapp and Blake Morrison as possible arts and books editors and James Fenton, Willie Shawcross and Tim Garton Ash as foreign and special writers. He was particularly interested in James and Willie. He then asked me what I thought of Miriam Gross because Frank Johnson had put her name forward. I said I didn't know her or her work but in my mind she belonged to a group of talented women who somehow managed to be too showbizzy. I associated her in my mind with Claire Tomalin, Miriam Stoppard, Antonia Fraser and such-like dames. I could be unfair to Miriam Gross but I felt more confident of Hilary Spurling or Suzannah for some reason.

Matthew said, 'I sort of know what you mean. They're too glamorous in a way.'

'Something like that. Glamorous blue-stockings. Claire once gave James Fenton a book of Antonia Fraser's to review. He thought the book was awful and instead of reviewing it he wrote about the photograph of the author on the back of the dust cover. It was a very funny way of dealing with a ridiculous book. Claire absolutely refused to publish it. I think she just couldn't bear to upset Antonia.'

I got up to go and was suddenly overcome by an extraordinary wave of nostalgia. It took a moment to identify what caused it. The conversation about staffing, presenting and designing the new paper was reminding me of the time I spent working in the theatre in the late 1950s and early 1960s. The curiously aimless, gossipy talk, the guessing at the future and what would work and what wouldn't was exactly like thousands of sessions I'd been part of years ago at the Royal Court Theatre, the Establishment Club and in Peter Daubeny's office. Matthew reminded me of John Bird, compulsively talking, reeling off statistics, tremendously ambitious, worried, self-centred, comical. But familiar though the atmosphere was, my role was now different. In my theatre days I always felt I wanted to be something I wasn't. I wanted to be wonderful and charismatic and exciting, like Orson Welles. Now I know what I am and have a pretty good idea of what I can and can't do. The moment of nostalgia was followed by a warm feeling of satisfaction that I no longer worked in the theatre and that it wasn't John Bird at Cheltenham rep but Matthew in a newspaper office who was sitting in front of me.

Before I left Matthew surprised me by asking whether I thought Tony Howard would talk to him. He wants to consult Tony on who to get as department heads, and to pick his brains generally. I said I had no idea what Tony would say but that if he liked I'd ring him up and ask him.

When I got to my office Stephen rang me. He apologised again for the disorganised day and said he was particularly pleased to hear of James Fenton's interest. I gave him James's telephone number. He's going to arrange lunch.

'Should I ask Matthew as well?' he enquired. I think James would be extremely irritated by Matthew, and, as carefully as I could, I suggested Stephen see James either alone or with me. As usual I felt

Stephen was already tuned in to my attitude as he said he'd ask just me and James.

He also said that I should be very frank about the designer and it was so vital to get the design right that no one's feelings should get in the way of criticism. I felt he was expressing doubts about the moustache and all that went with it. I tried to be diplomatic.

'Let's see what he produces. I have so little to go on at the moment. I have nothing against the guy but, er . . .'

'Yes, OK,' he said. We both knew what the other was talking about.

In the evening I telephoned Tony and put Matthew's proposal to him. He at once agreed to the meeting, indeed seemed keen. 'Mind you, I don't want a job with them,' he said firmly.

I thought, 'So you're thinking of joining them, are you?' I said, 'No, no, or course not.' I told him to ask Matthew about all the research into circulation and sales.

'Yes, I will,' said Tony. 'I may be quite wrong about it – it may well be they are going to win.'

I'd had enough of it for one day. Caroline was looking quizzically at me. 'I hope you know what you are playing at,' she remarked.

'I don't like you disapproving of me,' I said.

'I don't disapprove of you – I just hope you know what you're playing at. It makes me nervous.'

Wednesday 22 January
While waiting outside Bill Deedes' office for the conference, I met Rod Junor. He has a colossal belly now. He used to be rather dashing – always a cad, but a mischievous one. When I first knew him he wore a permanent self-conscious grin as if he was about to be discovered with his fingers in the till. Now he adopts a stern middle-aged frown, which is just as unconvincing. It's a great mystery to many people what Rod does. He is a leader writer and he comes to leader writers' conferences but he almost never writes leaders or takes much part in the discussions. When he does intervene it is usually to state, in a slow ponderous monotone, a point of puzzling irrelevance. He may repeat it once or twice, getting slower each time, and then the others go on talking round him. He always notes down the initials of all those present on his news-list. He writes them down with an expensive gold propelling pencil. I sometimes wonder if he files them or works out attendance averages from them or makes reports to someone. It's an odd thing to do.

Rod loves gossip and intrigue, so I asked him whether he had any idea what Conrad Black was going to do with the *Telegraph*. Boiled down and put briefly, his view was that Black might engineer a shut-down of the paper by deliberately confronting the unions and then after

"MIRROR, MIRROR, ON THE WALL..."

12 January, *Sunday Telegraph*

a huge and presumably expensive shake-out start up a smaller high-tech newspaper using the new plant in the Isle of Dogs.

'Do you mean do a sort of Eddy Shah but with a built-in existing readership of 1¼ million?' I asked.

'Yeah, something like that.'

I wasn't able to ask him any more about this wild idea because the conference began.

Thursday 23 January

Stephen rang this evening to say, 'Come to dinner with James at the Caprice tomorrow.' I accepted.

I asked him what he thought of Rod's idea and he said it couldn't be done because the unions would find a way to stop it. I put it to him that Rupert Murdoch seems to be trying something very similar with his new printing works in Wapping. Stephen thought he'd fail too. 'But,' he said, 'if they succeed then that's very bad for us.'

'Because if they can produce cheap papers they can offer even better terms to advertisers and better pay to the best journalists?'

'Precisely.'

As usual Stephen sounded worried. I very much like his instinctive and characteristic self-depreciation. He is always ready to be sceptical about the success of the adventures he's caught up in – a sensible and realistic scepticism which paradoxically gives me much more confidence than Matthew's booming certainty.

Friday 24 January
At 8.00 I went to the Caprice to meet Stephen and James. I was early and sat at the bar drinking orange juice. It is a rather ritzy place and when Stephen arrived I said it was obvious his new company had plenty of dough. He laughed and said, 'No, no. The point about this place is that you can eat terribly cheaply if you choose carefully.'

'What's "cheaply"?'

'Two people can eat here for £35.' He picked up a menu to point out the prices.

'OK,' I said, 'I understand. We've got to pick the cheapest dishes.'

'No, no,' he said.

When James Fenton arrived he was all excited about Leon Brittan's resignation. Stephen's comment was that it was awful having this great political scandal breaking all round but having no paper to write for or pick up all the gossip from.

When we sat down to dinner we began by wondering whether Murdoch would beat the unions with the new plant at Wapping. Stephen repeated to James that if he does that's very bad for *The Nation*. (It seemed that 'The Nation' is the name the paper will have.) I feel sure that Murdoch will beat the unions and very quickly too. Furthermore, I'm sure that once he's done it Black will try to engineer something very similar at the *Telegraph*. I don't know whether that will scupper *The Nation* but it seems the obvious thing to try to do.

Stephen asked James what he thought of the name 'The Nation' and James said that so long as the name sounded like a newspaper, an old-fashioned newspaper, it really didn't matter all that much because the name would very soon lose all its usual connotations and simply mean that paper.

'It's no good calling it "Newsday" or "Outlet",' he said.

'Or "The Daily Loss",' I suggested.

'Or "The Daily Dull",' said Stephen. 'That's what *Private Eye* has called it already.'

James spoke at great length, and very well, about what he thought *The Nation* should be and what traps it should avoid. I wanted to take notes but it seemed wrong to do that even though I knew much of what he said I'd forget. Stephen did jot down one or two things.

First of all James was against it being an SDP paper. He doesn't like the party or David Owen at all. (It was Tony Howard's suggestion, I think, that the paper should come out as SDP.) James said he would lose interest in it if it did. He felt the paper should be independent and have a clear idea about what each part of it was for. If I understood him correctly, he felt that at all costs features such as The Friday Page should be avoided, or any such vaguely named slot which just had to be filled. Each page must have its reason for existence and that reason must be remembered. He said he had nothing against, say, a Women's Page or Special Interest Page of one sort or another so long as they fulfilled that service. 'It's no good having a page with a regular feature "Miss Perrick writes". Who the hell is Miss Perrick and why should I read her? If I read her I'll have to read all sorts of other junk in order to understand what she's on about. I've nothing against columnists so long as they are good enough, but if it's "Woodrow Wyatt writes" it's just . . . it just becomes a . . . sort of brown hole . . .'

I laughed and said 'Ugh!'

James said, 'I mean . . . umn . . .' He laughed. 'You know what I mean, nothing escapes from it. As soon as you start reading you know you're in the shit.'

After a bit of this I said, 'I think anyone starting a paper would hope not to have dull slots – but producing a daily paper, can you be too ambitious? After a while aren't you more concerned with journalists who'll write to length and on time rather than with excellence?'

James thought the design of the paper could affect the contents. You never, never create a job or a slot just to make room for someone. You remember what the original purpose of the paper was. Listening to him I was surprised, as I often am, by how much he thinks about papers and how clear and strong his views are. He had opinions on layout, on staffing, on features and so on and it all came out as a long, coherent speech. He is sometimes slowed up after a few drinks, but tonight he remained quick and clear.

Stephen began to try to find out how he might like to work for *The Nation*. Would he like to be on the staff? Was his interest political writing? Foreign stuff? The arts?

James said he wanted to write longish pieces that would be of use to him later. I understood him to mean that could be collected into books. Stephen tried to tie him down a bit.

'Could you say how many pieces a year you'd like to write, on what sort of subject and how long?' he asked slowly.

James said, 'All that could be negotiated.' He made it clear he did not want a desk job and that he intended to live in Oxford, which ruled out too many visits to London.

Stephen tried another tack. He said that Andreas was obviously very keen that James should join *The Nation* and he suggested that some sort of arrangement could be made in which he joined the paper well before production started, perhaps in a month or two. The plan would be for him to have a say in the whole construction, design and staffing of the paper and his writing role would develop out of that.

23

James was interested but a certain vagueness crept in. Stephen thought that once they got their money, £16 million in March, he should join. The paper would then certainly come out whatever happened, and run for at least three years. They projected a loss for the first two. He also talked about the scheme for staff members to get a slice of *The Nation*. In the end the two came to a sort of rough understanding that this or something like it would be a good idea. James is going to be away for a month and I suppose they'll be in touch and meet again after that.

Stephen then turned to me. He said I too should join them, and asked whether Tony Howard's scepticism and doubts affected me. I said my doubts co-existed with Tony's and weren't particularly affected by them. I was being asked to take a colossal risk. If I joined *The Nation* and it floundered I'd be up shit creek.

'You'd find another job immediately.'

'You just don't know that,' I said. 'There aren't that many jobs going, for a start.'

Stephen said that Tony had suggested that he'd fix up work for me on the *Observer* and that, if I had both positions, if one failed I'd still have the other.

'Typical,' remarked James. 'Typical Tony plan.'

I said, 'There already is a political cartoonist on the *Observer*. I'm not going to try and take his job.'

'It would be like you and Arthur Horner on the *New Statesman*,' said James, recalling the nightmare time when Horner and I were both political cartoonists on the *New Statesman* and used to compete one against the other to get our work published.

'Anyway,' I told Stephen, 'the *Observer* pays peanuts and wouldn't keep me.'

'Look,' he said, 'you negotiate yourself a huge salary . . .'

'What's a huge salary?' I interrupted.

'£50,000,' he said.

'Mm, not bad,' said James.

'But a huge salary is no help if it suddenly stops,' I insisted to Stephen. 'What I need is a great big cushion in case I fall.'

'Yes, but we can't guarantee you fifty years' pay in the event of our going bust.'

'What about two or three years?'

Stephen seemed to think that might be possible so long as it was secret – they couldn't offer such terms to everyone.

'I'm keen to join you,' I told him. 'I want to jump – but you've got to narrow the gap. I'm afraid of falling.'

At about 10.45 James left to get a train back to Oxford and I told Stephen, 'The thing about James is that he's terrific and an immensely

24

valuable colleague, but you have to understand how to use him. It's no good expecting him to be a sort of fireman reporter – Tim Garton Ash can do that brilliantly, but James isn't really interested. You see, he wants something from you. He wants someone to make it possible for him to write and publish long, thoughtful pieces of a particular, personal kind. He wants to pick the places he goes and how long he writes, at least up to a point, and in return you must say what you want and need from him. Most people who employ James want him to bend to their needs too much and consequently they either lose him or get unsatisfactory work from him, like *The Times* who cut his space to make room for those awful illustrations. They are crazy not to let him just go on and give their readers a better read. James's advice and experience and intelligence and judgement would all be very valuable and you can get it if you understand what he wants from you.'

I wasn't sure I was saying anything particularly sensible but I think of James as an artist who should be given his head. If I had the money I'd just give it to him and hope for the best. I'd give money to Jonathan Miller in the same way – I'm fantasising about being a millionaire now – I'd have given millions to Orson Welles too. There are some people who shouldn't have to waste time thinking about money. For some people it's a useful spur and all that sort of thing; others are better employed practising their art or craft or science.

Monday 27 January
Stephen rang me at work. When I answered the phone he said, 'Hello, doubter!' He thought that at dinner on Friday I had sounded less confident than ever about joining *The Nation*. I said that I merely expressed reasonable and genuine anxieties because I felt otherwise it would somehow become established that I had thrown in my lot with the paper and it could lead to misunderstanding later. I was trying to keep my position clear. He laughed and said, slightly uneasily, 'Of course, of course – I was only joking.'

He wanted to know whether I thought it was a good idea for Andreas to write to James saying, 'Glad to hear you are interested.'

'Yes.'

I always imagine that the telephone operators are listening to these conversations and reporting them to Lord Hartwell. Guilty conscience, I suppose.

Wednesday 29 January
Spoke to James who said he'd heard from Andreas. James is going to the Philippines for three weeks and will get in touch with Andreas on his return.

I told him I had been very impressed by all that he'd said at dinner

25

the other night. It came as something of a surprise to realise that he thought so much about newspapers and had such clear opinions. With mock earnestness he said, 'I thought you were brilliant, too.'

'Oh, shut up.'

'No, really.'

I was worried by how little Stephen had said. It seems to me that the three *Nation* musketeers have extremely good ideas about how to raise money and get a newspaper under way, but become a bit vague about what the paper is for and what it should look like. James thought that Stephen was there to listen and sound out rather than discourse on *The Nation*, but still I felt a nagging doubt.

Thursday 30 January

Tony Howard rang this morning and I told him about the overture to James. He thought James would be unwise to flirt with them. He didn't seem to have any particular reasons, except that James was well off at *The Times*.

'Apart from the fact,' I said, 'that he wants to write different sorts of pieces – longer things that he can collect into a book one day. And also he wants to travel. They muck him about at *The Times*. He's not very happy there.'

Tony grunted, half withdrawing his remark but leaving me with the impression that at the moment he is not too enthusiastic about *The Nation* and its chances. It turned out that he hasn't seen Andreas yet. I'd like to meet him for lunch after he has. I think Andreas will convince Tony that the paper's chances of survival are better than he thinks.

This evening when I took my cartoon to Bill Deedes he said he was going for a drink with Stephen. I asked where, with half a mind to join them if they were going to a pub. It turned out that he was going to a party at Stephen's to which I too had been invited. I'd had the card some days ago and completely forgotten about it. Bill said that if I wanted to I could come in the office car. He, Sue Davy and her husband were going to pay a 45-minute visit and then come back to the office. I accepted the lift gratefully. Stephen lives in Greenwich and I didn't fancy going all that way on my motor bike.

Squashed up in the back of the car, Sue and I talked about the new paper. I tried to pretend I knew less than I do but Sue is sharp and I soon became aware that I was giving away more than I had intended. I said that my doubt turned on the fact that nearly all the conversations I'd had with Stephen and Matthew (I didn't say I'd met Andreas) were about the technical side of producing a paper. I felt I'd like to hear more about what they wanted to put into it or what they wanted it to look like. I tried to make it clear that I was sure they had ideas about that sort of thing but I hadn't heard them yet.

Sue listened thoughtfully and didn't say much. Bill turned round from the front seat and said, 'I can't quite hear your conversation. Are you talking about Andreas's paper?'

'Yes,' said Sue. 'Nick is telling us what he knows about things.'

'Well,' said Bill emphatically, 'I think the important thing about this evening is that none of us should be recruited.'

'Absolutely,' Sue replied. She sometimes adopts a comical *faux naif* manner to express perfectly serious thoughts. 'We'll have to watch out for Nick, you know. They're bound to be looking for a cartoonist.' She looked at me with wide eyes and an innocent smile. I looked right back at her.

'Bound to be,' I said, smiling.

Bill seemed unaware of any special meaning attached to this exchange and I continued to chat with Tony about Stephen and Matthew's plans but I guarded my tongue carefully and remained aware of Sue's beady intelligence judging and interpreting everything I said.

At the party I didn't get a chance to talk to Stephen who was moving around with drinks, but I did have a few words with Matthew. The first thing he said was that Rupert Murdoch's brilliant manoeuvre in shifting *The Times*, the *Sun*, the *News of the World* and the *Sunday Times* to Wapping was a godsend to *The Nation*. I wondered why, because Stephen had obviously felt that Murdoch's success would be a bad blow to their own plans. Matthew said that so many *Times* journalists were outraged by Murdoch's attitude, and anyway hated working beseiged by pickets behind barbed wire in Wapping, that *The Nation* was overwhelmed by people looking for work.

'We'll have the best editorial line-up in Fleet Street,' he boasted. He grinned all over his face.

'It would be nice to have a talk,' I said. 'Let's meet for lunch some time when you have a minute.' We half arranged to meet the following week.

The party was mostly hacks. I talked to Serena (who used to work for Peter Utley) and to Charles Moore and Jock Bruce Gardyne and one or two others, but then I saw Bill and Sue looking as if they were going, and I left with them soon afterwards.

As we drove back Bill said, 'Well, that was very good, we got there and out in perfect time.'

'Yes,' I said. 'Thank you very much; I'd never have made it without a lift.'

'You got some brownie points for turning up, and I showed there were no hard feelings,' said Bill. 'That's why I wanted to go. I thought Stephen looked pleased and somewhat surprised to see us. But I wanted to show there were no hard feelings.' He meant that he had no bitterness about Stephen and Matthew leaving the *Telegraph* the way they did.

FEBRUARY

9 February, *Sunday Telegraph*

Sunday 2 February

In the *Observer* today there are stories of resignation and misery among the journalists employed by Rupert Murdoch. Claire Tomalin has resigned from the *Sunday Times*. Neal Ascherson has written a passionate article on the humiliation of the unions and the journalists. Things are hotting up.

About a year ago I was offered a job by *The Times*. There was no particular reason at the time why I should think of leaving the *Telegraph* and I said as much to Peter Stoddart who had taken me out to lunch. He said that he understood, but he added a rider: 'Remember, at the moment we want you when you have a good job already, and you are negotiating from strength. But the *Telegraph*'s future is uncertain and you may not be in such a strong position in a year's time.'

If I had been persuaded by this rather disagreeable threat, which is how I took it, I might now find myself being bused to Wapping each day. (Which all goes to show something or other.)

Tuesday 4 February

I heard today that Hugh Lawson the *Telegraph's* general manager has resigned. Everyone I've spoken to is jolly pleased to hear it. Only Bernard Foyster, the picture editor, had a kind word to say about him. He said, 'Under that horrible exterior, and behind that bullying, pompous, unpleasant manner, he wasn't so bad . . .'

I've always disliked Lawson because I used to have to go and beg him to give me a room of my own. When I first worked at the *Telegraph* I was given a desk in the features department. The noise of the telephones and the then features editor Brian Harvey's whining bad temper, sub-editor John Sparks's rhythmic sniffing and the way a chap called Norman answered the phone, still echo dismally in my memory.

Norman used to say, with exactly the same intonation, thirty or forty times a day, 'Ullo! Fleet Street four-two-four-twoooo – Can yer relp meh?' He had a north country accent and after about eight or ten phone calls I used to get near murdering him. He always took my newspapers and left them all messy on his own desk, and he usually had a heavy cold. One day he hung his sodden handkerchief on the radiator directly in front of my desk, about three feet from my face. Steam began to rise in the air and I quit for the day, swearing I'd never work in that room again. The next day Lawson, as always, told me there was nothing he could do.

The first thing I did when Bill Deedes took over was to plead with him for a room of my own. Lawson then offered me a place with no windows, a sort of filthy cupboard. I said no. Later that afternoon I was given the very nice little room that I still occupy. It had been empty for some time and I've always felt Lawson was thoroughly pissed off that he had to allocate it to me. He never greeted me in the corridor or lift after that.

Once, during the strike that brought down Edward Heath, some miners marched down Fleet Street. The march was orderly and even good natured and I stood outside the *Telegraph* watching with some interest. Suddenly Lawson burst from the swing doors behind me and strode across the pavement. He is a huge, heavily built man and, squaring his shoulders, he walked diagonally through the line of marchers. The first one or two men managed to step out of his way but he collided with a tremendous thump with a third who was thrown backwards and sideways by the impact. Without a glance or a murmur Lawson walked on and away. One or two miners made as if to go after him but were restrained by their comrades. Several looked coldly at me and the *Telegraph* building and I felt embarrassed. Lawson had deliberately used violence against a peaceful demonstrator. He is an awful man and by repute the worst negotiator in recorded history. He could enrage people just by the way he greeted them, let alone how he dealt with their complaints.

His departure is the first good news I've heard from the Conrad Black regime.

Wednesday 5 February
I had lunch with Charles Moore today. I had been looking forward to asking him about *The Nation*, its chances and my involvement with it.

'I want to talk to you about my future,' I began.

'That shouldn't take long,' replied Charles, quick as a flash.

I told him that Stephen and Matthew had both made me offers of work and said they'd pay me well and leave me free to do all sorts of freelance work, travel and so on.

Charles's reaction was cool and dismissive. He thought *The Nation* would most likely survive, 'But your problem is not the danger of finding yourself out of work but finding yourself working for a boring little small-circulation paper which no one reads.' This was a completely new idea to me. Charles said, 'Suppose you were offered lots and lots of money to do covers for some provincial weekly magazine – you'd be much better off working for the *Spectator* for less because your work must be seen by your friends and colleagues.'

I said that the *Telegraph* had become boring and lonely. 'I have no friends left there.' We made a list of the people who have quit the *Telegraph* in the last few years. Frank Johnson, John O'Sullivan, Colin Welch, Stephen Glover, Matthew Symonds, Charles himself.

'Don't forget how quickly the fortunes of a paper change,' added Charles. 'Not so long ago the *Telegraph* was riding high and *The Times* seemed finished. Now the *Telegraph* is in trouble. They've taken hardly anyone on, at least as special feature writers, for ages. But that's bound to change. Andrew Knight will begin recruiting soon. There'll be a new editor and things may look up.'

'Um,' I said.

'I think you ought to go and see Andrew Knight and talk to him like you've talked to me. Say to him you've had this offer, it's extremely attractive and ask what you have got to look forward to at the *Telegraph*.'

'What if he tells me to push off?'

'In that case your dilemma is removed: you join the *Daily Whittam*. But he won't. He won't want you to go. He may even make you a counter offer to make you stay. Either way you have nothing to lose.'

This sounded like good advice and I said so. Charles said, 'It's Alexander Chancellor's idea really. He's bored and fed up at the *Sunday Telegraph* and so he went to Knight and said more or less what I'm telling you to say.'

'What happened?' I asked.

'I'm not sure,' said Charles. 'I haven't seen him lately.'

I tried to get Charles to talk about Stephen and Matthew but he wouldn't be drawn much other than to say that Matthew had a personality problem ('He puts people's backs up') and that he didn't think they, including Andreas, were capable of producing a good paper. I think he meant none of them has the flair or style that's required.

I said that Tony Howard has some far-out idea that I might be able to work for the *Observer* as well as *The Nation*. Charles said this was not a good idea. It would look odd to work for two national papers. In his opinion I'd be better off doing more work for the *Spectator*. It turned out that Charles's idea of doing more work for the *Spectator* meant doing a comic strip. He might even write it himself and suggested that the hero might be a young fogey like himself. I'm not sure I want to do another strip. The trouble with strips is that it gets a bit dull doing the same character over and over again – unless it's really superbly written like Barry McKenzie was.

This conversation made me feel like making contact with *The Nation* people again. I am in an awful uncertainty about everything. The more people I speak to the more confused I seem to become. So I rang Stephen this evening. His friendly voice and generally optimistic and cheerful mood made me feel better, if not more clear in my mind about what I want, or should do.

We arranged for me to come and see some dummies on Wednesday evening. Matthew and Andreas will be there too, probably.

At work today things went badly. My mind was not functioning at all well and no ideas came, so that I failed to do a cartoon and as usual felt bad about it. But whatever badness I feel comes from me. The paper does not put any pressure on me at such times. In fact sometimes it may even be easier for all sorts of people if I *don't* do a cartoon. This means that I don't suffer too much if I occasionally fail. But what if I was working for someone else? What if it was a new paper that had invested a lot of money in me? Then the pressure would become difficult to bear. Such calculations weigh heavily on me these days.

Thursday 6 February
I heard from Stephen today that Peter Paterson, the industrial correspondent on the *Daily Mail*, had expressed considerable interest in *The Nation* (or the *Daily Whittam*, as I now think of it). Peter had given Stephen the impression that not only did he think the paper had every chance of survival and of being a success but that he was interested in working for it.

'What sort of position did he have in mind?' I asked.

'Sort of home editor, I think,' said Stephen.

'What's a home editor?'

'Well, doing what that bloke Green does on the *Telegraph*. In charge of everything, er . . .'

'Hmm,' I said.

'Do you think he'd be any good at that sort of thing?'

'Well, I'm still not quite sure what "that sort of thing" is, but, um . . .'

I found it hard to express my doubts about Peter as an editor. He can write well and he knows a great deal about unions and politics – or at least he knows how they work, what goes on behind closed doors, and so on. He has good contacts. He sees through the way politicians have to talk, and can understand what they mean. He has an attractive lack of solemnity about politics. But . . . his qualities all go towards making him a good and dependable journalist rather than an editor. I can't see him being tough enough on people who are not shaping up; or clear-thinking enough about an issue to be able to direct people towards different parts of it. I can see him attempting to muddle through problems rather than tackling them. I see him laughing ruefully at a balls-up rather than agonising over it and manoeuvring to avoid it happening again. Peter was my lifeline when I began as a cartoonist on the *Telegraph;* without his support and help and advice I probably would not have survived. Remembering this debt made it hard for me to criticise him behind his back.

I tried to give Stephen a diluted version of my doubts. After a bit he interrupted and said, 'Peter himself seemed aware that he might find being an editor difficult. I said to him, "Do you think you could handle the organising and running of an office?" and he laughed and said, "If I had a brilliant No. 2 and a very good secretary." '

I smiled at this example of Peter's frankness and perceptive self-assessment, and commented, 'At least it sounds as if he knows as well

33

as anyone what the problems might be. On the good side, he's an enthusiast, and very experienced. He's an entertaining and agreeable companion. He is obviously aware of his own organisational weaknesses, and I suppose he may have changed quite a bit since I last worked with him. If he says to himself, "Now I'm going to be an editor", perhaps that's what he'll make himself into.'

Trying to sum up this rambling conversation I said, 'Whatever his drawbacks, on balance Peter would be a serious contender for such a job.' Stephen obviously agreed.

Sunday 9 February

This morning I walked through the slowly melting snow to have a drink with Lennie Hoffman and his wife Gill. We talked for a bit about the *Daily Whittam* and I explained my hopes and fears about it. Lennie said he recently had dinner with an ex-colleague of Andreas's who had spoken of Andreas as being a first-class journalist but perhaps not so good at admin.

How on earth does one make up one's mind about anything? I tend to listen to other people's assessments and rely on them to a great extent. There are few issues on which I feel very clear. I once made a list of all the political questions of the day: pay rises, education, Common Market, North Sea oil, inner cities, GLC and so on. I found that I was more or less completely ignorant about the whole lot, and had absolutely no opinions on any of them. All I had was a rough idea of who from the political or journalism world supported which side of any given issue. I also had a clearish idea of which politicians or commentators I usually agreed with. So I make up my mind about things by seeking out who said what about them – looking not so much for arguments as for conclusions.

What is emerging about the *Daily Whittam* is that it will probably survive but also probably be rather boring.

Oh lumme.

The *Telegraph* is already boring.

Oh cripes.

Monday 10 February

This morning I had to ring Peter Paterson about an article he had written for this week's *Spectator*. I have to illustrate it. In the course of a few minutes' conversation I became acutely uneasy. He had not finished it and therefore couldn't be much help to me. His attitude to it was that it was a dull subject (the TUC and the EEPTU) and he'd dealt with it dully. I asked if Norman Willis was mentioned and he said 'No' but he'd mention him towards the end if I liked. It could be one way of completing the piece. His whole manner was curiously bored,

34

uninterested in both his work and my difficulty in trying to find a way of illustrating it. He is not unfriendly and quite prepared to be accommodating, but even his willingness to change things around or add bits reflects his fundamental lack of concern. For some reason he goes out of his way to give the impression that the whole thing is a drag and a kind of interruption of something else that he'd rather be doing.

I asked him how his lunch with Stephen had gone. He said that Stephen had more or less offered him a job, a very good job.

'As home editor,' I said.

'How do you know?' he said, surprised.

'Not a sparrow falls . . .'

'He told you?'

'Yeah.'

He went on to say that others had advised him to take the job. His friend Peter Campbell had said, 'There's no more risk in you working for them than in you taking all the risks that you usually take.'

Wednesday 12 February
I arrived at my appointment with Stephen at the London Wall office at about 6.30, half an hour early.

The atmosphere was exactly the same as my last visit except that there were more people around. Several shirtsleeved men I'd never seen before were walking about from office to office with important-looking pieces of paper, and there was an atmosphere of pally and energetic activity.

Matthew appeared to be interviewing a possible recruit from the *Observer*'s management side. Stephen was away having a drink with someone and Andreas was, like last time, on the point of going out. I was disappointed that I would not get a chance to talk to him. I think my joining or not turns now on my assessment of him.

I sat in Linda's office and sipped a weak whisky and soda and chatted to two men, one of whom was seated at a typewriter and was obviously a staff man; the other was a visitor who, I gathered, had been active in the early days in helping raise money in the City. Both were friendly and talkative and it was pleasant to sit and watch the comings and goings. The paper feels more real each time I visit this place.

When Matthew's visitor pushed off he took me into his office where we sat at a sofa. Two other men were conferring together on the other side of the room. I must have looked disconcerted by their presence because Matthew said, 'I'm afraid we'll just have to talk through that,' nodding to indicate the other two.

This was very different from the session I had hoped for. I had been told by Stephen that Andreas, Matthew, he and I would discuss the dummies that had been produced and it was understood that the conversation would also become more general. We sipped our drinks and looked at a number of newspapers lying in an untidy heap on a low table in front of us. From amongst them he picked out a curious-looking paper with a blank where one would expect its name to appear.

'The first thing this teaches us,' he said, 'is that we need a new designer.'

'Is this the dummy I'm here to see?'

'Yes . . . It's not right.'

He was right. In fact it was so bad that there was no point in even talking around it.

'What does Andreas think of it?' I asked.

'He thinks it's awful too – perhaps not quite as awful as Stephen and I do.'

He flicked over one or two pages. Some had a quite ludicrous number of different-sized headlines in different type faces. Some were strangely divided by thick black lines. Here and there a photo clung awkwardly to the page like a mountaineer on a frozen cliff.

Matthew began a spiel about how a list of absolutely first-rate newspaper designers was now being made from which truly great things could be expected. I wondered but didn't ask, why make the detour through the original designer?

Andreas passed by the open door, buttoning his overcoat.

'Don't be too unkind,' he said with a smile.

'No danger of that,' replied Matthew crisply.

Stephen came in after a few minutes. 'He thinks it's absolutely great,' said Matthew to him, holding up the dummy and nodding at me.

Stephen looked at me, incredulity and tactful interest at war in his expression. 'Really?' he said, unable to hide the shock he felt.

'No, not really,' I said. 'It's terrible.'

'Phew!' said Stephen. 'Thank God.'

Matthew went off into fits of laughter. I don't find tricks like that comical. I can be pleased to see someone I dislike made to look silly, and I can laugh at them to increase their humiliation, but I don't ever think it's funny.

We talked about the *Telegraph* and I told them how things were. I listened to myself describing Bill telling the leader writers' conference about an advertising supplement the *Telegraph* is producing at the end of this month. I was being catty about Bill, Godfrey, Adrian Berry, the science correspondent, and Nigel Dudley. I was really only joking about them all but I felt a pang of conscience, and disliked myself for sneering at the *Telegraph* while still working for it. It felt wrong.

Matthew began putting down Nigel and I weakly came to his defence. 'That's a bit hard,' I said.

'I agree,' said Stephen.

'Yes, you're right,' said Matthew, still laughing and withdrawing what he'd said.

'Well, Nick,' announced Stephen. 'It's time to talk turkey.'

'OK,' I said briskly. 'Let's.' But I didn't feel like talking anything. I felt muddled and uncertain and rather miserable.

'Right, when are you going to join us?' said Stephen.

I made a little speech about how I felt they were asking me to take quite a risk. I mentioned my children's education and my mortgage. This cut very little ice with Matthew. He said he had a mortgage three times the size of mine, and a son.

'Yes, I know,' I said lamely. 'But you could start earning a living tomorrow in the City if you had to. You've got other strings to your bow.'

'Nick, be realistic,' said Stephen. 'You are the most easily employable man here. You don't even have any rivals.'

I tried to be practical and matter-of-fact. I asked about holidays, pay, pension and travel.

Stephen said, 'Look, go and talk to Tony Howard, or whoever you like, and write yourself a contract, whatever you want to put in it. You know that he's hard' – he pointed his thumb at Matthew, who grinned modestly – 'but I'm soft, and Andreas is pretty soft. Tell us what you want. Drive a hard bargain. We can work out a deal.'

They asked me when I felt I could join, supposing I was going to. I explained that I'd be away for all August but I could come over in June or July in order to work myself in and be ready to go into full production round about 1 September. They expected to launch at the beginning of October.

'I don't want to join too soon and spend too long not doing cartoons,' I said.

'You should come in the middle of June,' said Matthew.

We left the office soon after this and I walked with them until I reached the bay where I'd left my motor bike.

'Be in touch,' said Matthew.

Stephen smiled. 'Did you know you're twenty times as likely to have an accident on a bike than you are in a car?'

I said, 'But you are twenty times more likely to have an accident on a bike if you are 19 or 20 than if you are an old gent of 50.'

'Anyway,' said Matthew, 'riding a bike is at least twenty times more risky than working for us.'

We all laughed and they walked away while I put on my reflecting Sam Browne belt and my helmet and gloves, and unlocked my Honda. Before leaving, Matthew told me the name they had decided on. The *Daily Whittam* is going to be called the 'Independent'. I felt very pleased about that, and I knew Caroline would be.

At home I tried to describe to her my feelings about the *Independent*. I find I am less and less anxious about whether it will succeed or fail and more and more worried about how good it will be. I told her that Matthew had told me they were going to have sport on the back page. I thought this was a mistake. Matthew explained it was because they could have colour on that page and not on the immediate inside back pages.

I had said to Matthew, 'Only the pop papers have sport on the back.' He then spoke the sombre words: 'We will be in competition with the *Mail* – we're aiming at their readers too, you know.'

'Would you want sport on the back if colour didn't come into it?'

'Yes, I prefer sport on the back. Most people do.'

'I don't.'

Caroline thinks my position is increasingly awkward. She feels I must talk to someone on the *Telegraph* and explain my dilemma. Or perhaps just make a decision and stick to it.

But who can I talk to? Bill would just waffle and anyway I don't trust his judgement or advice, and I don't know Andrew Knight. And I couldn't go and see Andrew Knight instead of Bill – it would seem too rude to Bill.

I rang Tony but he's away until Tuesday, damnit.

Friday 14 February
I wanted to get away from work early today but I met Bill in the corridor round lunchtime and he told me there was a meeting of the entire staff at 3.00 in the newsroom. Andrew Knight was going to address everyone.

'Pass the word around, will you? You'd be doing me a great favour.' It's somehow typical of Bill to ask you to do something quite useless, just to flatter you and make you feel important. I knew perfectly well that all heads of departments would have been told about the meeting and would make it their business to tell their staffs. Me 'passing the word around' was quite unnecessary, but of course I said I would.

I met Godfrey Brown, the agricultural correspondent, in a coffee bar and asked him if he was going. He said he was and we guessed at what we might be going to hear. 'Bad news, I should think,' he said. His cheerful parting shot was, 'See you at the St Valentine's Day Massacre.'

I asked Ricky Marsh, the foreign editor, and Bernard Foyster whether the meeting was worth going to. 'Will we learn anything?' I enquired. 'The last time Bill addressed the staff it was a ridiculous exercise in waffle.'

Ricky looked pained. 'Of course we'll learn something.'

'I bloody well hope so,' said Bernard. 'I've come in on my day off to hear this.'

These great big meetings are fun. As the huge newsroom filled up everyone was grinning and joking quietly. Sarah Jewell stood by me for a minute. She works in the Foreign Department. I've known her since she was about 10 years old.

'This is like school, isn't it?' she smiled.

'Yeah. How are you? Have you found another job yet?'

'Not yet. I'm still looking.'

'So are most people in this room, probably,' I said.

One of the newsroom staff clapped his hands and stood on a chair. 'Er – colleagues,' he called, 'Mr Knight will address you from that end of the room.' People began pressing down in the direction he indicated. I pushed through a group and near the front found an edge of a desk to sit on. There was a pause and a low murmur of conversation. Cigarette smoke curled up here and there. Most people looked serious and thoughtful.

Earlier in the day I'd had a brief chat with John Miller who had said quite savagely, 'We'll smash Whittam Smith.'

'How?' I said. 'What do you mean?'

'We'll smash him because the *Telegraph* is going to be so good and it'll get better.'

I had been surprised by his passion and apparent anger at Andreas. I wondered how many of this huge crowd of hacks crammed into the newsroom would be together after the Black Axe fell – if it was going to fall.

A door opened and, looking rather self-conscious, Andrew Hutchinson, John Thompson, Bill Deedes, George Evans, the managing editor of the *Sunday Telegraph*, and Andrew Knight emerged. Knight looked extremely young and rather tense. He was wearing a nice three-piece green tweed suit and his shirt collar was awry, giving him a boyish appearance.

Bill made a short introductory speech and then Andrew Knight spoke for about an hour. It was an odd sort of speech and it impressed me more retrospectively than it did at the time. He came across as an intelligent, decent and very tough young man. He made me think that although he would take no pleasure in being hard he would act decisively if he had to. And if people had to bite the dust, that was just too bad.

He made no bones about how serious the economic situation facing the *Telegraph* was. He said he hoped and expected us to survive but that it would need change. Everyone had to ask themselves whether they were prepared for and could face things. He praised much about the existing *Telegraph* and spoke warmly of Lord Hartwell and very warmly of Conrad Black.

Central to his theme was the threat posed by Murdoch, Shah and Whittam Smith. I was glad he spoke so seriously about Whittam Smith.

He said at one point that if the *Telegraph* faltered then Whittam Smith would be well worth investing in.

He announced this to be the year of Murdoch. 'Murdoch has changed everything. He has said he is going to double the circulation of *The Times* and when Murdoch says he'll do something he usually does it.'

The message in brief seemed to be: We may not survive; whether we do or not depends in considerable part on our efforts, our goodwill, loyalty and readiness to adapt. Potentially the *Telegraph* is perhaps the finest paper in the world, but at the moment it's all over the place. Right now the primary concern is with management problems but soon we must tackle the editorial difficulties. This whole process could take up to eighteen months or more to complete.

Once he was interrupted by the tannoy broadcasting a test transmission. The whole room rocked with laughter as the technicians solemnly counted up to ten and back again. The sustained guffaws and chuckles measured the tension in the air. Everyone was relieved to express some feeling at last.

After his speech Knight took a few questions. They were good questions and in them you could read acute anxiety about the future. Among other things he tried to reassure people about the safety of retirement benefits and future managerial interference in editorial decisions.

Then, somewhat subdued, we all traipsed off to our offices.

Back in my office Morrison Halcrow called to discuss some drawing I'm doing for him. He was full of admiration for Knight and thought his speech terrific. He too was gloomy about the future – and, incidentally, the present. He said Bill had taken an almost unendurable amount of punishment over the last few months. I wasn't clear what he meant and he explained that Bill's power had all flowed from Hartwell. As Hartwell's power had waned and his attention drawn away from editing the paper, Bill had been left in a hopeless position. Things simply happened all round him, about which he could do nothing.

'Why doesn't he just go, then?' I asked, more brutally than I felt.

'I suppose he will soon. He wanted to stay on after Eastwood left to help over the period of transition, but it's all gone wrong.'

'The trouble with Bill is he'll do almost anything to avoid a confrontation,' I said.

Morrison agreed. 'He used to change his mind every few days,' he said. 'Now he changes it every half hour.'

I felt more and more morose and bad tempered. 'I think all that stuff of Knight's about thinking first and foremost about what's good for the *Telegraph* is bullshit,' I said. 'He came here because he was offered a good job with lots and lots of money, not because he's in love with the *Telegraph*. The bloody paper doesn't give a sod for all the poor bastards

40

it's going to sack or move to boring jobs. Why should it? It's a tough old world, not a Boy Scout camp.'

Morrison was taken aback by my bitterness.

'Knight tells me,' I went on, 'that the *Telegraph* may fold under me and will I please make its survival my absolute priority. What crap. I'll make *me* my absolute priority. Everyone else will be the same, including Andrew Knight.'

'What would you say if you were him?'

'The same, I suppose. I'd have to. But it's nonsense. I've had offers of jobs from several people,' I said, my mood making me reckless, 'and I have to think about them seriously. What am I to do if someone says, "Nick, you're gold, we want you, we'll buy you, you can have this income, that perk, this pension scheme"? Am I really supposed to put the *Telegraph* first? Why? The *Telegraph* says bugger-all to me except, "Sorry old boy, tighten your belt, we may fold." I am told: no more foreign trips, my cartoons are cut down from four columns to three – and all I get is a pep talk.' Morrison gazed at me thoughtfully while I rambled on. 'I'm not saying I think of myself as gold,' I said, feeling a bit silly, 'but that's what people say and . . .'

Morrison said, 'Some weeks ago I went to Bill and said to him we must make a list of the dozen or so people we want and need to keep if we're ever going to get the *Telegraph* going again.'

'What did he say?'

'He just said "No." He didn't seem to know what I was on about. Anyway, nothing happened.'

'It's stupid,' I said. 'It's a bad leadership.'

'But what can we do anyway with no money to offer?'

'I'd be much more inclined to stay if I felt someone on the management side really reckoned me, or if Bill or someone simply said personally, "Please don't go, we need you. Stick around and we'll make it worth your while if we ever get out of the shit." '

Morrison grunted Scottish agreement. 'I don't know what Bill thinks he's doing. I think he felt he could use his great diplomatic skills.'

'It's no good going into a controversial situation with just diplomatic skills. You've got to have a purpose – and something you want to achieve with your diplomatic skills.'

'You need someone to talk to. It's a pity there isn't anyone. Bill's no good, and who else is there? Of course, there was a time when people in your position used to go and speak to Lord Hartwell. But he always took a rather high and mighty view. It was a matter of, "If that's how you feel, farewell." '

'Yes,' I said. 'I've heard that, and it's inhibiting. There's no point in going to discuss things if the very act of discussing them means you are no longer welcome aboard.'

I was in a funny mood, sounding angrier and more worried than I felt. Mostly I felt a sort of flatness but Morrison brought out in me something bad-tempered. I think too I was sending a message to Bill perhaps, or Andrew Knight even, to say: Make it easy for me to stay or harder for me to go.

Matthew said when I saw him on Wednesday that although there was a risk in joining the *Independent* there was also a risk in staying on the *Telegraph*. This remark makes me keen to stay rather than the opposite. I hate being scared into doing things.

Sunday 16 February

The Sunday papers all carry stories of how Murdoch has smashed up the unions. My jaundiced view of the whole of Fleet Street, including the *Independent*, continues. The weather is bitterly cold. I've arrived at that time of winter when I long for warmer weather. Roll on spring.

Monday 17 February

I often have an early-morning telephone conversation with Chas Moore on Monday because it is then that we discuss details of work that I may be going to do for the *Spectator*.

This morning, in the gossip that accompanies the practical side of these chats, I learnt that John O'Sullivan had been offered jobs on both the *Daily* and *Sunday Telegraph* heading his own department on both papers and assured of the editorship of the *Sunday* in due course. According to Chas, John had refused the offer and is going to *The Times* instead.

I wondered what this indicated about the intentions of the Black/Knight axis. I considered it a mark against them because I think John's political views are too peculiar. He is far too attached to the United States. He is someone who has shifted his interest in the destiny of his own country and centred his emotional loyalty and interest to another. I have heard Peter Utley describe those of our contemporaries who unthinkingly support the US as traitors who belong in the same category as the left-wing fellow travellers of the 1930s. This judgement Peter delivered with his own delicate mixture of self-mockery, knowing exaggeration and real seriousness.

I said to Charles that I thought something along these lines and he made a little speech which included a knockabout attack on Black and a swipe or two at Knight and concluded with the comment, aimed at the latter, 'You have to remember that he's an American ideologue.'

Friday 21 February

For some reason or other today was very difficult. I had one or two extra drawings to do for the *Sunday Telegraph*. Chris Fildes found it hard to think of a way to illustrate his Monday City page article and the day slipped away with nothing achieved. On top of everything else, Charles Moore telephoned to give me an impossible brief for next week's *Spectator* cover and I sat in despair, unable to think of a cartoon for Sunday and unable to get on with anything else until I'd done that fundamental task.

The *Spectator* piece I'm supposed to illustrate is to be written by Perry Worsthorne and I went to have a chat with him in the afternoon to see if he could give me a lead. As usual he was friendly and pleasant and useless. I don't mean he is incompetent or even uncooperative but his efforts to describe what he is going to write and how it might be illustrated do not help me. He talks in a sort of airborne, floating style, catching the thermals of an idea and soaring miles from his starting point. The return journey is so slow and indirect it is terribly difficult to remember where it was originally heading. You listen with drowsy pleasure to his nasal voice and watch the light catching his white hair, but your own thoughts are far away. Today his theme was falling standards in Fleet Street. Oiks became editors because proprietors think oiks can make more money than educated, cultured people with high intellectual standards. He seemed to hope for a time when the low cost of newspaper production would create a return to a 19th-century ideal, when distinguished gentlemen edited important newspapers from booklined studies.

I said that modern proprietors would keep popular editors on their low-cost newspapers and simply make a bigger profit. Perry vaguely agreed but insisted that nevertheless something was made possible by the new technology. I gave up after a bit having, as always, enjoyed listening to Perry even though spending time with him is like bunking off to the movies – great fun but it doesn't butter the parsnips.

It was not until nearly eight o'clock in the evening that I handed in my last drawing. Only Stuart Read was left in the office, subbing some article. He was bending over his work frowning and resting his forehead on his hand.

'What do you think of the news?' he asked.

'Mm?'

'You haven't heard. They've appointed the new *Daily* and *Sunday* Editors.'

'Really?' I was suddenly very interested. 'Who?'

'Perry to do the *Sunday* and Max Hastings to take over from Deedes.'

First of all I began to calculate whether Stuart was sending me up. Both appointments were possible but both quite unexpected. Perry has for so long been a failed contender that it didn't seem likely that at this late stage he'd be given the job of revitalising the ailing *Sunday*. In a sense it seemed like a continuation of what's been before. Hastings is obviously an interesting appointment but it struck a dread in my heart. I think of him as intelligent, ambitious, crudely insensitive, self-centred and arrogant. It's an awful mixture. He's the kind of guy you can't write off and you can't like. You just have to lump him.

Stuart convinced me that he was not kidding. I felt absurdly as though Black/Knight had made a clever chess move against me, and I looked hard at the board to find a response.

Perry's appointment doesn't really matter. I can get on OK with him if I stay. Max Hastings is the problem. I barely know him and the two contacts I have had with him do not warm me to him.

The first came about on the day Nick Tomalin was killed in Sinai. I was sitting with a number of journalists including Max in El Vino's. Everyone was talking about Nick in a way that irritated me. They were saying that a very great journalist had been taken from us. His achievements were being preposterously over-praised and he was being spoken of as a figure of towering importance. I had heard Max earlier on the radio speaking in the same vein. I felt Christopher Isherwood had set a good example when someone stuck a microphone in his face and asked for a capsuled comment on the news of Auden's death: he'd said he was far too unhappy at the news to say anything.

But I remember Michael Frayn's speech at Nick's memorial service with pleasure. He spoke about Nick very well without any hyperbole or nonsense and expressed properly the sense of loss Nick's friends and colleagues felt.

Years later when Max Hastings was the most famous man in the world for his derring-do in the Falklands, I drew a caricature of him for the cover of the *Spectator*. He asked the then editor, Alexander Chancellor, if he could have the original. Alexander asked me and I said yes. I did not charge him, partly because I did not particularly want the drawing myself and partly because I admired him and giving him the drawing was a kind of inarticulate salute. He never acknowledged either the gift or the salute. He seemed to assume the drawing could just be his, and it has bugged me ever since.

On the whole Stuart seemed to think the two appointments were good. He could live with them.

Back in my office I wanted to talk to someone about this hot gossip. It was about 8.30 by this time. I tried Tony Howard, Matthew Symonds and Stephen Glover but none of them was in. At about 9.30 Stephen rang me at home and we talked about the new editors. In fact we had little to say because neither of us knows Hastings. Stephen had come from having a drink with Frank Johnson who felt Hastings was a very clever appointment.

I asked Stephen whether Miriam Gross who'd been with Frank was going to be the *Independent*'s literary editor. He said maybe but that my reservations expressed to him and Whittam Smith told against her. A chill of real horror went through me at the idea that my casual and unsubstantiated remarks could actually affect her career. It seemed terribly unfair. Undeterred by this moment of anxiety, I went on to plunge a dagger into Peter Paterson's broad back. Stephen made it clear that while Peter seemed keen to come to the *Independent* as home editor, he (Stephen) and Andreas were beginning to have doubts. Peter was obviously an experienced useful industrial correspondent but could he handle a bigger editor's job?

I added my doubts to Stephen's.

Stephen was, as usual, carefully optimistic about the *Independent*. He felt everything was cruising along OK. He urged me to put in with my demands. He said Matthew had disapproved of him saying to me, 'Write your own contract'. Psychologically what Stephen said was absolutely correct and far more likely to set me on the road to the *Independent* than Matthew's trying to frighten me into leaving the *Telegraph*. Stephen instantly moved to heal any breach between me and Matthew.

'Yes, well – he expresses himself badly,' he murmured. 'He wants you here just as much as I do. You know that.'

He's a good chap, Stephen.

Saturday 22 February

Tony rang this evening, having heard I'd rung yesterday.

He was delighted for Perry and said, spluttering with laughter, 'But it shows they've written off the *Sunday*.' He felt the appointment could only mean they wanted and expected no real change there, I suppose. Tony believes the *Sunday* is unsaveable anyway. He had no instant reactions to Hastings' appointment except to say that when the man had edited 'Londoner's Diary' on the *Standard* he had been disliked by his staff to a quite astonishing degree.

'They absolutely loathed him', he repeated in emphasis. I could sense the grin all over his face. The whole point of the anecdote was to alarm me, and it did.

'Oh God,' I said. 'What does it all mean?'

We agreed to meet next week. I look forward to that.

Monday 24 February

Charles Moore and I spoke this morning about the cover drawing for Perry's piece. He thought the new appointments at the *Daily* and *Sunday Telegraph*s were excellent. I asked him if he knew Max Hastings. He said not well but that he was 'nice'.

I said, 'I thought he was self-centred, insensitive and arrogant.'

'Yes, he is arrogant and a bit insensitive and self-centred. I mean, he

45

knows what he wants and just goes for it without any thought for anyone else in a way . . . but he's nice.'

'Sounds absolutely ghastly.'

'No, because he is good-natured.'

'That sort of good-natured loner who is tough and single-minded makes a good journalist – you need other qualities as well to be an editor.'

'But he is responsive and appreciative. He'll say, "That's jolly good, Garland" when you show him a cartoon. Mind you, he'll also say, "That's terrible – take it away", as Bill never would.'

'Oh cripes!'

'No, he's a good chap. I like him.'

I asked Sue Davy what changes the new editors meant to her – apart from the fact that Bill would go. She said she hoped to keep her job. 'I need it – to keep my family.' She asked me whether I knew Hastings. 'Is he nice? People say nice things about him.'

I reported what Charles Moore had told me.

She laughed. 'He rang me up at 10.00 this morning,' she said. '*Ten o'clock* – we can't have that.'

'He's obviously a hard man.'

'You can see that from his face,' said Sue, gesturing with her hand over her own face. She grimaced slightly.

I left the building after work with the literary editor David Holloway. We asked each other about Max Hastings.

'I had him on the phone at 10.30 this morning,' he said, 'about some book.'

'Crumbs,' I said.

'Mm. He cheerfully called me by my first name although I don't know him. We've just been in the same room full of people once or twice.'

I pulled a face, half laughing. 'Oh well – we'll just have to see.'

'Yes, we'll see,' he chuckled and walked off into the night.

Friday 28 February

I've let nearly a week go by without keeping this journal up to date. I will try to remember as much as I can. On Tuesday I had another brief conversation with Sue Davy about the changes, this time asking her about Bill. She said that when the news of the appointment of the new editors came through Bill had been much cast down, but he recovered quickly and he seemed brighter now.

Several people have talked to me about Bill. Stephen Glover said that he found it in himself to feel sorry for him because his end was ignominious. Instead of a graceful retirement at the end of a long career, he just got the bullet.

I too felt sorry for Bill for the same sort of reason, but I also felt that Bill's peculiar character was well suited to dealing with setbacks. He would discover a way of presenting the circumstances of his departure that reflected some sort of glory on himself. Facts don't really bother Bill too much. He is an actor and a fantasist and he always casts himself in the leading role. His favourite part is the flannelled fool, the Bertie Wooster sidekick; but in this episode he'll play a different role – probably the grizzled veteran who has seen it all before, who stayed loyal and true, and stood his ground until the new order swept him aside. Perhaps he'll comfort himself with the thought that the day will come when his editorship will be looked back upon with yearning by the people who leave him behind now. I'm one. I have never suffered particularly at the hands of Bill's fatal unwillingness to make up his mind about anything, or his desperate need to avoid confrontation at all costs. He could not possibly have been more pleasant to work for, invariably amiable and tactful and flattering; but I have watched with a strange remote sort of gloom as the paper has wallowed and yawed and eventually driven herself on the rocks while Bill has grinned and joked and lingered at his desk.

John Thompson came to return a book to me on Wednesday evening and I told him I was sorry he was leaving. I have always liked him and found him enormously helpful. His political views have influenced me and he is one of the few people with whom I can discuss possible cartoons and find my ideas clarifying instead of clogging up.

He said he was glad to go and that he'd had enough. He'd offered to retire a year ago. He didn't feel sorry for Bill; not out of lack of sympathy, but he believed Bill too must feel it's time to quit.

I spoke to him about my own anxieties and hinted broadly that I was thinking about leaving. His attitude was what I knew it would be. He quietly and reasonably argued against doing anything precipitate. He said the future on the *Telegraph* could be very exciting. But I didn't want advice. I was telling him what I was telling him because I want him to let someone know that I may go. I want someone from the establishment to come to me and say please stay. I really want to be offered more money and be flattered and be made to feel part of it all. That's why I have not hidden my interest in the *Independent*. I feel humiliated by this need for reassurance. I like to feel that I'm tough and confident, but the smooth young men in suits with their bland expressions and clipboards who are moving through the *Telegraph* depress me. I don't feel part of it, and even worse I don't want to be. I think they look self-important and phoney.

At lunch with Stephen and one or two others yesterday I heard an interesting story.

When Alexander Chancellor heard that Perry had got the editorship

47

of the *Sunday Telegraph* he got into contact with the *Independent*. They let him know they wanted him to join them and he expressed some interest – or at least left that door open. Perry then begged him to become deputy editor of the *Sunday* with such feeling that it decided Alexander. He agreed to stay but first he went to see Andrew Knight. He said he wanted an extra £15,000 per year and a car.

'Done!' said Knight.

Alexander later telephoned Andreas and said he was staying on the *Sunday Telegraph* but also that, should his position prove less agreeable than he hoped, he'd get in touch again round about April to reopen negotiations.

'April?' I marvelled incredulously.

'That's what he said, apparently.'

We laughed at the amazingly short time Alexander felt he needed to make up his mind.

Stephen also reported that everything was proceeding smoothly at the *Independent*. He showed me the prospectus, which is very badly designed. It looks dull. I can't help feeling this is a bad sign. They got their original designer to do it, and it's not good. They have also let him design a second dummy which Stephen says is about 30 per cent better than the last, which means it's still absolutely terrible.

'He's on his way out,' he said.

'What's keeping him?'

Just as I was leaving my office on Wednesday evening Morrison looked in and said would I come and see him for a moment. I thought he had some extra work for me but it turned out that he wanted to know whether I'd heard anything. He was clearly very anxious about his future. He's got two weeks' leave coming but he's cancelled it and is taking a long weekend instead. Poor bastard.

I had nothing to tell him. In fact he told me one or two things. For instance, that it is rumoured that Lord Hartwell took no part in the choice of Max Hastings and opposed him when he was told. I wonder if that's true. Probably.

Last night when I took my cartoon in to Bill he was sitting at his typewriter doing a leader. He looked at my cartoon and as usual in his friendly way he smiled and said something nice about it.

I said, 'Bill, I'm very sorry you are leaving. I'm sure you go with mixed feelings, but for me it's sad.'

He swung round in his chair and fell at once into a chatty mode. He said it was very nice of me to say that but he at once put distance between himself and recent events and began talking about the need for change and expressed confidence in the new order. He said people would react with relief at the speed things had happened. 'You know, a few months ago it was really quite likely we wouldn't survive at all.'

I cut across what he was saying. 'I'm sure there is truth in all that,' I said, 'but that's not what I'm talking about. I have very much enjoyed working with you. This has been a happy time for me and I'm awfully sorry that it's coming to an end.'

MARCH

14 March, *Daily Telegraph*

Monday 3 March

When by nine o'clock this morning Charles had not telephoned I assumed that he did not want me to do a cover drawing for the *Spectator* and I started to do a lino-cut for myself.

At 10.00 he rang to say he did want one. It turned out I'd have to go and do it at my office. By about 2.30 I was about half way through and was just painting in a bit of green when someone came into my room saying, 'Aha! Just the man I want to see!'

'Hang on,' I said, 'I must just finish this.' I glanced round and there was Max Hastings.

'I won't be a sec,' I said. 'I have to finish the wash or I'll leave an ugly mark across it.'

'That's OK.'

When I looked up he was sitting on a high stool grinning at me. We shook hands and I congratulated him on his new job. He thanked me and made some remark about it being an enormous undertaking but that he thought it was possible. He laughed and said, 'We'd better make it work or we'll all be taking a long walk.'

In one hand he held a cigar and in the other a writing pad. His manner was extremely friendly, almost conspiratorial. It was as if he were engaged in a huge game or joke and was inviting me to join in. At least, it was half like that. It was also like an officer going round the barracks meeting the men for a friendly chat.

He told me that he'd brought someone called Don Berry from the *Sunday Times* who was going to be Number 3. His title was going to be Assistant Editor, Features. I asked who was Number 2. He said Number 2 was Andrew Hutchinson and he was going to be called Deputy Editor. Anyway, Berry was a superb layout man and was going to be in charge of the 'New Look'. This would involve me because a special slot was being invented for the cartoon opposite the revamped leader page. He said he thought I was wasted on Page 2 where I usually appear. We discussed this arrangement for a while. I don't think I have any objection. In fact it is probably to my advantage to have a special place rather than be dodged about the paper. I hope it doesn't mean I can never change the 4-column format. When I asked Max he said he'd send Berry to talk to me about it.

He added, 'He's very nice. No one could quarrel with him. I hope if I ruffle anyone's feelings he'll go and calm them down.'

'You've been reading your own profiles,' I said, referring to recent articles in the *Observer* and *Spectator* in which his abrasive character had been described.

He laughed loudly and said, 'I've never heard of anyone quarrelling with Don.'

I was curious to know whether he'd appointed, or fired, anyone else.

Max said there would be others coming in and some would have to go, but he couldn't tell me about them because the changes had not been finally decided yet. He praised Andrew Knight, saying that although the economic situation was catastrophic, each time Max asked for money for some new person or plan Andrew had instantly agreed. Knight's attitude seems to be to give Max absolute freedom – at least for the time being.

Max said that he would have preferred to spend a month 'doing nothing' while he learnt the ropes but Andrew had insisted there was no time to lose. Whether this is because our rivals are leaving us behind and we've got to improve the product at once, or whether it's a question of ramming through what changes can be thought of before the money runs out and there's a general freeze, I don't know, but Max referred several times to the ghastly cash problem and more than once said, 'I think we can make it', in a way that made me think the total collapse of the *Telegraph* empire was imminent.

'I'd rather have my job than Perry's,' he said with feeling.

'Perry's job is different, I suppose,' I replied. I meant that Perry's task was to hold the fort rather than go on the offensive, which was Max's mission, but Max just grunted. I didn't feel I should draw him into a conversation of that kind. I had a strong impression that I was only one of many such calls he had to make.

In spite of the fact he was rushed off his feet he did discourse a bit on the shambles he is now in charge of. He seemed genuinely amazed at the cackhanded way the features are organised. I asked whether he was going to continue the leader writers' conference and he said yes, and he was going to call a morning conference as well for news and features staff. I said I had been surprised when Matthew and Stephen left that they had not been replaced because the leaders writers' conference needed more and better people.

'Absolutely,' said Max, and shrugged as if to say 'The place is a mess – no one's been doing anything about anything.'

After twenty minutes or so he stood up.

'Do you know the *Telegraph* – from before, I mean?' I asked. Suddenly it seemed such an extraordinary and loony institution.

'Not a bit,' he said with a grin, again giving me the impression it was all a bit of a jape. 'People keep stopping me in corridors. You know, putting out skinny hands.' He gestured like an ancient mariner. 'They drag me into corners and tell me the strangest things.'

The impossibility of 'understanding' the *Telegraph* amused me. It must be like trying to understand the Church of England from scratch.

Before he went he said, 'Look, is there anything you want to tell me or anything that's a problem for you? If there is, please feel absolutely free to say.'

I understood him to mean straightforward work problems left over from the old regime rather than wanting vast sums of money. I also thought that he could not give my career too much thought right then and there. Anyway, I was not prepared for such a discussion and had to think of finishing my cover drawing so I just said, 'No, there's nothing I need to say at the moment. I had a good and happy arrangement with the old regime, and have no retrospective complaints. The new order is unknown to me . . .'

'OK, fine,' he said. 'I must be off. Nice to see you, and look, as I said to Peter Simple, just go on doing exactly what you have been doing – and – er . . . well, you know . . .'

I called 'Good luck' after him. He called back 'Thanks'.

I liked him very much. He could not possibly have been more amiable. He seemed quite frank. I liked his grinning manner and odd mixture of playfulness and seriousness and he gave off an unaffected air of enthusiasm and energy that was attractive.

I couldn't say he did or said anything that irritated me or even jarred. As Charles Moore had said, he's a nice chap.

Tuesday 4 March

I met Tony Howard at the Gay Hussar for lunch. He asked me at once about the *Telegraph* and reactions to Max H's appointment. I said that there were two things I was bursting to talk about and that was the second, but first I must hear about his own reactions to lunching with Andreas a couple of weeks ago.

Tony's description of the lunch was disturbing. He said it had all gone off all right but in the middle of it something peculiar had occurred. Andreas and he had been talking about the *Independent* in a friendly sort of way although Tony had been surprised now and then by things Andreas didn't know about newspaper production and design, and even more surprised by well known newspaper names of whom he had never heard. Then, all of a sudden, he had begun to attack Tony, accusing him of being a wet blanket and of expressing doubts about the success of the *Independent*.

Tony protested that he was not being pessimistic or cautious for any other reason than that he felt the hurdle Andreas was setting himself at was very high. He had simply given his opinion that the theory of expanding the market by introducing a new product was unconvincing and that pinching 100,000 to 150,000 readers from the *Telegraph* was also a bit much to hope for.

Andreas abruptly became maudlin. Tony mimicked him: 'I expect you are right – I'll probably be a sub on some boring little newspaper in a year's time – I'm finished – I've mortaged my house – oh dear! oh dear!'

I was surprised by this account, but Tony assured me he wasn't exaggerating.

We talked as well about the damp squib effect produced by Eddy Shah's *Today* hitting the streets – or rather, failing to hit the streets. Distribution had been dreadful; I had been unable to buy a copy. 'Anyway,' Tony said, 'the thing is no good. They've got a column by Derek Jameson, for God's sake. The colour is all pale and pastelly. There's better colour on the front of the *Mail*.'

Tony went as far as to say that if the first issue is anything to go by Shah may even fail to keep the thing going. This also will have a bad effect on potential investors in the *Independent* – the logic being that if they see Shah steaming away with a lively attractive paper, City chaps will think, 'I'd like a piece of something like that.' On the other hand, if they see a flop they begin to hum and haw.

I began to tell Tony about Max and the *Telegraph*. It's very difficult to tell Tony gossip because he's always heard it already and usually knows the next chapter too. I gave him my version of A. Chancellor's flirtation with the *Independent* and his big raise from Andrew Knight. Tony said it wasn't quite like that and gave a slightly altered story that he'd got, I think, from Perry.

When I told Tony how impressed I'd been with Max he listened carefully, and at last he said, 'Well, you've made my job easier than I thought it would be. You're obviously moving away from involvement with Andreas. What I came here to say to you is you'd be out of your mind to join the *Independent*.'

'You'd put it that strongly?'

'Yes.'

I turned my attention to what I could get out of Max in the way of a raise for myself on the strength of the offer from the *Independent*. Tony asked what I got at the moment and thought I was seriously underpaid and should certainly be able to get more.

'What if they just tell me to push off?'

'They won't. That's not in Max's character. And I told Perry you were a bit unsatisfied and restless. I told him to massage you a bit and he said, "It is essential to keep him." '

Tony's advice was to go to Max and be quite frank. 'Say you've had this offer, you don't want to accept it but it's so generous you must consider it seriously. It's very important that you let him know this is nothing to do with his arrival on the paper, that it all began months ago. I think he'll come to terms. Don't say the *Independent*'s offer is impossible to turn down because if in the end you do they'll think, "Aha, we'll never have any trouble from him again", and they'll never give you a raise.'

'There's something daft about an offer from a paper that doesn't actually exist yet. The *Independent* may not even get the money to start.'

'Mm, that is a problem. But you can't wait. I think you should see Max this week. Once he's there and you've accepted things as they are it will be much harder to shift him.'

'Can I say I've also had an offer from the *Observer*?'

'Yes,' he said. 'In fact I think you should.'

I was beginning to feel nervous. 'I told Max yesterday that I was quite happy with my job at the *Telegraph* and had no complaints.'

'That's all right. It would have been quite inappropriate to have said, "I want more money" at the moment he comes in to say hello. Just say that you have this delicate matter to raise with him and that you feel it must be settled now.'

I was grateful to Tony for his advice and found all his stories and gossip helpful. I determined to go straight to find Max and deal with all this.

When I got back to the *Telegraph* Sue Davy told me that Max was on the fourth floor 'seeing people', but that he was calling in on her at 4.30. I said I'd try to catch him then.

She told me that Max had given her the ridiculous task of making her own office 'absolutely 100 per cent secure', because he intends to install some expensive equipment in there. He had issued this instruction one day and the next he'd said to her, 'Remember, I want this place secure by Monday – and if it's not I'm going to blow up.' The way she told me this made it clear that in a thoroughly disagreeable way Max had been threatening her. She pulled a face and I made a sympathetic noise.

At 4.30 I returned to Sue's office and through her window I could look across an open space and into Morrison Halcrow's window twenty-odd yards away. Morrison had his back to me and across his desk I could see Max. They were talking.

'I'd like to listen in to that conversation,' I told Sue.

'Mm,' she said.

'Poor bastard,' I said, meaning Morrison. He could hardly survive now that a new features editor was being brought in. Sue told me he was not getting the bullet but being offered a choice of other positions on the paper.

After a few minutes Max came in. He said 'Hello' and sat in a chair smoking his cigar and studying a notebook.

I said, 'If you've got a minute I'd like a word with you. If not now, some time soon.'

'Fire away,' he said.

'Here – in public?'

'Mm.'

I felt this put me at a considerable disadvantage. It's always difficult to talk about your own value, and almost impossible in front of an audience. As we talked several people, including Bill, came in and out of the office.

As exactly as I could, I did what Tony had suggested, including the bit about it all pre-dating Max's own arrival.

He pulled a face when I told him I'd had an offer and asked at once who from. I told him. I said, 'The offer is so generous that it has altered my attitude to my own value.'

His first response was, 'Do you want to go?'

'No,' I said. 'Although in saying that I think I weaken my position.'

'No, you don't,' he said. 'I believe in the market principle. It's a great relief that you don't want to go and it makes it easier for me.' He went on. 'Look, it's essential that we keep you. Frankly, when I looked through the salaries list when I arrived I thought yours was too low. Give me a few days and we'll work something out. I'm sure we can come to a satisfactory arrangement.'

It was all over very fast. I felt he was being absolutely straight.

'OK,' I said. 'Thanks – let's leave it like that.'

Wednesday 5 March
At midday today I went to an exhibition of Ronald Searle's PoW drawings at the Imperial War Museum. There was much about the exhibition and many of the people I met that was extremely interesting, but it was a short chat with Michael Foot that interested me most. After remarking on Searle's brilliance he said, 'Well – how are things at the *Telegraph*?'

I described the turmoil and what I knew of the proposed changes and how desperately short of time the new management felt. Michael said it was inevitable death to a paper if it tried to change its look and/or content too radically too fast. He mentioned several papers that had tried and consequently come to grief. He was going back a bit, as is his wont – one of the papers he spoke of was the *News Chronicle* – but even so he sounded convincing.

I told him that Max agreed with him but the management said there was no time.

'Rubbish – they are insane. What absolute nonsense.'

'On the other hand,' I said, 'change – and very radical change – does seem to be necessary.'

'Why?'

'Because the paper is losing readers fast.'

'Why?'

'Death, mostly,' I said. 'The readers get older and older and no young ones join.'

'Mm,' said the elderly journalist thoughtfully. 'That's what did for the *Herald*.'

'There is one good argument for doing things fast. If Max Hastings leaves everything as it is for, say, a month, he will find that he has slipped into the old way of doing things. People he could have sacked as strangers would have become colleagues and much more difficult to move. That's what Tony Howard says, anyway.'

Michael listened and asked other questions about the *Telegraph*. He spoke of it with affection and interest and with his very attractive cheerfulness, as if he enjoyed the drama, and the expectation of exciting developments and possibility of disaster, all without any malice – or very little.

Back at the *Telegraph* there was the now familiar air of revolution and anxiety.

John Miller told me that Peter Birkett, the editor of 'Peterborough', had come out of his office and seen Alan Rusbridger, his opposite number on the *Guardian*, passing by.

'Hello,' he said in surprise. 'What are you doing here?'

'I've come for an interview,' said Alan.

'What?' said Peter, staggering aback. 'What's going on?'

'Like I said, I've come for an interview. Must fly, in fact. See you.' Alan headed off towards Bill's office.

Cold with fear, Birkett got back to his desk and began making frantic telephone calls. It turned out Alan *had* come for an interview: he was seeing Bill because he's doing a profile of him.

John also told me that John Keegan had been made defence correspondent, and that David Holloway was going. I'm sad about that. He had heard that Morrison had been offered several jobs, but that he was turning them down.

The best part of the conversation with John Miller was when he spoke about Matthew Symonds. He hates him because he believed Matthew had tried to prevent John getting the job of foreign leader writer and had nearly succeeded.

'He didn't, did he?' I said, feigning amazed shock at Matthew's behaviour. 'Good heavens!' I remember several times talking with Matthew and others about John; the general feeling was that John was OK but no more than that.

'I had to really argue with Bill,' said John. 'He told me my appointment was being reconsidered and I told him – I told him – "You promised it to me." '

Next, Martin Ivens came to my room and we discussed events. He is inclined to see how things develop here before planning to go. He has had offers from Whittam Smith and others. I told him about my position and my recent conversation with Max about money. We both said we feel retrospective anger at being underpaid. He told me that Jock Bruce Gardyne is getting over £30,000 for a couple of leaders a week and a column on the *Sunday*. Good luck to him, but that makes my pay look rotten considering how much more I produce.

I feel what I am paid by the *Daily* is held low because I also get paid by the *Sunday*. My *Sunday* pay is likewise held low because it is considered to be related to my *Daily* pay. Thus both papers get a cheap cartoonist. Furthermore, my *Sunday* pay is marked down as *Daily Telegraph* overtime and does not appear as salary so my pension, calculated as a percentage of my pay, is artificially low. Grrr.

At lunchtime I learned that Michael Hogg had been made letters editor – the Fleet Street equivalent of being put in charge of a Mongolian power station in the Soviet Union.

At the leader writers' conference Bill was working on a letter to *Private Eye*. In this week's edition of the *Eye* there is a silly little story about Bill and John Thompson, the editor of the *Sunday Telegraph*, not being told soon enough about their dismissal. Bill told Nigel and me, the only two people at the conference, that Knight had asked him to write saying the story was untrue.

When he'd typed out the letter Bill, giving appreciative chuckles, handed it to me. 'What do you think of that?' he said.

I cannot remember exactly what he'd written but it went something like this: 'I don't mind being misrepresented in your feature "Dear Bill" but I draw the line at your story in the current issue saying that announcement of my departure was made public before I was told. It wasn't. I should know.'

I said, 'It's too long. Leave out the bit about "Dear Bill". Just say, "In your last issue you state that I was not told about the change in editorship until after the news was made public. Shome mishtake, surely." '

Bill laughed, and quickly typed it out again with Nigel and me dictating it to him. Then someone was called to take the copy to Knight. Within a few seconds they came back saying, 'Andrew thinks this is not a strong enough denial. He has added, "This is not true. I should know" at the end.'

I said, 'Why is he taking this so seriously? It's nonsense. No one ever believes anything in *Private Eye* and no one ever believes denials either. It's all nonsense.'

Bill said, 'They (meaning Knight and co.) are very sensitive.'

Nigel said, 'He's spoilt the rhythm of the joke. The letter must end with "Shome mishtake, surely." '

Bill suddenly cried. 'All right! I've got it.' He switched the end round so that Nigel's proposal was used. The letter was now a few words longer but still OK.

'They're losing a first-class editor,' he said as he marked up the page.

I was puzzled that Knight should make such a fuss about such a trivial matter.

Thursday 6 March

I wanted to give Bill a drawing as a going-away present. I've done caricatures of leader writer conferences for Maurice Green, Colin Welch and Peter Utley in the past, but for some reason or other I found it very hard to do the same for Bill. It was partly that there are scarcely any leader writers left and to leave out Matthew and Stephen seemed in some way to draw attention to them. And characters such as Colin, Michael Hilton, Charles Moore and Ray Steed have all left too long ago. In the end I chose a drawing of Bill taking a conference that I did from life a few months ago.

I took it to show Sue Davy to ask her whether she thought Bill would like it. The drawing shows Bill chewing the end of his specs, with a cigarette in his other hand. 'I know that mood so well,' she said. 'He's just thought of something.'

Then she said, 'About this time of day (3.30) I get a bit weepy.'

'At the thought of Bill going, do you mean?'

'Yes,' she replied, turning down the corners of her mouth. 'A bit weepy.'

I gather there is anxiety in the new management about Lord Hartwell going to Bill's farewell drinks tomorrow. It is rumoured that he may express his pain at recent events, or possibly his disapproval.

In the evening, when I took my cartoon to Bill, I also took him the drawing crudely mounted and a letter in which I thanked him and expressed my regrets that he was leaving.

Perry and Jock were there, all three of them drinking whisky and looking a bit like naughty schoolboys having a jape. I congratulated Perry on his new job and he waved my words aside. 'Oh, no – too kind, dear boy . . .'

Bill okayed my cartoon and then I gave him the envelope with the drawing. 'This is a prezzo,' I said.

He took it, protesting and thanking me. As he opened it I felt it was not quite the right drawing. I should have chosen something more light-hearted.

He didn't read the letter but made suitable and appreciative remarks about the drawing. The others glanced at it too.

'This is going home with me tonight,' said Bill. I said, 'So long,' and he blew me a kiss. 'My dear boy . . .' he said.

Friday 7 March

Today was an important day. This was the actual end of the old regime. Both Bill and John T had their farewell drinks, speeches and gifts. It was like the end of term at school.

Before I left to go to work I spoke to Charles Moore about next week's *Spectator* cover and naturally we gossiped about the *Telegraph*. I told him all the rumours I'd heard. Talking to him I realised how radically my attitude to the *Telegraph* has changed in the last two weeks. Where I was bored, irritated, fed up and depressed I am now, suddenly, interested, even excited, amused and curious. This means that my interest in the *Independent* is proportionally diminished. The *Telegraph* appears to be in the hands of decisive professionals and the *Independent* is still a vague dream of unbelievable wealth for Matthew, Stephen and Andreas. If I think only of the designer Andreas is still proceeding with, my heart sinks.

Tony Howard once told the board of the *New Statesman* as they debated his successor that they should go for 'excellence'. He meant that James Fenton and Neil Ascherson were both excellent men. Both had great achievements in various fields to their credit, but neither of them was the most obvious contender for editor as far as their experience or political views went. The *New Statesman* chose Page, and simply collapsed. If I apply Tony's rule to the man at the *Telegraph* and at the *Independent*, it's no contest.

James Fenton returned from four weeks in the Philippines a couple of days ago and at once asked me about the *Independent* and Fleet Street news generally. I found myself slagging off the *Independent* dreadfully. Everything I had to say was critical and expressed my growing doubts. I told him I was aware that I was sounding more pessimistic than I really felt, and he kind of grunted. All the changes at *The Times* during his absence have deepened his depression about it, and the *Independent* had therefore assumed a great importance in his plans for the future. He complained bitterly about the philistinism at *The Times*. I was sorry to be the bearer of gloomy news.

He told me that Tim Garton Ash had been contacted by someone from the *Independent* and that when Tim asked, 'Who have you got joining you?' the reply was 'James Fenton'. James paused and I said, 'Oh dear! That's not good.'

'That's no good at *all*,' he added with considerable emphasis.

I went into the *Telegraph* at about midday. The weather has suddenly become quite mild and gentle after weeks of freezing easterly winds and bitter frosts. I had thought that the basement room at the Cheshire Cheese, where Bill's farewells were being held, would be full early, so I went at quarter to one, fifteen minutes before the scheduled start. The drinks were laid out and the sandwiches and pies, but only John Sparks and Keith Heron were in the large chilly room. Both were drinking pints of beer.

A few minutes later Peter Utley arrived with Sarah Compton Burnett who was carrying the presents Bill was to be given. I chatted with Peter who told me that as far as he could gather the new editor wished him to continue writing his column and leaders but had relieved him of other duties. This suited Peter perfectly. I was not sure, and neither did Peter seem to be, whether he would continue to sit in the editor's chair at weekends.

Gradually the room filled up. Bill came in. He was slightly flushed and excited. He talked in staccato sentences, and stood in his eccentric way sticking his tummy well forward and tucking his chin into his chest.

Many people came up to him. Some he stuck his tummy out at and smiled, some he clasped around the shoulder. By the time the room was full Lord Hartwell came in and Sarah showed him which boxes contained which presents for the presentation. He looked overweight, his features puffy and rounded with fat. He stood like a prisoner in the dock, his arms limp at his sides.

The atmosphere in the room was peculiar. I felt that no one quite knew whether this was an occasion to express loyalty to the old order and disrespect for the new or whether it was a kind of carnival time when, as we were all likely to go down the plughole, we might as well go laughing and drunk. There was an uncertain tension in the air.

Peter spoke first. Someone banged an ash tray on a table and quiet fell. I was standing beside him and could look over his shoulder at the faces of my colleagues. Peter's job was to introduce Lord Hartwell and he did it beautifully. He described Bill taking a leader writers' conference. It wasn't exactly true to life in a documentary way, but it delicately conveyed exactly the quality of Bill's casual and deceptive style of editing. Peter had people laughing good-naturedly at his sketch of Bill; it was brilliant and set the tone for what followed. From that moment the atmosphere of the occasion settled down. It was instantly clear we were just to say goodbye to Bill, and whatever his drawbacks we liked him and wished him well.

When Lord Hartwell came to speak it was as if he coasted in on the wave of warm feeling that Peter had started. Hartwell's mode of speaking is extraordinary. He is a big man and he addressed his employees in a monotonous whisper. It was so softly spoken that his words were often hard to catch; but his very reserve gave strength to the meaning of his speech.

He spoke warmly of Bill, calling him a great editor. He said this was a most unusual farewell and marked more than the end of an editorship. He spoke hopefully of the future. Several times his dry humour had us laughing. It was impossible not to feel part of a family or gang. I felt more than ever that I was part of the *Telegraph* and that it was the strangest institution I'd ever joined. It has always been a home for eccentrics and oddballs and it is itself therefore an eccentric organisation. It's why everyone likes it, I suppose; no one hates the *Telegraph*.

When it came to presenting Bill with his gifts, to everyone's surprise Lord Hartwell began opening them. The beautiful shiny purple wrapping paper was ripped aside and the first box opened. Each layer of tissue paper that fell to the floor produced a delighted laugh from the staff as it revealed more tissue underneath. 'It's like Russian dolls,' said someone. A manic smile played across Lord Hartwell's face. He looked like Tommy Cooper attempting an impossible trick. At last with shaking hands he uncovered a gold travelling clock. He said, 'The thing is, it sort of comes apart.' He began to unscrew it while Bill mumbled, 'Good heavens, wonderful, I say.'

The clock was so made that it could be used either as a fob watch or a travelling clock. Lord Hartwell struggled clumsily with it but then said, 'Someone will show you later.' While Bill tried to react graciously to the first gift Lord H was already turning to the second. This time the whole room was keyed up for the comedy of the layers of wrapping paper but the added excitement of knowing that the parcel turning over and over in the old man's hands held a fragile glass decanter with a crystal and silver base. The regular gasps of laughter turned into rhythmic roars as paper and plastic, ribbon and cardboard were flung in all directions. When the decanter at last emerged the tension was awful. Shakily Bill and Lord H handed the delicate and beautiful thing to and fro, Bill actually muttering that he was damned if he was brave enough to hold it.

The act was pure farce and quite brilliant. It produced a mood of light-hearted wildness. Then Bill stepped forward to reply and a new and expectant silence fell.

He paid generous tributes to several of his colleagues, including Peter and Morrison. He spoke very warmly about Lord H now standing in his stuffed dummy pose staring at the floor, mentioned Max and said he'd return to say a few words about him later (which he never did). He said that there was something he was going to tell us that even Conrad Black didn't know, that although he'd been helped by various fellow journalists the paper had in fact been edited for the last few years by Sue Davy. I saw her smiling with pleasure at his compliment, and the assembled journalists laughed and murmured 'Hear, hear.'

Touching lightly on his own long career on the *Telegraph* and frequently referring to the fact that he'd made no notes and was speaking unrehearsed, Bill moved towards his peroration. He spoke of the difficult times the paper was going through and then admitted that he had in fact jotted down something he wanted to say. He drew a piece of paper from his pocket and unfolded it.

'It was written by a great journalist,' he said. 'Charles Dickens. And it comes from *A Tale of Two Cities*.' He glanced down at his paper, paused, and said, 'It comes towards the end of the novel, a novel of which I'm particularly fond, and the words are spoken by Sidney Carton.' A ripple of laughter swept through the room. He can't be going to say, 'It's a far, far better thing . . .'? Bill looked up in mock surprise and milked the moment for all the pleasure he could. Then, timing his words perfectly, he read, ' "I see a beautiful city and a brilliant people rising." ' He interrupted himself to say, 'I'm talking about Fleet Street.' Then he said again, ' "I see a beautiful city and a brilliant people rising from the abyss . . . in their struggles to be truly free, in their triumphs and defeats, through long years to come . . ." '

It was an odd quote to use. I'm not sure whether he meant he and the old guard were an 'abyss'. I think he intended to strike a blow for the future of the newspaper that had dismissed him somewhat peremptorily – you never really knew with Bill. I looked at Edward Steen, to see if it was harder for him to leave the *Telegraph* now after Bill's appeal. I've heard that he's claimed by the *Independent*, but his face was inscrutable.

Bill's final words were, 'I wish you all well, and want you to know my heart will always be with you.' He stopped speaking and, turning away, put the paper back in his pocket.

'That's it,' he said.

Prolonged and warm applause broke out and swept over him. When it eventually died away, the silence was at once filled with a lively roar of talk and clink of glasses.

Bill examined his presents again and Sarah showed him how the clock came apart. A moment later McManus came up and showed him a second time. Bill registered exactly the same incredulous delight and surprise to both of them. 'I say – that's really something . . .'

I didn't stay long but did talk for a moment with David Holloway the *Telegraph's* literary editor. One of the rumours I'd heard was that he is leaving. He told me he'd been asked to stay on. 'Touch wood,' he said grinning.

I found myself standing next to Andrew Knight at one point and said, 'Hello, I'm Nick Garland.'

He said, 'I know who you are.'

'We met briefly in Bill's room – I thought you might have forgotten. There were so many people . . .'

'We met many years ago,' he said looking at me with his cool, disconcerting smile.

'Oh God, really?' I said, braced to hear of some awful *faux pas* from the past.

'Twenty-five years ago I was married to someone called Victoria Brittan.' This was a relief – I'd only met Miss Brittan once or twice in my life. 'And we met in the City office with her. I was hanging about on the fringes.'

'That's very clever of you to remember,' I mumbled. 'I'm afraid I . . . er . . .'

'It was long before you achieved your present eminence,' he said with more than a touch of irony.

I didn't know what to make of this exchange except that it left me feeling obscurely uneasy.

Round about 4.30 a girl came into my room and said that she had come from Don Berry who would like to see me some time. I said what about now, and she took me to his office.

We shook hands and he said, 'Well, my job is to . . . er . . . well, several things – but mainly . . . um . . . I'm here – I'm not sure why I'm here, sometimes.'

'I do,' I said. 'Max told me.'

'Really?' he said. 'Can *you* tell me why I'm here?'

'You're here because you are enormously charming and when Max upsets people you can make them feel better again.' He laughed.

'And you are going to redesign the whole paper and you are a features supremo.'

'Yeah. That's the sort of thing,' he said.

We began to talk about the centre pages and where on them my cartoon could find the best permanent home. He was extremely charming just as everyone said, but what was really impressive about him was the way he talked about newspaper layout. I have never heard anything like it. He talked about the different uses of a page given over to comment and one used for news stories. He praised parts of the existing *Telegraph* layout and pointed out 'frayed' and messy bits. I asked him whether, if I had a permanent slot, that meant all my cartoons had to be the same shape. He said, not at all, it would simply mean he'd have to redesign the page.

'I like designing pages,' he said, and picking up a pad sketched in his proposed layout with a four-column, shallow cartoon then changed it to suit a three-column, deeper cartoon. It was a pleasure to watch him work.

'What if I fail to do a cartoon or it is turned down or I'm away?'

'Then we can always use a photograph or possibly an American syndicated cartoon or' – once again he began changing the layout – 'we could move this up here . . .'

His manner was direct and good-natured and he really did seem to like solving the problems he'd set himself. I liked him very much.

At 5.30 I went to John Thompson's farewell do. It was very different from Bill's. This time there was no uncertainty about the occasion. John is well enough liked but he wanted to go, and I don't think anyone felt awkward about saying goodbye. And he is handing over to Perry who is well known and liked by everyone.

John's own reserved and formal personality had an effect on the whole proceedings. Perry spoke well and introduced Lord Hartwell who once again went through his routine with various presents, this time holding them up as well for everyone to look at, like an auctioneer's assistant. He was kind about John but there was not much feeling as the ritual was gone through. John spoke too, without really saying much.

Once again, I found myself standing next to Andrew Knight. When the speeches were over I said to him, 'Phew! Quite a day.'

'Mm,' he said. 'Especially when you feel responsible for it all.'

'Do you fell responsible for it all?' I asked. I was surprised because I would have thought Conrad Black or possibly Lord Hartwell were the only ones who could claim responsibility for the day's events.

'Yes, I suppose I do,' he said.

Saturday 8 March
This morning I read the appreciation of Bill that Charles Moore had written for the *Telegraph*. Some years ago Charles said to me, 'I'd love to write a profile of Bill, but no one could write it honestly without being too critical.'

In that sense the article was not honest. It didn't tell lies; it simply didn't tell the truth. It said Bill was a first-rate, spiffing chap through and through. It noted affectionately some of his little eccentricities but avoided all criticism or suggestion of imperfection. Of course it could hardly have done otherwise, but all the same I felt disappointed. Charles would like to think of himself as unsentimental and that's what one should be even though one is forced at times to sound harsh. But he has written a kind of whitewash.

Monday 10 March
I spoke to Charles this morning and chided him about the piece on Bill. He agreed that the piece was all half truths and actually misleading, but said it was impossible to write it any other way.

I asked how Bill had been on Friday evening.

'Oh, he was fine – his usual self. Kept telling me things in the strictest confidence. You know: thish one musht go no further, old boy. Then he tells you something of absolutely no importance at all. He did tell

66

me one quite funny thing – shrictesh secreshy, thish one. Sue Davy has decided not to say "Editor's office" when she answers the phone. Now that Max has taken over, she's going to say, "Hello – Bomber Command".'

Max gave a pep talk to the assembled staff today. I missed most of it and couldn't hear very much when I did get there because I was too far back. The gist was that times were hard and everyone's task difficult. He expected to make mistakes and begged everyone's patience while he and others sorted things out.

He also announced that he's appointed Marc to do a daily front page pocket cartoon. This is excellent news.

At the leader writers' conference I thought Max was nervous. He was not able to start any discussion going; the conference proceeded with short bursts of question and answer. Everyone made allowances and we got through it OK.

It was a thin day and Max puffed on his cigar. Rod Junor turned up and introduced himself. Max said, 'Oh, hello, Rod.' I was surprised to realise this was the first time they'd met. Rod unwrapped and lit a cigar of much the same size as Max's. I've almost never seen Rod smoking at a conference before. Can he have been feeling nervous?

The first thing I noticed in the editor's office was that he had caused pictures to be put on the walls. A portrait of a lady on a sofa, his wife I imagine. Not a good painting. Also one or two small drawings, one by E. H. Shepherd of First World War soldiers. It is from *Punch*, I would guess; there is a caption about the troops having stopped firing because they've run out of ammo and their sergeant is saying, 'All right then, cease fire!' The worst picture is a truly horrible painting, presumably of the Falklands, of some warships sailing about on an awful white, yellow and black sea.

In the evening, Max gave drinks to leader writers and heads of departments. When I passed by the room, Sue said to me, 'Hey! You're supposed to be in there. If you look behind that ghastly Falklands picture you'll find a glass.'

The painting is hanging on a door to a hidden cupboard. She put an enormous amount of feeling into the remark.

Max has shifted the leader writers' conference to the morning, 12.15 instead of 3.45. It means I won't even see leader writers any more. It's rather a pity. I see few enough people as it is. Cartoonists can be rather isolated.

Wednesday 12 March
Stephen rang, ostensibly to ask what I thought of Tom Sutcliffe of *Kaleidoscope* at the BBC because James F had suggested him as a possible arts editor.

I felt Stephen really just wanted to keep in touch because he asked how I was getting on with Max and sounded his usual mildly anxious self. I tried to hedge but could not hide the fact that Max seemed to be doing OK and the atmosphere at the old place was quite different from anything he had known. He'd heard that the leader conference was now held in the morning and I wondered who had told him. He said James Fenton was coming to see them on Friday and added, 'Perhaps the *Independent* could take you to lunch soon?'

'That'd be lovely.'

'OK. I'll fix it – and bring along a contract,' he said.

Thursday 13 March
I asked Charles who was keeping Stephen informed about the *Daily Telegraph* and he said, 'Peter [Utley] probably.'

'Are they trying to get him?'

'Yes.'

He didn't know what post they had in mind.

I saw Bernard Foyster at the picture desk talking intently to one of his colleagues. I wandered in to glance through the day's pictures and Bernard said, 'It's long knives day – have you heard?' He told me that sackings had been going on all day. He'd lost one photographer, a man in his middle fifties. He was called in and told his services were no longer required and that if he went to a certain office he'd be told what his redundancy pay would be. In his case it was a year's salary. plus a pension of £50 per week which would be (I think) £90 if he waited until he was 65.

The woman's page editor has been made travel editor. The fashion editor has gone.

When I took my cartoon to show Max he wasn't in his room so I talked to Sue Davy.

'Cheer me up,' she said.

'What's the matter?'

'Oh, I don't know . . .'

'This is the time of the day you told me you miss Bill.'

She smiled. 'Yes,' she said and acted feeling nostalgic.

A moment later Max came bustling in, as usual in shirt sleeves and carrying a cigar and notepad.

'Hi, Nick – have you come about your affairs or with a cartoon?' he said, brightening as he saw I was carrying a drawing.

He passed it with a flattering and warm remark.

'Thanks,' I said. 'How are you doing?'

He relaxed for a moment and looked quite troubled.

'Well – it's been a rough day. I've been sacking people.' He paused for a moment and looking straight at me he said, 'I've never sacked anyone before in my life. It's awful.'

'Mm,' I said.

Almost as if to convince himself he went on. 'Everyone agrees it's got to be done. They've all known it had to happen.'

'Yeah.'

'It'll be over soon. I'm sure it's right to get it all over.'

I've been reminded time and again during the last few weeks of accounts I've read of revolutions and purges and the falls of governments and collapse of empires. In microcosm the *Telegraph* has been like that. Bemedalled generals hanging on aimlessly, not yet realising their power has gone. The palace rooms invaded and redecorated. The summary executions. The quick switching of allegiances. The genuine sorrow at the passing of an order loved for all its faults, and the equally genuine excitement at the arrival of something new. There are even little knots of strange men wearing suits, in earnest conversation at the corners of corridors, like the guards of the new authority, glimpsed passing through the city going about their secret and momentous business.

Max clearly found this part of his job very unpleasant. I've no idea what Andrew Knight, the *éminence noir*, feels but he looks cool and aloof. I guess he is a real party man and a very tough apparatchik. He seems to say it has to be done, and done now. It's pointless grizzling about it.

Max told me my memo about more pay had gone to management and they are agreed something must be done for me. Max hopes the *Sunday Telegraph* will cough up the main bulk of the raise. I'm not sure that's entirely in my interest. What if they then close the *Sunday Telegraph* . . . ?

Willie Shawcross rang this evening to ask whether I thought he should accept an offer from the *Spectator*. I said, 'Yes – leap at it.'

We gossiped about Fleet Street for a while. He said things are nearly collapsing at the *Sunday Times*. The NUJ chapel are on the point of passing a resolution that 'This chapel has entirely lost confidence in the editor.' Murdoch is trying to stop them. Willie thought Neil may be fired.

Friday 14 March

Rod Junor got the bullet today. No one is in the least surprised. He's been a bit of a joke around the *Telegraph* for years but even so all the people I spoke to had words of sympathy for him though it is rumoured that he got a fairly hefty golden handshake. I thought to myself how much I'd hate to be in his position. Perhaps his dad will find him a job but it won't be easy. I said to someone, 'What will he do on Monday?' and they replied, 'Same as he always does – bugger-all!'

Perry told me he hoped the management would find me some more money and that they can persuade me to stay. If they knew how nervous I am at the prospect of going they'd be very relieved. I feel I have lost most of my confidence in the *Independent* and the idea of working for both the *Independent* and the *Observer* appals me. In fact I don't think I could.

Saturday 15 and Sunday 16 March
Over the last two days I've been having a long and frequently interrupted telephone conversation with James.

On Friday he had a meeting with Stephen, Matthew and Andreas. The last time we'd spoken I'd said that I was worried about whether these three could create and edit an interesting newspaper. How one makes up one's mind about such a matter is difficult to say; in the end it's a matter of faith. But nothing any of them has said has ever made me have much confidence in them as editors, however charming or intelligent or ambitious they are.

However, James said very firmly that after talking with Andreas on Friday he felt he was certainly capable of producing a good paper. He had come away convinced that he'd like to join the *Independent*, and impressed by Matthew as well.

The main problem for James is making up his mind what he wants to do and therefore what sort of a job he wants them to offer him. 'I've got the wanderlusts again,' he said mournfully. 'I want to go straight back to the Philippines but I don't know whether I want to go back just to avoid cleaning up the mess in the sitting-room left by the thieves.' (He was burgled while he was away.)

I spoke to him like a Dutch uncle. 'You must complete the work on your first trip before you contemplate a second. You are addicted to travel, but you mustn't let it separate you from your country, your home and your friends. You must beware of the Gavin Young syndrome.'

'Mm, I know.'

Gavin Young, sometime foreign correspondent for the *Observer*, had often discussed the problem of spending long periods abroad. James had once put it like this: 'When you have been away for a long time and you come back, some part of you makes the absurd assumption that all your friends' lives have remained suspended in your absence. You say to them, "Well, what's been happening?" as if they could tell you. But their children are a whole year older, huge changes have occurred, friends have changed jobs, wives, homes – there is too much to tell. The traveller has to find a way of easing himself back into circulation and not resent the gap that has opened up and isolated him from his own background. It's like astronauts coming back from space – if they come in too steep they burn up and if they come in too shallow they bounce off the atmosphere and disappear into space. A traveller's return must be timed and angled with great care.'

I told him, 'You must remember what you went to the Philippines for and write the piece you undertook to do. Just as on a newspaper you must always remember what a page was originally intended to contain, and never let it just be a slot. When you've done your piece then you can think of travelling again.'

I told him to consider other papers besides the *Independent*. Even the *Telegraph*.

'The *Telegraph* is not sexy,' he said.

'The *Telegraph* has changed out of all recognition. It looks the same still, but just behind the façade there are new people planning and designing a new paper.'

'I don't think you are going to the *Independent*.'

'Well, before this new lot took over I thought I was going to leave. I realise now how completely fed up I had become. The *Independent* offered a change and more money. Now the *Telegraph* seems to offer the same – but they also offer more security and some continuity.'

'I don't think you're going to the *Independent*,' James repeated. 'And I don't see why you should.'

'When you see them again don't tell them anything I've said. If I break off negotiations with them, *I* want to tell them.'

Monday 17 March
I finished my cartoon early today and when I took it in to Max he said that there was a memo on its way to me from the management in response to my letter about the *Independent* and the *Observer*.

While I was hanging around finding things to do until this exciting document arrived I went to see Don Berry. I want to take a holiday for two weeks at Easter and I had to make sure this would not clash with the introduction of the new-look centre pages. My cartoon is to be a central part of the new design.

To my horror he plans to start the new look on 2 April. In other words, I cannot take an Easter break this year. Apart from the fact that I really need a rest Caroline is going to be away and the boys will be off school. It's going to be a difficult time for all of us.

By 5.00 pm I couldn't stand waiting for Max's memo any longer and went and asked Sue Davy if she still had it.

'Yes,' she said, 'but it isn't signed yet.'

'Can I look at it?'

'I suppose so – you'll be getting it eventually anyhow.'

The letter said they wanted to keep me on both the Sunday and the daily *Telegraph*s and that both were putting my pay up. The total raise was worth £8,000 a year, all of which would be pensionable. I chuckled at one passage in which Max referred to 'jealous competitors'.

Sue Davy said, 'I don't know why you are laughing – I didn't see anything funny about it.'

I couldn't tell whether she was cross because I was getting so much money and giggling about it or whether she was joking and saying, 'Christ, that much money is no laughing matter.'

I mumbled some explanation and said I thought I'd accept the offer.

'Who wants you?' she asked.

'The *Independent*.'

'Oh, don't go there – oh, I hope not,' she said.

'I had another offer too.'

'Who from?'

'I'll tell you but you must be discreet because – '

'Discreet,' she butted in, definitely nettled. 'How do you think I kept this job?'

'I know – but I have to emphasise discretion because it was the *Observer* and they already have a cartoonist. I couldn't bear it if he discovered they were looking for someone else. I don't want him to get the idea I was after his job.'

'Mm,' she said, slightly less crossly.

While we were talking Max came in and saw what I was reading. He asked whether it was OK and I said that I thought it was.

'Give us a reply soon as you can,' he said.

I found to my irritation that I was not particularly bucked about the hefty raise. Somehow it had no meaning for me. I assume it's all window dressing really because it'll all go in tax. I felt flat.

It also meant the end of my flirtation with the *Independent*. I'm not sure what my feelings about that are. Mostly I think I dread telling Stephen I'm not coming over. He will be disappointed and depressed. Somewhere it will be like a personal rejection and as if I'm saying to him you made the wrong decision, you should have stayed on the *Telegraph*. It will seem like a criticism – at least, that's what I fear.

I suppose too it will mean a similar difficulty with Matthew and to an extent Andreas. I enjoyed being welcomed by them, to the extent that I was, and don't fancy being out in the cold.

But there's no getting around it. I'm staying on at the *Telegraph*.

Wednesday 19 March

On my way to work I stopped at El Vino's in Fleet Street to buy some wine for Tony. If it hadn't been for him I'd never have got round to facing up to the decision about the *Independent* or the *Telegraph*, nor would I have known how to deal with asking for a raise.

It's a long time – six or seven years, perhaps more – since I was a regular lunchtime and evening drinker at El Vino. A group of journalists used to meet at a certain table where Philip Hope-Wallace always sat. Included in this group at various times were Alan Watkins, Tony, Perry, Geoffrey Wheatcroft, Corinna Adam, Chris Hitchens, James

Fenton, Dick West, Peter Paterson and Peter Jenkins. The barman who served me today greeted me and remarked that they didn't see much of me now. I said I'd got out of the habit of drinking at lunchtime – or the evening, come to that. It's partly because I ride a motor bike, which is scary enough as it is, let alone when one has had a few drinks.

I was always surprised by how much my colleagues drank. It is difficult to say how it affected them. Sitting at Philip's table was always fun. The conversation was merrily spiteful, and often extremely interesting. Philip had a set of stories, reminiscences of old theatrical days, that were wonderfully well told and delightful to hear. He was also a great gossip – everyone told him everything and sooner or later he passed it on. The journalists would argue about politics and I learnt an enormous amount from them.

Bottle after bottle of burgundy, or champagne if Watkins was there, would be consumed, and time would slip by. I was always worried about getting too tipsy because it made it impossible for me to draw, but I'd see my friends hammering away at their typewriters in the afternoon apparently still able to think. They might have drunk five whiskies or most of a bottle of wine – enough to make me quite incapable. I once drew a cartoon of Peter Paterson, Ian Waller, Richard Bennett and me drinking beer in the Cheshire Cheese. Peter is shown draining a glass and saying, 'Well, we can't stay here drinking all day – let's get down to El Vino!'

As I chatted with the barman we looked around the crowded bar. It was about 1.30. Peter's son Graham was at the centre of a noisy group. Many faces were new to me, but the smoky, boozy lunchtime atmosphere was unchanged.

'I don't know how they do it,' said the barman, looking almost pityingly at the endlessly rising and falling elbows.

I agreed with him. 'You'd think they'd all have to go and sleep for several hours – but they'll all be at work again soon.'

'Yeah, and by six o'clock some of them'll be back here and starting again.'

I chose three bottles of Margaux. The barman said, 'Tony will like that. It can be drunk now or kept two or three years. If it's drunk now it must breathe for a bit – he'll know that – he wouldn't just open this and knock it back.'

I thought Tony would be pleased to hear himself spoken of in this way, the cool wine buff knowing when to open and drink the stuff.

I dropped off the bottles at the *Observer*. Three seemed too many when it came to it, so I kept one.

When I got to the *Telegraph* I wrote Max a short note. It just said that I was happy to accept the new arrangements that he had proposed.

When I took it to him he said, 'Good – it'll take a couple of days to go through – you understand.'

I said, 'The note merely says that I formally accept your offer. I didn't say thank you and express my gratitude and so on, but I am very pleased . . .'

He waved my remarks away and smiling said, 'Of course – of course . . .'

He told me to go and see Don Berry because there are some new layouts of the centre spread and it seems likely that my cartoons are going to be printed considerably bigger in the future as well as prominently featured there. I didn't go to see Don. Instead I dropped in on Bernard Foyster on the picture desk. He is an excellent source of information and from him I learnt that Max had tried to get my cartoon on the front page last night but failed. It was encouraging that he'd tried, but mildly alarming that he'd been overruled. Does that mean conservative pressures will keep the *Telegraph* in its old mould? If so, is that a good or bad thing?

Bernard then told me, his voice dropping to an ominous mutter, that the *Telegraph* was losing 4000 readers per day and had done for the last ten days. This statistic shocked me. I asked him where he thought the readers were going.

'*The Times*, I suppose. A few to *Today*. *The Times* is so much better than us. We are grey and dirty and a mess. Look at today's front page.' He held it up. It was column after column of figures about yesterday's budget. 'It puts you off just to look at it.'

I asked him what will happen if these losses continue.

'I don't know. The City said if we lost another 50,000 we'd had it. Well, we're nearly there. I suppose we'd go bust and Black would have to sell the title.'

Bernard's No. 2, Ronnie, said, 'We all get paid a week's salary for each year we've worked here.'

'And hope to get taken on again the next day by the new owner,' I said.

'Yeah – ideally . . . whoever that is.'

'The Australians,' I said. 'The guys who bought the *Spectator*.'

I thought of Matthew trying to frighten me into joining the *Independent* by cheerfully predicting the collapse of the *Telegraph*.

After work I went to the Blackfriars El Vino where I know Tony often goes. Sure enough he was there. It was like a trip down memory lane. Alan Watkins was at the table with a glass of champagne in one hand, a reeking cigar in the other. Peter Hillmore, the *Observer* columnist, was with them. Tony spotted me through clouds of smoke. He called out thanks for the wine and said I should not have bothered.

Peter at once asked, 'What is he thanking you for? What have you done? What's he talking about?'

With instinctive distrust for a columnist I said, 'I was indebted to Tony. He did me a favour, so I gave him some wine. A debt of honour. . . .' Peter was still mildly curious but let it drop.

It was like being back at Philip's table. It's odd to have avoided El Vino's for so long and then find myself visiting both in one day. Nothing had changed except that at the next table a young couple gazed into each other's eyes and from time to time caressed each other. The girl's hand stroked the man's ear and she ran her fingers slowly through his hair. This was not something I remember seeing in El Vino's before. I half expected the barman to come out and order them to stop it. The girl bared her teeth in a smile, or rather an erotic grimace that resembled a smile. She pulled the man's head towards her and licked his lips. They had both forgotten they were in a crowded room.

As soon as I could speak to Tony privately I told him what I'd been offered. He whistled and nodded appreciatively.

'You couldn't possibly refuse *that*,' he said. 'You'll be happy to know you now earn as much as the deputy editor of the *Observer*.' His face collapsed into laughter.

'Do I? How wonderful – but you earn so much extra from radio and TV.'

I told him about the *Telegraph* losses and he seemed puzzled. He had no theories about where the readers were going. He and Alan discussed the *Independent*. Their view was that Shah's failure – and they consider *Today* to be a disaster – means that the *Independent* will now never appear.

'They simply won't get the money to start,' said Tony. He'd been talking to some old Fleet Street hand and he firmly believes the *Independent* has had it without even starting.

Alan, who has been asked to write for them on Rugby League football, agreed.

'It'll be like old Paterson's – what was it called? – the *Globe*.' They both laughed at the memory of Peter trying to start a paper in about 1975 or 1976.

Tony said the trouble with *Today* was that the editor wasn't up to the job. 'Nice enough bloke – just couldn't do it.' He sometimes sounds like Clem Attlee is reputed to have spoken. He likes to express judgement in a final and confident brief statement. 'But the Sunday *Today* is better. Tony Holden has done quite well.'

Alan blew out a smoke screen and through it could be heard chuckling and wheezing. 'Oh, really,' he said ironically, 'I'm not sure I'd say that. These old comrades stick together.'

Tony laughed. 'I made that boy,' he boasted. 'I recognised his talent.'

'He hasn't got any talent,' said Alan. 'Somehow or other people simply assumed he had and began bidding for him. As soon as James Fenton appeared and I read a few words by him, I knew, this young man was a very good writer. I knew at once. Holden is not like that. No, no, he's no good.'

They both laughed – and laughed at the way Harold Evans had bid for Tony Howard.

'He just got more and more expensive each time round,' said Tony. 'It was very funny. Anyhow, he and wife are set to make a fortune translating operas for the ENO, where James once was,' he added.

Alan mentioned that young Graham Paterson has gone to the *Sunday Telegraph* as political editor. 'Alexander Chancellor told me he shares a room with him.'

'Why? Does the deputy editor not have his own room?' interrupted Tony.

'Apparently not,' said Alan. 'Alexander is not happy with the arrangement because young Paterson has got an extremely loud voice. He shouts down the telephone. When Alexander is dictating letters to his secretary she is taking down what Graham is saying.' Off they went into fits of laughter again.

Before I left Tony told me that I must tell the *Independent* what has happened at the *Telegraph*.

'I know. I'm going to call Stephen tonight – I'm dreading it.'

I did call him but Celia, his wife, told me he was in Germany and not back until tomorrow. I wondered whether to call Matthew instead, but didn't.

Thursday 20 March
I am increasingly affected by the isolated way I now live at the *Telegraph*. Today I went to see Nigel Dudley after work to see whether I could pick up any gossip. John Miller was also in the room. I asked whether Rod had ever surfaced again. John said, 'No, I put through a call to him today but I only got his answering machine.' I thought to myself, you don't 'put through' a call to someone in London, you 'ring' them. John is using foreign correspondents' language. You 'put through' a call from Kiev to London or from Bali.

Neither of them had any news. They merely reported that leader writers' conferences now take ten minutes and no longer involve any discussion.

I wonder whether to say to Max that he ought to encourage a little argument and chat amongst his colleagues. It would make them feel more a part of something, it would create a sense of comradeship and anyway some good ideas come out of casual conversations. However, neither John nor Nigel would be drawn into a criticism of the way Max takes the conference.

Nigel said he'd had to write six leaders in the last five days. This was said as if it was a really remarkable score. In five days I will always have done at least seven drawings, and usually ten or eleven.

I work too hard.

Friday 21 March

Today I did a cartoon for the *Sunday Telegraph*; a cover (in colour) for next week's *Spectator*; an inside drawing (in colour) for the *Spectator*; an illustration for an article for Oliver Pritchett; and an illustration for Monday's *Daily Telegraph* City page.

Before doing all this I telephoned Stephen and asked if I could meet him this morning. We agreed to rendezvous at the *Independent*'s new offices in City Road at 10.30.

'Do you want to see Matthew too?'

'No, I don't think so – I've always talked to you,' I said.

'OK. I'll meet you downstairs.'

We went to a workman's café across the road and ordered tea. As we sat down Stephen said, 'If a working man from the 1920s walked in here now, he'd feel completely at home, wouldn't he? There's nothing that would surprise or puzzle him.'

I looked around and agreed. The shiny water-boiling machine looked extremely old, the window had a lace curtain, the walls were bare and covered in vaguely flowery wallpaper.

'He might be surprised by the formica table tops,' I said, 'and possibly the neon strip lighting.'

'Mm – not much else.'

I plunged directly into telling Stephen that I had felt I must speak to Max about the *Independent* before Max actually took over. I said that I had been worried that the longer I left it the more awkward everything became. And if I was eventually persuaded to stay on at the *Telegraph* the less likely I was to be able to negotiate myself better terms if I once allowed the present state of affairs to become established. It was even possible that the *Independent* might never appear and my bargaining position be completely undermined. I reported Max's quick and generous response and told him that I'd accepted it.

Stephen was as friendly and sympathetic as he could possibly have been. 'Of course,' he said. 'You were quite right. In your position I would have done exactly the same.'

I said I was extremely relieved to hear him say so because I felt uncomfortable playing the two sides off against each other.

Stephen said, 'It's all because the timing got wrong. By next week we would have been able to offer you the money.' He correctly understood that by now the question of financial security was really the only issue that prevented me joining them.

77

'Is it true,' I asked, 'that Shah's relative failure is going to prevent you getting your money from the City?'

'No, not at all. In fact, between you and me we've already got it. That is to say, we are about three million short but we expect to get that early next week.'

'That's good,' I said. 'Anyway, I'm sorry if you feel I've led you on . . .'

'Don't be silly. We shouldn't talk about newspapers as if it was a question of joining and leaving a regiment or the Brigade of Guards. We're talking about newspapers. If the *New York Times* offered Max £250,000 a year to edit it, he'd go.'

'Mm,' I said.

'So you feel quite committed to the *Telegraph* now, then? Your decision is final.'

'Well – yes. I've told Max I accept the offer.'

'Supposing we made a better offer?'

'Oh, Christ,' I said. 'Look, I wanted to get this settled. I felt uncomfortable auctioning myself to you both. It's not a situation that one can stay in too long. If you mention a new offer I divide in half. One side of me says, "You've made a decision – stick to it", the other side says, "Hear, hear! But it might be interesting to know what they'd offer." '

Stephen smiled. I went on, 'If things were simply left as they are I'd be happy to go on at the *Telegraph*. It's rather like working on a new paper. There are new people, new looks, new styles – it's exciting. But I suppose it's possible that something may happen to make my life there intolerable. Perhaps the management will begin to interfere in editorial decisions. Perhaps the new-look *Telegraph* will be plain awful, all slick and packaged and dull. It may even fold.' I told him about the falling circulation.

In his view none of these possibilities would become real for at least six to eight months. 'By then it will be too late – we'll have had to find another cartoonist.'

'Of course,' I said. 'You'll find it bloody difficult, by the way. They don't exist.'

'I know,' he said.

He asked me how much Max had given me and I told him and asked him not to tell anyone because it made one feel odd for some reason if people know what you earn. I also know that actually people don't keep secrets. Everything gets discussed. It's good fun knowing more than other people, such good fun that sooner or later it all gets blurted out. For example, Stephen told me about the *Independent* long before he should have done. Matthew even told Ed Pearce. I told Tony Howard and Lennie Hoffman. However, in one way it remained secret. *Private Eye* never heard about it.

Stephen said, 'Is it OK to talk to Andreas about this conversation?'

'Of course – that's why I'm telling you. You don't have to tell him exactly what I earn, but of course talk to him.'

'OK. I will – and then we'll see what happens.'

I was left with the impression that I could expect a new and gigantic offer from the *Independent* and he was left with the impression that I have my price just like everyone else.

I tried to say to him again that I had committed myself to the *Telegraph* and that it was mostly plain curiosity that prevented me from telling him it was useless to try to tempt me now. But he only smiled and said, 'Of course, of course.'

'Come and see our new offices,' he added.

We walked back to the hideous building they occupy and went up to a large open-plan room on the first floor.

'This is the newsroom. Home down there – foreign in that corner . . .' He waved his arms about. The room was freshly painted and unswept. Sawdust, odd nails and sheets of plastic lay about. Like a dreamer who wakes up to find his dream come true, he looked about in some wonder. 'It's all real. It's all going to happen.'

'Yup,' I said.

'There's even a room for the cartoonist,' he said. 'He's one of the few people who gets a room of his own. It's up one flight in the graphics department.'

We discussed the changes that are happening at the *Telegraph* and he impressed me very much with a speech about what an extraordinary and unique institution the *Telegraph* was. 'There's no paper like it in the world. And no readership like its readership.'

He went on to praise the old-fashioned, messy, quirky, dependable thing that it was and said it could be a catastrophe to change it too radically too fast.

When I left we shook hands and I told him I much appreciated the way he'd listened to me and responded.

He said, 'We'll be in touch soon.'

I got a charming letter from Bill today thanking me for the drawing I'd given him. He also amazed and pleased me by saying that in the last turbulent days he'd spent at the *Telegraph* he'd come to look upon my 'reassuring figure as the one anchor in the harbour . . .' I was very touched.

I also got a memo from Max thanking me for my note and adding that he hoped our arrangement would last at least several years because they couldn't stand giving out raises of this order too often. It was as if he'd been listening to my conversation with Stephen earlier.

Tuesday 25 March
James resigned from *The Times* today, which I suppose makes it likely
that he will finish up on the *Independent*.

Wednesday 26 March
Through the post today came a statement from the *Telegraph* management. In effect they were saying the same old thing. We were at rock
bottom. The situation was desperate. We had no more assets. We hoped
to make generous redundancy payments and to survive until the
autumn when we could start production at our new super-duper modern
plant, but you must all be good boys and girls until then or we would
go down the chute.

There were a number of new developments about dividing the
company up into satellite printing units and shifts of staff but the biggest
and saddest news was that we were going to move out of Fleet Street.
They hoped we would not have to go right out to the Isle of Dogs,
although that would be the cheapest arrangement. Somewhere in
Waterloo had been suggested.

I don't use Fleet Street all that much. That is to say, since I started
riding a motor bike to work I rarely go to pubs and I have never spent
much time in restaurants. But I love Fleet Street. I always like arriving
in it by road or stepping out of the *Telegraph* back on to it. I love the
view up Ludgate Hill and all the local street names such as Shoe Lane,
Chancery Lane, and Bouverie Street. I like to look back at the bus-
loads of tourists who gaze down at the busy pavements as they pass
through on their way to St Paul's and the City. Their somewhat blank
scrutiny makes me feel alive and real, and that I belong. No one who
works there ever steps into the street without seeing someone they
know. Often I try to avoid familiar faces because they bore me or
because I dislike them, but I'll miss them when we go. I even like
saying, 'I work in Fleet Street.' It makes me feel special – as if one
belonged to a somewhat disreputable club, or a dashing, unconventional
regiment.

I heard that Nigel Wade has been made temporary foreign editor. It
seems a strange appointment. Why not leave Rickie March doing it, if
it's only temporary? There's nothing wrong with Nigel, of course –
except his ridiculous beard – but is he an editor? His beard is one that
requires a lot of attention; most of it is shaved away, leaving a narrow
strip from ear to chin, which joins up with a carefully trimmed
moustache. I like beards, but the whole point of them is to avoid
shaving. Nigel's beard actually makes shaving more difficult.

I met Tim Garton Ash for lunch at the newly designed Bertorelli
restaurant. At least, it's newly designed since I was last there ten years
ago. It now looks like the set for a musical based on the adventures of

a *flaneur* in *fin de siècle* Paris. I asked him why he had not gone to the *Telegraph* when both the daily and the Sunday made overtures to him. The reason was that he had a perfecly good set-up already which gave him plenty of money, the opportunity to travel and freedom. But he said there was one remark that Max had made to him that decided him definitely against the *Telegraph*. He was told that *Telegraph* readers could not be expected to read feature articles that were 1000 to 1500 words long, and that shorter, more pithy pieces were therefore required. Tim felt this was not the writing that he wanted to produce and that a paper that was going in for such journalism was not for him.

If anything, he seemed to think that what the *Telegraph* needed was longer, heavier, more erudite articles. It may be that this is what I think and that I foisted my views on him – I can't remember exactly; but we agreed that as Murdoch steered *The Times* down market in search of more readers, the *Telegraph* should aim upwards. If *The Times* was going into competition with the *Mail* it was probably that many of their supporters would drop away and they should all come to the *Telegraph*. But they wouldn't if we tried to beat Murdoch at his own game.

It is an awful shame we didn't get Tim. He is the best writer on Eastern Europe and communism generally these days. We desperately need better foreign writing, and reporting.

Back at the *Telegraph* David Holloway came to my office with a couple of books on Indian architecture for review. I asked him whether new looks and staff changes were affecting him at all.

He knocked the door with his knuckles and said, 'Not yet, touch wood.' He said he had feared that Morrison might get his job at one time but that no longer seemed remotely likely. Otherwise all the changes were still in the future and unknown. He intended simply to bash on as usual.

Thursday 27 March
I did a cartoon for the *Sunday Telegraph* today so that I could take tomorrow, Good Friday, off.

When I took it in to Perry he was as usual sitting at his little side table and not at the editor's desk. The only difference was that now he has turned his chair round so that his back is to the door. It is as if he has symbolically removed himself a stage further from editing.

He was complimentary about the drawing and then said, 'If you have any ideas about how the *Sunday Telegraph* could be improved or made more, er, lively, do let me know.'

I thought, 'It's a bad sign when editors are asking cartoonists for ideas for brightening up papers,' just as I had thought when talking to Andreas months ago.

He discoursed a little about falling standards of writing. 'It seems to have become a lost art. I don't think anyone under the age of – say – fifty can write these days . . .'

It was one of those remarks that cry out for contradicting. I should have thought at once of Frank Johnson, Simon Hoggart, Martin Amis. I said, 'James Fenton can write.'

'Yes – but he's a special case,' said Perry vaguely.

This evening Caroline and I went for a drink with M. J. Akbar and his wife Mallika. Akbar asked what was happening at the *Telegraph*. His own Calcutta-based paper is also called 'Telegraph' and he brought out a copy to show me how he solved a certain problem. Immediately he began talking I felt, 'Here is an editor'. The design and content of the paper are his. He knows the mix he wants of news and features and he knows how he wants it presented. He made the complex, abstract problems of design and presentation sound clear and simple. Above all, he sounded confident and enthusiastic. And his paper looked good.

Later Alexander Chancellor came in and while he drank whisky and chain-smoked he talked about his new job as deputy to Perry. First of all he said how devoted to Perry he was and that he intended to make him the best and most terrific and wonderful editor in Fleet Street. This ambition was made rather more difficult than it should have been by Perry's eccentric idea of what editing is. He seems to believe it means sitting in the editor's office and by his simple presence attracting excellent contributions and raising standards generally.

Alexander's view is that the editor should take an interest in the presentation of news and the balance of comment and features too. He told me a long story about how Perry was going to allow a photograph of Mrs Aquino illustrate a front page story about the escape from extradition of Evelyn Glenholmes, the IRA suspect.

'I mean, I could be wrong, probably am, but I'll say it anyway,' Alexander had remarked to Perry. 'But it occurs to me that possibly a picture of – sort of – Glenholmes, or someone, might be the more obvious choice . . . given the main story. Or not.'

Perry had been enormously impressed.

'I took him down to the picture desk,' continued Alexander, as if Perry were a new bug who needed showing around, 'and asked Sidney what's-his-name to find a photo of Glenholmes. Perry became extremely excited and said, "Look here, we must use that, harumph! First class – er – kill Mrs Aquino, as it were, and – yes – use this. Excellent." '

I couldn't entirely grasp Alexander's mood. He seemed to be saying that at the Sunday absolutely bugger-all is happening – apart from what he can get done. His style of talking is very roundabout and hedged in with self-deprecating qualifications to every statement, but like Akbar he sounded like an editor. Behind the jokey anecdotes you could see he knows the difference between editing the *Spectator* and editing a national paper ('. . . if the *Sunday Telegraph* is a national paper – sort of almost is, in a way . . .').

His veiled criticism of Perry spread to Max Hastings. He said there should be a much more clearly established relationship between the *Sunday* and *Daily*.

'Max suggested a weekly lunch,' he said laughing, as if to say, 'Sitting around boozing once a week will not do the trick.'

He also said that contributors to a paper must know *what* they are writing for. 'Contributors to the *Spectator* didn't have to be told *how* to write, they knew the journal so well it wasn't necessary.' He was saying the *Sunday Telegraph* (and possibly the *Daily* too) had not got a clear enough personality.

He left me with the impression that he didn't have a very optimistic view about the future of the *Telegraph* but that he was committed to working as hard as he possibly could for the survival of both.

I asked him why Max had discussed my future on the paper with him instead of with Perry.

'I dunno,' he said. 'Perhaps he did talk to Perry too. I just said, "Give him lots of money".' He went off into his hissing, spluttering laugh. 'You get more than me now – I know.' He waved his finger at me accusingly.

'But you get a car,' I said.

'Oh yes – the car.' This levelled things out.

Monday 31 March

I find that my attitude to the *Daily Telegraph* has gone through a complete revolution since Bill's departure.

It is clear that I had become fed up with the paper over the last year or so. As disaster slowly overwhelmed the old order I had grown increasingly depressed by the lack of reaction from the editor or the management. Once Lord Hartwell sold out to Conrad Black my sense of belonging more or less vanished. Self-interest might keep me working on the *Telegraph* but all fondness for it and loyalty had gone.

As soon as Max appeared on the scene everything changed. His energy and enthusiasm and buoyancy were infectious. He gave off a sense of adventure and excitement. At once his appointments were encouraging. Don Berry was obviously impressive and a personally delightful man. As far as I could tell, those of my colleagues who bit the dust or were moved quickly sideways and downwards deserved their fate. I found that I was waiting with high expectations for these changes to manifest themselves in improvements in the look and content of the paper.

At the same time the large pay rise I received boosted my morale, and gave me a sense of being wanted and therefore belonging. I felt once more that I was a *Telegraph* man and committed myself to its survival and success for tribal as well as self-interested reasons.

However, there were one or two small details that bothered me. The first was the shifting of the leader writers' conference to 12.15 pm. This meant that I did not attend it any more, and consequently lost contact with my colleagues. The only person I see is Max but he is always preoccupied and in a hurry. Unfailingly friendly and courteous though he has always been, he is too busy to exchange a few words or to chat for a moment, as Bill always did. This increases my isolation. I talk to Sue, and to Bernard Foyster and John Burgess at the picture desk, but I miss the rambling discussions of news and politics I used to hear.

I am afraid I will get more and more out of touch.

As bits of new design began to appear they had the raggedy look of pointless change that tinkering with layout always seems to produce.

The new layout of the centre pages that Don Berry and Vic Clark worked on so hard also gives me a serious problem. Don decreed a permanent size for my cartoon. From now on it is either a wide shallow four columns or a more-or-less square three columns, each shape covering exactly the same amount of square inches. The deep oblong that I used to use (and that Vicky and Low and most daily cartoonists have used) is now denied me. And I miss it. Figures tend either to get lost in the wide format or squashed up by the square one. But I'm battling on with this difficulty.

As the dust settled after Max's arrival an awful realisation began to dawn on me. The revolution had not solved any problems. I began to feel irritated with myself for having believed the new rule would bring about improvements. It is fundamental to my attitude to life that nothing much changes and when it does it is an immensely long process.

I began to see that Max was being pushed to move much faster than he wanted. In a sense, he was not in charge; he was being directed by the management, and they in turn were held in the grip of outside forces. Like wolves prowling outside, falling circulation, falling advertising revenue, fear of bankruptcy, Murdoch, Shah and recruiting officers from various competitors all terrified Knight and his advisers. Panic was the most powerful force around. For all its grey suits, clipboards, neat haircuts and shiny shoes, the new order could not hide its alarm.

When I talk now with colleagues their attitude is a wry 'wait and see' but all express misgivings. Bernard Foyster and John Burgess are particularly comical about absurd discussions they have been part of about the use of logos, graphics and photographs. They describe Max and Don endlessly discussing with designers, layout people and their numerous assistants little matters that should be settled by one man instantly.

So I face the future full of doubts; somewhat world-weary, still committed to the *Telegraph* and wishing Max well, but suspicious of the management.

APRIL

15 April, *Daily Telegraph*

Tuesday 1 April
General reaction to the newly designed centre spread somewhat cool. Most people say, 'Give it time to settle down.'

I thought it looked as if it were trying to look like the *Sunday Times*, and failing.

In an article published on the centre spread Max described me as 'perhaps' the outstanding political cartoonist of the day. I have been teased about it all day long. Everyone also noticed that he described Marc as 'the wittiest pocket cartoonist'.

'No perhaps there,' declare my kind friends.

John O'Sullivan telephoned me this afternoon from *The Times*. He wanted to know whether he could tempt me over to Wapping. I said, 'No – but let's talk.' We'll have lunch together soon.

Wednesday 2 April
Second day of the new-look centre spread. It looks neat and orderly but oddly dull. I miss the old junk-shop quality the news page opposite the leaders used to have. Now that it has feature articles on it I turn to it with a sense of duty rather than expectant irresponsibility. The new order is heading directly away from one of the old *Telegraph*'s finest qualities. Max has set in motion, for sensible and well-meaning reasons, the destruction of the frayed rag-bag side of Bill's *Telegraph*. Lord Hartwell's home for dead-beats and eccentrics is closed.

I met Godfrey Barker in the corridor late this afternoon. He appeared on the front page this morning writing about the fire at Hampton Court, and billed as arts editor.

Yesterday Sue told me that her arms were aching from typing out rockets from Max to Godfrey.

'What's he being ticked off for?'

'Oh, I don't know,' she said. 'He's never around – you can't find him. He thinks he can still nose around the House of Commons and be a parliamentary sketch writer. He's hopeless.' She spoke without irritation. You can't be cross with Godfrey. He is not wicked. He wishes no harm to anyone. He's just on the make, and assumes everyone else is too – which in many ways we all are. Such men test our morality more sharply than decent, upright citizens can do. Every sensible person hates to be preached at. Goody-goodies make one want to go out and punch someone smaller than oneself. But before you condemn the Godfreys of this world you have to consider the wide-boy in yourself.

As we met he took me by the arm. 'We must talk – I must have a word with you.' Godfrey habitually talks in quotation marks. He is a perfect example of the middle-class wide-boy. Tucked away behind his tasteful shirts and matching ties are the padded shoulders of a 1940s spiv as well as the flowery waistcoats of an Edwardian cad. Grinning and joking, and occasionally pretending to care, he revels in his act.

Before he left Godfrey and I discussed the arts pages and he asked whether I'd be interested in doing theatre criticism. I said that I couldn't, I was not qualified, and anyway it was a full-time job and I already had a job.

He then suggested that I might do some pieces on fine art, covering exhibitions around Cork Street and Bond Street. I said probably not.

I did not get a very clear idea of what he wanted to do with the pages. The only idea I offered was that they should sometimes use huge pictures and give generous space to an article or profile that deserved it. I remembered a piece in *The Times* about the RA Exhibition of 20th-century German art. They used a big photo of a painting by Max Beckmann and in the text mentioned several little satellite exhibitions of German art timed to coincide with the main show. Because of the generous space allotted to the subject, one was left with an abiding impression that the paper cared about fine art.

Thursday 3 April
I found I turned to the centre spread at once today. It's not because my cartoon appears there. It is because it is new, and it provides a special sort of commentary that is pleasant with an early cup of tea.

Later to the Reform Club where I had agreed to meet John O'Sullivan for lunch. I arrived dead on time and was mildly surprised to find he wasn't there. There is something so orderly and grand about big London clubs that you expect everything in them to go unusually smoothly.

Twenty-five minutes on it began to dawn on me that perhaps I'd got the wrong day so I asked the doorman whether Mr O'Sullivan had booked a table for lunch.

'Which Mr O'Sullivan is that, sir?'

We sorted this out and John had indeed booked a table for that day so I found a *Times* and sat on a big leather settle under a big shiny Victorian portrait painting and waited. Men in suits looking relaxed and at home passed in front of me across the magnificent hall. Servants passed by; they also gave off a pleasant air of everything being all right. The atmosphere was very male. Although there were two women chatting and smoking with separate groups of men, when a homely middle-aged servant lady waddled past, her huge gently moving bust looked almost shocking in this splendid and formal and masculine interior.

John arrived, apologising about being 35 minutes late and saying it was just impossible to get anywhere from Wapping.

I thought at once of the sadness I felt about leaving Fleet Street.

Telegraph staff will be puffing across London from somewhere south of the river soon. It doesn't seem right.

Over lunch we discussed the new-look *Telegraph*. On the whole John was fairly sympathetic but he did say he'd felt quite a pang of nostalgia for the old paper when he'd seen Don Perry's new centrefold for the first time.

He thinks the op-ed page is not right yet. It's partly the layout, but the mix of articles is dull.

He edits a similar spread on *The Times* as well as writing a leader each day, and he told me that when he got the job Murdoch had said to him that he must recruit a team of the most amusing and intelligent writers he could find for this part of the paper. John said he'd not actually taken on any new people yet but he was looking around.

I told him I thought everything was being done too fast at the *Telegraph* and that Max was not in control. Andrew Knight appeared to be the nearest thing to an authority in the place but even he gave off an air of closely reined-in panic. They have hit the ground not running so much as toppling forward madly trying to find their balance.

John thought that might be about right. He told me that he'd met Andrew and Max in a restaurant a couple of weeks ago and he and his guest were invited to join the *Telegraph* men for port after dinner. They had a delightful time, the conversation had been extremely frank and of great interest. But at one moment John had offered Andrew a thought on some point that Andrew had quickly taken up. 'Yes,' he had said, 'you're quite right. You know Max, we ought to . . .' As he went on to enlarge on the theme John noticed to his amusement and surprise that Max took out a piece of paper and began taking notes.

'He actually began taking it down,' said John, chortling at the idea. What he meant was that it was as if he was seeing, in miniature, the way the *Telegraph* was run. We agreed that Max was a nice bloke but Andrew was a real cool dude, and very formidable.

At this point John said, 'I'll go into my spiel,' and he began to say how his editor was a great fan of mine and how much he, John, wanted me on *The Times*. 'We all do.' He laid out the offer, which was to pay me more money, guarantee annual travel ('You can put it in your contract if you like') and also space to write on the op-ed page on various subjects that took my fancy. His pitch was good. Flattering, relaxed and saying in the end, 'There's no hurry – this offer is just on the table . . .'

I repeated to him what I feel has become *my* spiel. 'I don't want to mislead you. I am not thinking of leaving the *Telegraph* at the moment. If anything dramatic changes there I'll let you know. Thanks very much indeed for the offer. I am very flattered.'

John likes, and admires, both Murdoch and the editor Charles

Wilson. He says Murdoch is fun to work with. Unlike most newspaper owners Murdoch doesn't seem to give a sod for research and statistics when trying to boost circulation in one of his papers. He comes bustling in saying, 'I think we should do such and such, because it's lively/interesting/challenging/dramatic.'

I sought John's views on the *Independent*. He thought it should probably be OK. It would all depend on who they could recruit. I told him my anxiety about the apparent absence of ideas from Matthew, Stephen and Andreas about what the newspaper should look like and contain. It's no good, I said, them repeating that they're going to get good people and a good designer, they needed a personal touch, something idiosyncratic. The paper must eventually exist to express their personalities and views.

'Yes,' said John. 'Otherwise you finish up with something like *Today*.'

John clearly wished them well. I think on the whole he wishes everyone well. He's one of the least envious and vindictive people around.

It was after three when we strolled out of the Reform. As we walked towards the bay where I'd left my bike John said, 'I think we should just offer you lots of money.'

I said nothing, and he smiled.

'What is a lot of money?' I asked. 'How much does a highly paid journalist get these days?'

'I suppose a Frank Johnson gets about £30,000, something like that. How much do you want?'

'I was advised recently never to say how much I want – people always offer more if left to make their own calculations.'

'That's right – that's good advice. Just give me an idea, then – something that you'd want more than.'

'Well – on the understanding that all this is quite academic anyway – a lot more than you've said already.'

He pulled a little face expressing respect. 'Forty thousand.'

'Even more.'

He laughed out loud. 'OK. If we get you I think you'll get more than anyone else – apart from the editor.'

'Really?' I said, surprised.

'Editors are easy to find. Cartoonists are rare.'

I felt I should explain to him that my inflated salary was because it represented payment from two papers.

'Oh, yes, of course,' he said. 'In that case you're underpaid!'

We parted chuckling merrily at the ludicrous amounts of money we were airily discussing.

When later I took my cartoon in to Max he was sitting at his desk with a huge pile of letters to sign. He puffed on a cigar and looked tired. He glanced at the cartoon and passed it without comment.

'How's it going?' I said.

'I've just been to see Hartwell.'

'Do you do that every day?'

'*De temps en temps* – under duress. It's pretty awful.'

'Why?'

'He doesn't like what we're doing. He doesn't like the cartoon on the leader page.'

'Does that matter?'

'No – not really, but . . .'

'What sort of reaction are you getting generally?'

'Negative. People don't like it. We haven't got it right yet. We're losing readers like *that*.' He tilted his pen to indicate a downward move on a graph. 'And I think we're going to go on losing them all through the summer.'

'But we were losing them before you came.'

He took the point quickly. 'Yes – and the riposte to Hartwell's criticism that remains unspoken is, "Well, look what a mess you made of it." '

He was speaking gloomily with no sense of triumph or excusing himself. He went on: 'Even if we get it right, it will take ages to show in the circulation figures.'

'Well, for what it's worth, most people have told me they like my cartoon where it is now. Also, although there is criticism of the changes, everyone around the place recognises the need for *something* to be done.'

Max looked up. I said, 'Do you get much reaction from your colleagues? Do you know what people here are saying?'

'To tell you the truth there's been no time,' he replied. 'I am completely rushed off my feet all the day every day.' His eyes flickered to the clock as he spoke, letting me know that I was using up valuable seconds. I ignored the hint. I was trying to cheer him up.

'Yeah, I remember you saying you wanted a month to look around and get the feel of the place before you did anything.'

'Yes, I did. But there's been no time.'

I ventured to suggest a change in the centre pages and he said, 'We agonised over that, but we can't change it now or it will look as if we are continually tinkering. We'll leave it for a few weeks.'

He spoke of the need for a lighter note to be sounded somewhere in the centre spread and said he could see why *The Times* used Miles Kington.

I was seeing Max not as the star journalist from the Falklands, nor as the over-confident young Hooray Henry he sometimes seemed to be. He looked uncertain and baffled and frankly unhappy. When he said that Andrew Knight was giving him a lot of support and freedom, I could almost hear him saying, 'Won't someone tell me what to do . . . ?'

Could it be that Max won't last the pace?

I quoted Stephen Glover to him without attributing the remark. 'You know, the circulation of the *Telegraph* is so huge you can afford to lose quite a few readers while you get everything right. There's surely no need to panic yet.'

'Absolutely,' he agreed. 'If we can keep our nerve we should be OK.' He looked forward with touching hope to the autumn, when the paper would come crisp and clean, and sharply black and white, off the new machinery in the Isle of Dogs.

I got up to go. He smiled and said, 'Everything you've said is very helpful – keep in touch.' It was as if our paths had crossed in some remote railway station. Keep in touch? I saw him every working day.

'By the way, I had lunch with John O'Sullivan today, and he was quite nice about the new look.'

Eagerly Max asked, 'What did he say? I'm a great admirer of his. I wish we'd got him.'

'He said more or less what you said, that the opposite page is not quite right yet but the leader page is fine.'

'Oh good.'

I was feeling pretty down-hearted as I walked down the corridor. All is not well.

I met Clive Barrow in the loo and we chatted as I washed my paint brushes. I found myself explaining how I missed the leader writers' conference.

'It makes me feel out of touch, isolated.'

'Don't we all?' he said cheerfully.

I handed in my cartoon to Bernard in the art room and described to him the scene of Lord Hartwell helplessly telling Max he didn't like the changes.

'It's pathetic, isn't it?' said Bernard. 'I heard that at the board meeting where Max's appointment was being discussed Lord H strongly opposed the choice. After a while someone handed him a bit of paper which he read and fell silent. I think I know what was written on that paper.' He scrawled something on a pad, tore off the page and handed it to me. On it he'd written '80%'. The message to Hartwell was brutal: 'We've got 80 per cent of this place – shut up.'

I could enjoy the story without believing it. It dramatically put Lord Hartwell's position very clearly even if it never happened.

Bernard was pretty scathing about the Don Berry regime. He showed me a list of pictures Don had asked him to provide that morning. 'Look at all that,' he said incredulously. 'I had a list like that yesterday – all for the centrefold. They finished up using one pic, or rather a part of

93

one. I said to him, "Look mate, hang on. I'm giving all my resources to one little bit of the paper. I've got nothing left for all the rest." It can't go on like this.'

Friday 4 April
I did two cartoons today for the *Sunday Telegraph*. I chose the one I liked best and handed it in. On my way back to my office I asked Vic Clark, a designer and layout man who works with Don Berry, whether he'd like the other for tomorrow's *Daily Telegraph*.

In the old days I'd always offer extra cartoons to the *Daily* and usually they'd be glad to use them. Vic was thrown into a loop by my offer. He began to do calculations in his head as he tried to work out where it could go. Anxiously he muttered that we could, he supposed, cut down the depth but that left the – no, that wouldn't do – and the letters must be spread tomorrow so there was nothing to be gained there. At last he said, 'I'll ask the Don and see what he says. He's not inflexible . . .'

'Look,' I said, 'I offered the cartoon in case it was helpful. I don't want to be troublesome. Why not just forget it?'

'I'll ask the Don.'

The new-look paper has a rigidity we never had before.

I took the cartoon along to Don anyway and said, 'It's here if you want it. Otherwise it will last until next week quite happily.'

Max happened to be in the room and said it might make a good front-page cartoon some time. He and Don set aside the work they were doing when I came in and began to plan when it might be used. Slightly embarrassed, I said again, 'I'll just leave it with you and if it's useful OK – if not, forget it. I don't want to be a nuisance.'

'God, you're not a nuisance,' said Max. 'We're grovelling in gratitude for being offered it.'

Just before I went Max suggested a slight change in the cartoon, a fairly simple piece of redrawing that was a definite improvement. I thanked him and took the drawing away. On my way back to my room I met Morrison and sat in his office for a while talking about the new look, with which he is closely involved.

He asked whether I'd be interested in producing a column to appear on the leader page. What he wanted was a fairly light-hearted topical treatment of any matter that caught my attention. I thought I couldn't have a column that appeared right next door to my cartoon, and he clicked his tongue and said, 'No, I never thought of that.'

I suggested it might be possible if I used a pseudonym but the fact was I already had too much work and knew I could not fit in any more. I agreed to think about it – either to do it myself or think of a possible alternative contributor.

It occurred to me that any humorous column introduced into the *Telegraph* would have to stand comparison with the mighty Peter Simple.

'Yes,' said Morrison, 'but he will not be there for ever.'

'You probably should get someone like Richard Ingrams, who is established and – '

'We've been through all that,' he interrupted.

Saturday 5 April
Spoke with James Fenton on the telephone. He sounds as if he is on the point of joining the *Independent* in some role or other. I think he is still uncertain quite what he wants to do.

While I told him how I was growing disillusioned with the *Telegraph* I had to fight against an impulse to add disparaging remarks about the *Independent*. It was as if having opted for my own paper I felt envious of him for being part of a more exciting team.

I told him my doubts about the *Independent*'s editorial skills and he mournfully acknowledged his own lack of confidence. I said he should join up now and take part in the recruiting and shaping of the thing. I told him about the overture from *The Times*, Morrison's suggestion that I write a column, and Godfrey's idea that I become a critic.

He just laughed at the absurdity of it all.

'It's nice to be wanted, though,' he said.

'It's all unreal. I suppose the offers from the other papers are pleasant to have in the background.'

This evening Max appeared on TV being interviewed by Clive James. James is like one of Martin Amis's more brilliant inventions. He is indescribably awful. The utter banality of his opinions and the monstrous self-satisfaction with which he delivers every word is painful to watch. I prayed for him to stop smiling at his own jibes as he tilted indiscriminately at Fergie, the Pope, Prince Charles, Marcos, the government, Prince Andrew and Prince Philip. When he did put on a serious face and drop his voice a tone or two, he simply added great dollops of self-righteousness to the act.

I guessed that Max was on as part of a *Telegraph* move to become better known. *Telegraph* people complain that we are never on TV and radio. He looked ill at ease as he tried to sound modest about his career as a war correspondent. The only paper he mentioned was *The Times* and he made no use of the opportunity to put in a pitch for the *Telegraph*. He came over as honest and straightforward, but not an editor. He hardly expressed an opinion of anything apart from a long-winded statement that newspapers could do some things better than TV and vice versa. He was asked whether his new boss interfered in the running of the paper. Almost plaintively he said that he'd expected to be given all kinds of instructions by Black and Knight, but had received none at all. The impression he gave was unmistakable. Clearly he wished someone would tell him what the hell he should be doing. Directions are useful even if they are simply ignored, because they act as a fixed point from which you are moving. Max is squelching round and round in a quagmire.

He spoke briefly about the death of Nick Tomalin and to my amazement and consternation I heard him say that he'd had lunch with Nick the day before he had been killed. I clearly remember having a drink with Max the day Nick died and chiding him for his remarks about the awful accident. If Max was in the Middle East, then I simply imagined the conversation. I suddenly had no hold on the truth. Had I heard Max talking on the radio that day and simply invented my conversation with him? Did I express my irritation with Max to someone else? Was the whole thing a fantasy that never happened at all? Hang on, did Max say he'd lunched with Nick a *few* days before his death? In which case he might have had time to return to London. Or had he lunched with Nick in London before Nick's departure for the Middle East? Hmm – very rum . . .

Monday 7 April

It was snowing when I woke up this morning. Large wet flakes that fell through the cold air and slowly melted as they came to rest.

I opened the *Telegraph* at the centrefold. It made me feel numb. Each part was OK – nothing special, mind, but not in itself bad. Yet the overall effect was deadly, like being in a padded cell.

I rang Charles Moore and bored him to death worrying about it. Charles was unwilling to be drawn into criticising Max's attempt to improve the paper. He kept saying that new looks were always awful at first. I said, 'It's not just a new look, it's a new paper. They've bulldozed the whole central section. What was a news page is now the sort of features section you'd expect in a Sunday paper.'

Charles hummed and hawed. He did eventually concede that nothing Max had done was an improvement, except perhaps for some of the hirings and firings. But if he'd got rid of some dull people and recruited some lively ones these changes did not brighten up the pages yet.

He said he'd had lunch with Martin Ivens the other day and he'd been optimistic. I pointed out that Martin had done well by the new regime. He'd been promoted and his talents recognised. Some individuals did benefit. I had, for instance, by getting more dough, and so had Graham Paterson by being promoted. But the newspaper . . .

Charles said, 'Give it time.'

Wednesday 9 April

John O'Sullivan rang me at home this morning and told me that the editor of *The Times* would like to have lunch with me. I am extremely curious to meet him and said yes. I also said that it would be on the clear understanding that I was staying on the *Telegraph* unless there was some new development there which made me wish to leave – and at the moment there was no reason to expect it.

John said OK. I asked him if he'd be coming to lunch too and he said maybe.

After he'd hung up it seemed to me that when I'd said I had no plans to leave the *Telegraph* at the moment and expected to make no such plans, John had become a little thoughtful. Perhaps this lunch will not come off. After all, why should the editor of *The Times* waste his time having lunch with the *Daily Telegraph*'s cartoonist?

Thursday 10 April

Charles Moore telephoned this afternoon to discuss next week's *Spectator* cover but spent most of the time telling me about a lunch he'd had *à deux* with Max yesterday.

He began by saying that the meeting had more or less confirmed everything I'd been saying lately about the state of affairs at the *Telegraph*. He believed that Max had sensible enough ambitions as editor but absolutely no idea about how to achieve them. His aim was to keep the *Telegraph* as the best and fullest *news*paper in Fleet Street while building up its features and arts coverage to attract younger intelligent readers. He does not believe it is possible to challenge successfully *The Times*' position as spokesman for the British establishment with its world-famous letters column and mighty reputation.

I think the main trouble is that Max cannot tell a good writer from a second-rate no-hoper, and doesn't appear to have the faintest idea about, or even much interest in, politics. He calls himself a Conservative, but that just means he has a nostalgic notion that we've always been a great nation so why change anything? And above all let us keep well clear of all that communist tommyrot in the Labour Party. This overall view lives quite happily with a straightforward dislike of all political nastiness. For example, he thinks the policy of apartheid is rotten and he is wet over Northern Ireland. As least, he won't let Peter Utley say what he wants to on that subject any more, and I'd guess he thinks we should get shot of the province as soon as possible. The complications of *how* to escape from twisting political labyrinths of this kind don't interest him.

He loved newspapers with the love of a foreign, or war, correspondent – the glamour of jet flights to faraway places, the thrill of living on expenses and the entrée through the back door to the corridors of power.

97

And later the drinks and jokes and reminiscences back home. What's more, he'd proved that he's good at that. But it's all got nothing to do with being an editor.

Charles mimicked Max's voice very well and gave me a funny caricatured account of Max arriving late at the restaurant and immediately bawling out the waiters. 'Christ! Can't you get any service around here? Get me some cigars. Bloody hell!'

In the same vein Charles quoted Max more literally on being editor: 'Christ! I dunno, I've never taken responsibility for anything in twenty years. Fucking difficult. Bloody Godfrey and Pearce writing letters all the bloody time fighting each other; bloody Morrison coming in every five mins moaning on, circulation going down all the time – going to go on going down too – bloody hell!'

'He's such a charger-in to everything,' said Charles. 'But you can criticise him and he takes it very well.'

'What did you criticise him about?'

Charles had accused Max of being mean to Peter Utley. The situation is complex. Peter wishes to leave the *Telegraph* and go to *The Times*. The pension he can officially take now from the *Telegraph* is pitifully low, for certain unfortunate reasons. Peter had been assured, some time ago, that his pension would be made up to a proper amount when he quit but he never got that promise in writing. Now the *Telegraph* are saying they'll make up the pension only on condition he does not go to *The Times*. It's really being dog in the manger. They don't want to keep him but they don't want a rival crowing about getting him.

Charles's criticism had another even more important side. 'They don't understand Peter's value. He is not just a leading writer and columnist, he is a first-class intellect and is marvellous to listen to on politics and the nation's destiny and heritage.'

Charles had tried to explain to Max the need to foster talk and argument at the leader writers' conference and to make sure to include in the team one or two formidable minds such as Peter's. In Charles's view the conference should be a 'powerhouse for talent'. It's influence should spread out over features, leader page, articles and letters. He said, 'It would be useless to hire a couple of Fellows of All Souls to write leaders but you need such men to test your arguments against.'

Max had cheerfully swept aside Charles's advice and declared that he wasn't going to waste time at the conference. This characteristic of Max's of never being available for a chat is very bad for everyone. It results in no one having a clear idea of what is going on. The editor should be a conduit through which information passed between departments, as well as a source of ideas and planner of directions.

I told Charles that the other day when I had asked Max to sign some expenses he did so at once but said to Ricky Marsh who was there, 'I don't think I should waste my time doing this. I mean – Ricky, you could do it, couldn't you? I don't think I should spend my time signing expenses . . . ' Ricky shrugged and nodded.

I said to Charles, 'But signing expenses is not a waste of time. It's contact and a chance to talk, it can be very useful.'

Charles interrupted. 'It's also more than that. The symbolic side of it matters. *Who* is distributing largesse is important.' We agreed that in our opinion Max had no understanding at all of this abstract and fascinating side of editing – or of leadership, I suppose.

Max had been generous with his praises of Andrew Knight. He told Charles that one particular incident had impressed him very much.

Recently Murdoch tried to run a full-page ad in the *Telegraph* and much to the advertising department's irritation Max refused it. For some reason related to this business Max found himself talking to Andrew's secretary. Andrew himself was away in the USA. Max asked the secretary what Andrew's attitude to the Murdoch ad had been. She didn't reply at first, and then said that Andrew had been in favour of running it but had instructed her not to tell him. Max was quite moved at not having his decision interfered with.

Max plans no more developments or layout changes until the paper starts being printed on the new machinery some time in the autumn. To coincide with that there will be more changes and a publicity campaign.

After lunch Max told his chauffeur to drive Charles back to the *Spectator*. The driver told Charles that things at the *Telegraph* were very difficult nowadays. He said he liked Max and found him a lively boss who was polite and generally agreeable to work for. Old Hartwell, on the other hand, was a shadow of his former self.

'I told him he should retire, just let other people get on with it.'

Friday 11 April
Martin Ivens rang me at home this evening and we had a long talk. On the whole he has benefited by Max's arrival, but he has criticisms of the way things are being organised. Martin has a curious jerky style of talking. His words come in a series of surging rushes which are punctuated by inarticulate pauses and stammers. He adds an interrogatory little 'hmm' at the end of his more dogmatic statements as if inviting comment. Everything he said was usual extremely intelligent and perceptive.

One thing he said amused me. Max is beginning to make a habit of spiking leaders that have been planned and written early in the day and asking Martin to write replacements at the last minute. This is a perfect example of Max's eccentric style of editing.

The object of moving the leader writers' conference to the morning was to get that chore over as soon as possible so as to clear the afternoon for other matters, and to give the writers more time to research and write their pieces. Martin doesn't mind being asked to write one little bit, but he can see the absurdity of the arrangement.

He gave me the impression that he was fairly optimistic about the future of the *Telegraph*. I tried to draw him out about the *Independent* but he wouldn't say much. I asked directly what he thought of Stephen appointing Ed Steen to his foreign staff. Martin replied that Ed's weird public manner of off-putting grins and jokes was deceptive. In Martin's opinion Ed was an outstandingly talented writer. He speaks fluent German and is very clever and well qualified for the job. I felt chastised for forming too strong an impression of Ed's abilities on the basis of his facial expressions.

Monday 14 April
I finished my work early this afternoon and when I took the cartoon along to show Max I found Bill Deedes talking to Sue Davy. He looked bronze from his holiday in Australia and he shook hands warmly.

Max was holding a conference in his room and I chatted with Bill and Sue while I waited. I showed Bill my cartoon because it was a golfing scene which I knew would please him. He smiled delightedly at it. 'Ah! gold – splendid – you never did *me* golfing cartoons. Max will never understand this, he's a shooting man.' As with so many of Bill's asides there was a sting in the apparently jovial remark.

Eventually I got tired of waiting and went away. When I returned Max was in Sue's room. His height always takes me by surprise. I am just under six foot but I had to tilt my head right up to look at him. As usual, he was harrassed and in a hurry.

My cartoon showed Mrs Thatcher unwilling to help President Reagan attack Libya, and I had some doubts about whether this would prove accurate.

Max was also uncertain. He frowned, then smiled and said, 'I'm a gambler – use it. We'll do this one off the seat of our pants. Risk it – I'm a gambler.'

'Shall I ask the news desk whether there are any indications . . . ?'

'No,' he said with utter finality. It was as if he were saying, 'No one questions or influences a Hastings decision.'

This evening I met Jock Bruce Gardyne to discuss the jacket for his book. He told me an odd story. Some time last January Bill had asked him to suggest some names for the job of City editor to replace Andreas Whittam Smith. Jock had done so and subsequently been invited to meet Lord Hartwell to take the matter further. As this meeting Jock had carefully but firmly raised the point that Andrew Knight should be party to the discussion. Both Bill and Lord H had airily waved his anxiety aside. Later, back in Bill's room, Jock had again pressed the point, saying it was out of the question to appoint anyone because they simply no longer had the authority to do so.

Bill had said, 'I think I'd better show you something. There are wheels within wheels.' He produced a letter written by Andrew saying that there was no need to hurry with the appointment of a new City editor and that time could be taken to find the right chap. Jock had handed back the letter utterly mystified, saying that it powerfully reinforced his point. Bill had just laughed and Jock had taken the whole incident to mean that both Bill and Lord H had lost their marbles or at least had not yet taken in the implications of the revolution that had engulfed them.

We agreed that the story vividly illustrated the pathetic and sad side of Lord Hartwell's position in particular. I repeated to Jock Max's description of his occasional visits to Lord H and how he listened passively to the ex-proprietor complaining about the way things are going until he felt he could decently leave.

Jock listened, nodding. 'It's pretty awful, isn't it?' he said.

He told me that Lord Hartwell has lost more than his authority and power. Part of his huge private apartment in the *Telegraph* building has been taken from him to be converted for use by the City office.

Tuesday 15 April
This afternoon I happened to be passing Peter Utley's office and saw him sitting alone at his desk. He was smoking a cigarette. As he is blind there is not much he can do to pass the time if he's waiting alone in his office, and I was glad to catch him when he wasn't obviously busy (although I now realise he could have been thinking deeply about a leader and in a sense very busy indeed). I went in and sat near him. '*Dear* boy', he said, with his usual warmth and comical greeting.

We began instantly to talk, in quiet voices, about the *Telegraph* and our own changed circumstances and attitudes to the new order.

After a few moments he rose and said, 'Let's have the door closed.'

He felt that in the end he'd come out of his negotiations well. He'd got a raise and a reasonably good pension. He can leave if he wants to on 31 December 1986 but Max has also let him know he can stay on. Furthermore, Max has begun to lean heavily on him as an adviser and general guru, asking his opinions about appointing new staff and so on.

I got the impression that Peter rather likes Max but he had reservations about his style of editing. Peter misses the discursive debates that used to happen at leader conferences, but also said that the conferences were getting longer and more chatty as time went by. His main anxiety about Max is that his compulsive style of decision-taking leads him into complicated situations and contradictory attitudes. Recently Max had rung Peter at home to discuss some matter and then had begun to muse on Morrison's position. He was obviously beginning to regret leaving him hanging about in an ill-defined position on the centre spread.

Peter's view was that anyone could have told him that was an error ages ago, and to finish up with both Don Berry and Morrison thinking they are in charge of the same department is nuts. He said he thought Morrison's job didn't really exist anyway. 'He's got bugger-all to do.'

Peter was puzzled by Max's editorship so far. Without bitchiness or anger, but with genuine incomprehension, he said it was impossible to see a coherent plan or shape that connected the various developments of recent weeks. He allowed that Max may learn. He was kind about the young fellow, and amused that Max should have apparently begun to value his opinions. At the same time he could see no reason for Max's change of attitude. It was just another perplexing switch.

I tried out some of my views on Peter, for instance that Max had no interest in politics, and that perhaps he rather wished he had more direction from the management. That he'd accepted the job in a spirit of adventure and fun and found the reality more difficult than he'd anticipated, and even unpleasant. Peter neither agreed nor disagreed.

Sarah, Peter's secretary, came in and after a little while I left. As I opened the door I looked straight across the narrow corridor and met the level gaze of Max who was just sitting down in Morrison's office. The expression on his face was one of surprise, and it seemed to me of enquiry. 'What have you been up to?' he seemed to ask. I felt a guilty look flash across my own face and thought wildly, 'My God! He's been listening to our conversation.' Then the impossibility of that struck me and I thought, '. . . but perhaps he heard our last few words.' I tried to think what we'd been saying as I had walked towards the door, but I couldn't remember.

On the way back to my office I wondered uneasily about my feelings of guilt about gossiping. Knowing that I am writing down as much of this sort of talk as I can remember, and that I am not telling my friends that I'm doing so, means that I am going in for sustained double deceit. Gossip behind people's back almost invariably involves breaking small confidences and a degree of damaging misrepresentation, and writing down confidential conversations is dubious, to say the least. I think my immediate flush of guilty feeling when I looked unexpectedly into Max's eyes was related to the dodgy position I'm in anyway and not caused by my conversation with Peter. Actually, on the whole, Peter and I had been speaking warmly about Max.

Wednesday 16 April
Caroline and I went to a party this evening at L'Escargot. I met Trevor Grove, who is the features editor on the *Observer*, and he asked about

the *Telegraph*. He's an old friend of Max's and likes the new *Telegraph*. He gave me a snapshot of Max from a few years ago.

'I used to have lunch with him quite often at one time,' he said. 'He used to embarrass me like anything. He had this great booming laugh, 'HUH! HUH! HUH!' and he'd say things at the top of his voice. I remember him saying years ago, "Trevor, isn't life wonderful? Isn't journalism just wonderful?" ' Trevor laughed affectionately. 'He used to say, "Trevor, never forget the journalism is fun. It's a great game – HA! HA! HA!" '

I said I thought the game had got a bit serious for Max now.

The high spot of the evening for me was listening to Martin Ivens attack Bernard Levin for the recent leader in *The Times* about Max, the *Telegraph* and the Murdoch ad which had been refused. Martin accused *The Times* of lying, distorting and general meanness of spirit. Bernard said Max had refused the ad simply because he was terrified of the union reaction and because his management had ordered him to.

I intervened to say I happened to know that wasn't true. In fact the management and advertising department had been in favour of using the ad. Max had refused it on the grounds he'd given, ie why should he help advertise a rival? Bernard said that was even more contemptible.

Martin said furiously, 'Are you saying Max is a coward? I would have thought that is a pretty difficult accusation to stand up. Mr Levin, are you calling Max a coward?'

Bernard blustered a bit. Shaking with rage Martin repeated, 'Answer me, Mr Levin – are you calling Max a coward? Are you calling him a liar? Tell me, did anyone from your office telephone Max and ask him how and why that decision was taken?'

Martin was magnificent and Bernard was awful. I could see him underestimating Martin's anger and intelligence.

We were interrupted for a moment by someone pushing past and Martin turned away. 'I've said what I wanted to say – I'm not going on with this. Fuck him!'

Thursday 17 April
The *Telegraph*'s criticism of Mrs Thatcher over the Libyan crisis is surely more robust that it would have been during Bill's regime.

At about 11.00 this morning while I was writing up this journal I got a phone call from a very brisk lady who announced that Charles Wilson, the editor of *The Times*, was expecting me at 1.00 at Wheeler's restaurant in Great Tower Street. For a moment I hesitated and she said, 'You are lunching with Mr Wilson today, aren't you?'

I said, 'John O'Sullivan suggested two dates to me and said he'd confirm one of them. As I heard no more from him I assumed the lunch was cancelled or indefinitely postponed.' I spoke sharply and accusingly, expressing the degree to which I was annoyed by her peremptory, bossy tone.

Her manner altered in a flash, 'Oh,' she said. 'That's very naughty of him.'

Having succeeded in putting her down I said, 'That's perfectly all right,' allowing a dignified hint of forgiveness to come through. 'One o'clock, then. Can you tell me where Great Tower Street is?'

'Somewhere in the City,' she snapped. 'Haven't you got an *A to Z*?'

I mentally tipped my hat to her swift and savage counter-attack, 'Yes.' She hung up with a triumphant and offhand, 'Good'.

I rang Martin Ivens to cancel the lunch date we had. It turned out he'd seen Charles Wilson yesterday.

'Crumbs,' I said, 'They're certainly trawling through the *Telegraph*, aren't they? What's he like? Is he as frightening and thuggish as he's cracked up to be?'

'He'll be gentle with you,' said Martin, and he packed an awful lot of sarcasm and curiously undirected contempt into the remark.

I laughed as much in surprise at his intensity as at the joke. 'How did you get on with him?'

'OK. I'll tell you later.'

I got to the restaurant and checked in my helmet and jacket. As I turned from the counter I saw a man standing by the door who had obviously just entered. It crossed my mind that he was Charles Wilson so I approached him. 'Are you Mr Wilson?' I asked.

I think for a moment he took me for a member of staff or perhaps someone he'd met before, because he seemed to hesitate and then said as if very surprised, 'Are you Mr Garland?'

'Yes. How do you do?'

'How did you know it was me?' he asked. He gave the impression that he couldn't quite work out how we'd managed to make contact.

'I dunno – perhaps I've seen a photo of you. Anyway, you looked as if you were waiting for someone.'

He has the reputation of being a foul-mouthed tough guy and an oaf, but his manner was quiet and courteous. His face, now smiling and relaxed, had a hard-bitten look. An urchin grin lurked beneath the polite expression and it was easy to see how his features could contort into a scowl. His soft Scottish accent had a similar two-sided quality. It is an extremely attractive accent in repose, but it lends itself all too easily to bellicose threats and violent abuse.

I declined a drink. He said, 'Do you never drink or like me do you just not drink at lunch time?'

'I never drink at lunch time and I'm here on my motor bike and I never drink when I'm on my bike.'

This remark led immediately to a lively conversation about biking.

He told me he'd long since given up motor bikes because they were too dangerous. He'd come off too often as a young man but he said, 'Unlike you, I often drank when I was riding.' He made this admission, as people often do when speaking of drink, wishing to give two contradictory impressions. While wanting to appear sensible and mature now, he was also quite happy to establish that in his youth he'd been a bit of a lad.

We discussed the extraordinary fascination of motor bikes and I told him how much I'd enjoyed a course in riding I'd taken. My instructor was an RAF man who had taught me to ride safely. His lessons in taking care, always knowing what you were doing and letting other road users know, keeping your bike properly cleaned and serviced and so on had great resonance for me. Metaphorically his instructions applied to life in a wider sense and not just to the problems of surviving a bike ride.

Wilson looked thoughtfully at me as I tried to describe this experience. He told me that he has a deal with his fifteen-year-old daughter that she'll get a car as soon as she's allowed to drive on the understanding that she cannot have a motor bike until she's twenty-one. 'If she hasn't been on a bike by then, she won't want one.' He spoke very sweetly about his small children and how his daughters would rush to kiss him and have a cuddle when he came home from work, while his little son was more likely to greet him with a flurry of punches. He smiled affectionately at the memory.

While lunch proceeded the conversation was entirely in this mode. We talked about our wives and children, about our general interests. He asked me about my interest in fine art and spoke at length about a 19th-century artist whose house he now lives in and whose work he collects.

'I love paintings and all art. I'm hopeless at it. I mean, I couldn't even write my name – do the ABC of drawing, I mean – but I love it. I love oil paintings, pastels, water colours, pen and ink, gauch . . .' I could have sworn he hesitated for a moment wondering if the last word had come out quite right; it hadn't.

Eventually I thought, to hell with this – I'm not going to spend a whole lunch idly chatting. So I said, 'I don't know whether it's appropriate to ask you, but I'd be extremely interested to hear your views on the *Telegraph* at the moment and Fleet Street.'

'You mean on Max,' he said.

'I mean on everything.'

He began to speak in a somewhat rambling way, then stopped abruptly. 'Start again,' he instructed himself. 'The *Telegraph* has begun to do what it should do, what it should have done in 1983 or perhaps even earlier . . .' He described how *The Times* had recognised the need for certain changes to be made and had gone about implementing them with energy and with a clear appreciation of what its goals were.

'We had an almost exclusively male readership so we went for female readers. It meant enlarging the paper, investing more money, developing new features. And we succeeded.' He described the way they'd gone for new readers elsewhere, all the time attacking the long-term interests of the *Telegraph* who let the years slip by without responding to the challenge. It was like listening to a wolf describing how it had taken a flock of fat lambs. I began to see that just because a man mispronounced the word 'gouache' it didn't mean he wasn't a formidable rival.

If he had expressed a pitying contempt for the old regime at the *Telegraph* he spoke of Max and Andrew Knight with a straightforward, good-natured and generous respect. He was also supremely confident that he and Murdoch could wipe the floor with them when it came to battling for readers – at least, that was the impression he gave me.

He recalled a conversation he'd had in Max's house in Leicestershire shortly after Bill Deedes retired. In the course of it Max had said, 'I suspect that like me you are not really interested in politics.' Wilson described how astonished he'd been by this extraordinary remark. To him it was nonsense to have an editor of *The Times* or of the *Telegraph* who was not interested in politics.

'I was very glad to hear him say that,' said Wilson, half smiling. 'I mean, from where *I* am,' he added, gesturing as if to say not himself personally but as a rival. He frankly said that actually he wasn't personally all that interested in politics in a way, but he bloody well was as an editor. He had to be.

He went on to talk about another side of editing. 'The editor must be the most commercially-minded bloke in the building,' he said, and discoursed for a while on management and his relationship with Rupert. I cannot remember all his words and themes but gradually he built up a self-portrait which fascinated me.

He is a rough and blunt man but his very lack of subtlety means that he concentrates his cunning and intelligent mind very powerfully on any given problem. He wastes no time projecting a smooth and urbane style, and makes up for his lack of sophistication with a dogged and single-minded ambition to win. I enjoyed listening to him, even as it chilled me to hear the opposition speaking with such unforced confidence.

He made only one slip. I had raised the subject of cartoons and cartoonists and we were discussing Peter Brookes who used to do political cartoons for *The Times* and has now gone back to illustrating features instead. He let it slip that one of the reasons Peter was not quite suitable as a political cartoonist was that on certain issues his views diverged too far from Mr Wilson's own. He had suddenly, and I think accidentally, revealed the really hard side of working for a Murdoch paper. I instantly expressed surprise that *The Times* should fine it necessary to curb the views of one of its cartoonists. I hoped to make it clear that I would not be happy working under such close direction. At once he rephrased what he had said. It was not that *he* censored the *cartoonist*, it was that the *cartoonist* did not feel at ease with the views of the *editor*. I was unconvinced by his subsequent waffling on this subject.

Wilson went out of his way to attack Max and the *Telegraph* management for their 'despicable' treatment of Peter Utley. He said it was one of the most unpleasant episodes he'd ever come across in a lifetime of working on newspapers. Peter had run into a problem when the new management of the *Telegraph* had not felt bound by a verbal agreement made between Peter and Lord Hartwell.

'I've worked with some real hard nuts – like David English, who is the biggest and best bandit I've ever met – but he would never have behaved like that.'

He sounded genuinely shocked at the way the *Telegraph* had been prepared to muck Peter about after he'd served the paper so well, simply to stop him going to a rival. He repeated several times, 'It's despicable – despicable.' What annoyed him most of all was that in his opinion the *Telegraph* hadn't even wanted to keep Peter until they realised *The Times* valued him very highly.

Finally he said that John O'Sullivan had explained why I couldn't leave the *Telegraph* at the moment and that he completely understood, even though he regretted it very much. On that friendly note we got up, agreeing that we'd enjoyed our lunch. He followed me up the stairs towards the street and began speaking in his quiet voice. I am quite deaf in my left ear and as he was on my bad side I had to turn my head awkwardly to catch the words.

'What I was going to offer you was £50,000, a car and three weeks abroad each year to write your illustrated journals for our feature pages.'

'That's extremely generous – I hardly know what to say. But thank you at least for the offer.'

I got my coat and helmet and we stepped outside.

'You know where I am,' he said, and raising his hand briefly he turned towards his car.

I rode back to the *Telegraph* unable to stop grinning to myself at the size of his offer.

Martin came to see me to fix up a new lunch date. I told him what Wilson had said to me. 'They'll pay that much to fuck us up,' he said grimly. I did not think this remark very flattering but it was probably true.

Later in the afternoon I had a disturbing phone call from Don Berry. In the most circumspect way imaginable he was ringing to pass on a message from Max. The burden of it was that the paper had come down very heavily on Mrs Thatcher during the last few days over the bombing of Tripoli and therefore Max did not want another cartoon hammering away on that point. In fact I had already begun to sketch out an idea which was on the theme of Gaddafi's survival, so Max's instruction was unnecessary; but nonetheless unwelcome for that. I said nothing to Don for a moment, then muttered that it was difficult enough thinking of cartoons on my own without having to take other people's ideas into account as well.

'Of course, of course,' he said, trying to pacify me and obviously not enjoying his job. 'It's just an idea Max had . . . er . . . he just felt that . . . er. . .'

'Well,' I said, 'I hear him.'

He laughed. 'That's what Max says when he doesn't like something – "I hear you." '

I made what I hoped was a good-natured snorting noise. 'OK then,' I said and hung up feeling less than entirely happy.

I did the cartoon I'd planned. It showed Gaddafi the terrorist as a phoenix rising from the fires of the bombing raid.

Max said, 'I don't like it. I don't like it as much as . . . er . . .'

I felt quite angry.

'I got a message from you,' I said coldly, 'and whatever you feel about the cartoon, it's what you wanted.'

'Yes, yes,' he said. 'Fine. OK.'

'All I'm saying is that Gaddafi has survived and is coming back fighting.'

'Yes, yes,' he said testily. 'OK.'

I thought, 'I'm going to have to watch you.'

I made my way to Don's room. He took the cartoon and smiled. 'Very good,' he said.

'Max didn't like it.'

'Why?' He sounded surprised.

'Dunno,' I said. 'It seems OK to me.'

Mike Green who was watching us said, 'It's fine', and Don also repeated, 'It's very good. I like it.'

Friday 18 April
The *Telegraph* continues to be outspoken against the government on the USA's bombing strike against Libya. I asked three colleagues about our line and all three approved of it.

18 April, *Daily Telegraph*

Don Berry was frankly opposed to the British having given permission for the American bombers stationed on British soil to be used. He was surprised that Max was so anti Mrs Thatcher. He told me that before the leader writers' conference Max had sketched out a leader on the subject criticising the government. When they all met at 12.15 his piece was handed round. Not a single voice was raised in Mrs Thatcher's defence.

That afternoon I completed my cartoon for the *Sunday Telegraph*. When I handed it in to Perry he was obviously not entirely happy about it. It showed Reagan and Thatcher as pilot and co-pilot of a bomber. On the fuselage near Reagan was painted a line of silhouetted bombs indicating successful raids. Near Mrs Thatcher was a similar line, only in her case instead of bombs there were four hostages' coffins.

Perry made it clear that he'd publish the cartoon whether he liked it or not but he questioned its justification and disagreed with the implicit attack on Reagan and Thatcher. We wrangled about it a little. He thought the raid a good idea and backed Mrs Thatcher's decision.

Alexander Chancellor came in while we were talking but on hearing what was going on he left at once. I called in to see him on my way to the features department with my cartoon. He thought Max's decision to come out against the raid was the correct one. However, it was the fact that Max should risk annoying the readers by his spirited condemnation of the American president and a Tory PM that really aroused Alexander's admiration. And even that example of Max's independence was insignificant alongside the fact that Conrad Black would almost certainly be extremely displeased by Max's line.

Alexander reminded me that Black once said that he was prepared to let his editors have a completely free hand except on one subject. He forbade attacks on American presidents in general and President Reagan in particular. Alexander lit another cigarette and gave out a burst of hissing laughter, acknowledging Max to be quite a chap.

I asked him about the *Independent* and he said he'd met Andreas that lunchtime quite by chance in the street. Andreas had seemed cheerful and optimistic but Alexander had not picked up any gossip about *Independent* recruits. I told him that James was almost certainly joining. He thought that was good for the *Independent*.

I said, 'I gather they failed to get Alexander Chancellor.' He laughed and said something about never knowing what that bloke would do, one could not be sure, never too late and so on.

I said that I discovered in myself a developing sense of belonging to this new *Telegraph* that we found ourselves in. 'I'm even beginning to think of the *Independent* as a rival,' I said. He agreed that a similar mood had gripped him. He said something about wanting to stay here to see it through to death or glory. We were half mocking ourselves because of course it's very uncool to admit one cares about anything – and most particularly that one might care about the survival of one's own newspaper. 'Makes one sound rather like a cub scout promising to do one's best – I mean, Christ!'

In the evening James rang. He said he had joined the *Independent*. That is, he had agreed to join in September. He is going to 'do' the Far East for them. First of all he'll revisit the Philippines and is contracted to stay out there, moving about as he pleases, for six months.

'And after that?'

'I'll cross that bridge when I get to it,' he replied.

'I'm glad for you if you've got what you want – and I'm glad for them. But I will miss you.'

'Six months isn't all that long.'

'One six months will lead to another.'

'We'll see.'

I said, 'I want to tell you what happened to me.' I related the offer *The Times* had made to me.

James laughed. 'That's very nice.'

I said I wasn't tempted but it had all been good fun.

'What sort of a car?' said James.

'Well, it wasn't a Mini.'

I asked him whether he had mentioned to Andreas and co. that I had heard that Wally Fawkes might be persuaded to join up. Tony Howard had told me that Wally was a bit strapped for money now that Flook was no longer running in the *Mirror*. He was even doing drawings for *Today* at the moment. James said slowly, 'Yes, I did mention Wally to them.'

'And . . . ?' I prompted.

'They said, "Mm, but the person we really want is Nick." '

I felt a small and slightly anxious wave of pleasure at this news – pleased that they still wanted me and anxious because it meant there were still matters to be settled in this area.

'OK,' I said. 'Tell me what they said.'

'Well, they said they wanted you, and I said that I gathered you had agreed to stay on the *Telegraph*. They just said, "Oh, it doesn't matter about that!" '

'Hmmm,' I said.

'In fact they said to me, "Now that you've joined, your first job is to get Nick" – so what do you want?'

'Is that why you asked me what sort of car *The Times* offered?'

'Yes.'

'Right,' I said. 'You know it's not a Mini and you *start* at £50,000.'

I could hear James chuckling down the phone but he said, 'No, seriously, where do we start?'

'I think we should talk seriously and at length. Not here and now.' (Supper was being prepared while I was having this conversation.) 'I'd like to have lunch *à deux*, and talk properly some time soon.'

'OK.'

Sunday 20 April

Over the last three evenings Caroline has read through this journal up to here. She said it gives a unique glimpse into the way men work together and talk to each other and plot. She said that, probably in a way I had never intended, a vivid and unusual portrait of modern males emerges. Actually, that is not so far from my purpose. I am trying to be as honest as I can, even though that means putting either myself, or others whom I am fond of, in a less than flattering light.

There is one story she reminded me of. When Max was addressing the staff on his first day in the editor's chair he said, 'No one will ever get stick from me for pointing out my mistakes; I expect to make mistakes. But I will come down like a ton of bricks on anyone who knows I'm making a mistake and doesn't tell me so, until it's too late. That I won't like.'

She has several times told me that on the strength of this statement of Max's I should tell him some of the criticisms that I have jotted down here. As a matter of fact I'd rather like to, but he's so damned elusive. I suppose Caroline would say, 'That's the first criticism.'

Monday 21 April

After three weeks of Max's new look, which has provided me with more space and prominence, I'm beginning to struggle. At first the excitement and challenge of the innovations stimulated me and I found my ideas flowing smoothly and easily. Good old stand-by political themes such as trouble with the Left in the Labour Party and Ronnie Reagan on the rampage in the Mediterranean helped, but today an awful kind of dullness came over me. I felt sluggish and tired and did a boring, rather confused, cartoon.

When I took it in to Max he was sitting at his desk talking to Peter Kellner of the *New Statesman*.

I was pleased to see Kellner because I admire him and always like to see lefties at the *Telegraph*, and I was also glad to see Max apparently having found time to sit and talk with someone. He was perfectly nice about my second-rate cartoon and said with a smile, 'Mm – nothing to upset Conrad Black in that.'

I remembered that Black was in town and said, 'Oh – have you been in trouble?'

'I had dinner with him last night.'

'Did he have a go at you about the *Telegraph*'s line on Libya?'

Max paused, grinning, and puffed his cigar. 'Let's say he greatly admired Perry's leader on Sunday.'

Perry had praised Mrs Thatcher for supporting the Americans in order not to weaken the NATO Alliance. 'Really?' I said. 'Well – right on, Max.'

'Just don't do anything too unkind about Reagan in the next few days,' he said.

'That's no good, Max. You've set the standard for independence and free criticism. You can't expect others to be more careful than you.'

He only half laughed because, I think, there was an element of seriousness behind his banter. He was not giving me a line that I must follow – but I guess he had been involved in a lively debate with Black, and perhaps did not altogether enjoy it.

Suddenly Peter said, 'No! I can't stand that sort of gossip, that sort of talk.' I thought for a moment he was chiding me for asking about what Conrad Black had said, but then it occurred to me he was continuing the conversation that my entrance had interrupted. 'It's like *Private Eye*. It's lies. I hate *Private Eye*. I think it is an evil institution. I won't buy it. I never buy it. I read other people's copies to find out what they are saying, but I don't buy it.'

Peter was spluttering with passion, and partly mocking his own strong feelings, but there was no doubting his anger and dislike.

More calmly, Max agreed with him.

'They really are the limit,' he said. 'They wrote a piece in the last issue that was simply untrue. They picked up the fact that I'd sacked Alfred Sherman and then said' – here his voice rose to an incredulous squeal – 'that I'd consulted Ed Pearce first.' He chortled contemptuously. 'As if I'd consult *Pearce* – about *Sherman!*' He and Peter shook their heads. 'I thought of writing them a letter, but what the hell – it's useless.'

'Agreed.' I said. 'Letters to *Private Eye* always come out wrong.'

Peter murmured, 'Yeah, it's no good doing that. They've got you somehow.'

Max went on, 'Peter Hillmore also wrote about the *Telegraph* on Sunday. Do you think he went to the trouble to pick up the phone and check the story? Pshaw!' He rocked back in his chair with one foot on his desk, and blew out cigar smoke. 'I think the principle "This story is too good to check" is just about OK in Greek Street, but it won't do elsewhere.'

This seemed a dubious statement. Deliberate carelessness with the truth is always bad.

I left the room puzzling over Peter's ridiculous position of refusing to buy *Private Eye* yet being keen to read it. The situation is obviously more inconvenient to Peter than the editorship of *Private Eye*; but paradoxically I like Peter the more for caring as much as he does, for being uncool enough to show it and for ruefully admitting that his attitude is fundamentally daft.

James rang and we arranged to have lunch on Wednesday. I hope he is going to try to get me to join the *Independent* because I will enjoy watching how he goes about it and I am intrigued to find out how much they want me. I don't suppose he has been given plenipotentiary powers but he might have some idea of what's on offer.

I met Martin Ivens as I was leaving the building, and he asked, 'Are you still smarting after your conversation?' I didn't know what he meant. 'I mean your scene with *The Times*.'

'I'm not smarting about that,' I said puzzled. 'I enjoyed it.'

'No – I mean – not smarting – I mean, it's all rather disturbing perhaps, mm? Unsettling, mm?'

'Not really. I know I don't want to go to Wapping and anyway, I don't want to work for Murdoch. I was scared by Charlie Wilson.'

'By him suggesting that the cartoonist's freedom of expression might be limited?'

'Yeah. He's a hard man. They're all hard men there.' A thought struck me. 'By the way, I hear the *Independent* chaps have got their money. Are they after you again?'

'Yup,' he said. 'As a matter of fact I'm seeing them again.'

'Are you tempted?'

'Maybe.'

'Let's talk about it on Thursday.' We're to have lunch then.

'Mm – OK.'

Tuesday 22 April
I think Max must be getting a bit of pressure from Conrad Black. My cartoon today was based on the news that the Labour Party is dropping 'The Red Flag' from its iconography and its song-sheet. When I handed the drawing to Max he said cheerfully, 'Oh, good – nothing there to make Black worry.'

I said something noncommittal and looked at him enquiringly.

'I think Conrad believes he has appointed a bunch of subversives,' he said with a broad smile.

I raised my fist in what I hoped looked like the Socialist salute and said in a jokey way, 'Well, he has.' The smile died on Max's lips and he turned back to continue his conversation with the foreign editor that I had interrupted.

Of course Max is not a subversive, but an editor who may make wayward political decisions or follow contradictory lines has a subversive effect in the end. Perhaps I was suggesting something like that with my frivolous remark, and Max picked it up.

Wednesday 23 April
James was late for our lunch. For half an hour I sat in the Café Pelican restaurant and tried to find something to read in *The Times*. My eyes skidded and slipped off the edges of articles on many different subjects. I glanced at the letters column and the leaders. I even worked my way down the gossip column until I hit a patch of Fantoni and finished up back in the middle of a great expanse of features.

Quality newspapers often have this effect on me. It is something to do with the paper's intention to instruct and inform. I become an idle schoolboy again, metaphorically gazing out of the window or doodling in the margin. The tabloids are easier to read when I am in this mood, but they quickly get tedious for different reasons. With them the attempt to entertain and hold the attention with ersatz emotion – 'Little angels in mercy dash' – can produce deep depression and boredom of a different kind. Even as a schoolboy I grew out of comics eventually.

I watched the restaurant filling up. Couples met and kissed, and pairs of men and groups of women all with cheerful expectant looks on their faces came and took their places. When James arrived bowing and pressing the palms of his hands together in an apology I said, 'Typical of the new high-tech-wizzo-go-go-go newspaper industry. Half an hour late.'

'Sorry about that,' he said.

I told him about an exhibition of expressionist woodcuts I'd been to recently when I had seen among many other treasures a Heckel landscape that I would have loved to own.

'Why didn't you buy it?'

'Because it cost £3,000.'

We ordered lunch and then I looked at him enquiringly as if to say, OK, make your pitch.

He sipped his wine and said slowly, 'Andreas told me to tell you he'd buy you that Heckel if you joined the *Independent*.'

'Done,' I said, and we laughed. 'Best bit of recruiting I've ever heard. We might as well stop now and go home.'

James said, 'Why don't you join?' and I made my usual speech about being settled at the *Telegraph*, being gripped by inertia, being uncertain of how long the *Independent* would last and how good it would be.

After we'd wrangled to and fro about this, I said, 'Why don't you tell me, "Andreas is a remarkable man. I am absolutely convinced that he is going to be an excellent editor and that the *Independent* is going to be a terrific paper"?'

James began to say very nice things about Andreas and about Stephen and Matthew as well, but he said there was nothing he knew about them that I didn't know already. 'All I can say is that when they have finished recruiting they will not look so exposed. Everything will change once they've got a staff around them. At the moment they're standing on the street in the drizzle wearing their white scarves and waiting for a taxi called the *Independent* to come by.'

This odd but pleasing metaphor had some truth in it.

In the end he said, 'The person you must talk to is Andreas. It turns on him really, doesn't it?

'Mm, yes.'

'And on Caroline. Talk to her and weigh up what she earns and what you earn, and see what she says . . .'

He's right about Andreas but I'm not sure I can go on playing silly buggers like this, leading them on and letting them down again. I said, 'It will be much clearer when they've finished their recruiting, I suppose.'

'Yes – but you can't wait until then. You are part of their recruiting. Each recruit plays a part in convincing other prospective recruits.'

'I know.'

He told me that Tom Sutcliffe has been given the job of arts editor. When James went to the *Independent* to negotiate his conditions and pay, Tom was talking to Andreas in one room while James was with Steven in another. They'd met as they came in and James said both of them felt like conspirators.

While James and Steve talked Andreas came in and said, 'I'm terribly sorry to interrupt – just want to clear something up. Steve, do you think that . . . er . . . the books page should be a satrap of the arts section?'

Stephen considered for a moment and said, 'Yes – yes I do.'

115

'Fine,' said Andreas. 'Thanks.' He turned to go but paused by the door and said, 'By the way – what *is* a satrap?'

'Well,' said Stephen and James, 'it's a sort of junior authority – literally, provincial governor in ancient Persia – a subordinate ruler . . .'

'Oh thanks,' said Andreas, and left.

Later over a drink with Tom, James mentioned this peculiar exchange, and Tom laughed and said, 'That sort of explains something. What happened was that while I was talking to Andreas he suddenly said to me, "Should books be a satrap of the arts?" and I didn't have a clue what a satrap was, so I thought for a while – and then realised I'd thought for so long I could not now admit to not understanding the question. So I said, "Well, I think it follows from what you're saying." I thought a puzzled look went over Andreas's face and he left the room. I suppose he must have been thinking, "Christ! What have I been saying?" '

It is a perfect example of a moment I am only too familiar with, when you realise you no longer understand what anyone, including yourself, is talking about.

I only know what satrap means because at school I once played Darius in Terence Rattigan's *Adventure Story* and the word crops up once or twice in the play.

Thursday 24 April

I had lunch with Martin Ivens today. He was talkative enough, but I thought he seemed preoccupied. He made very clear statements of approval and disapproval about Max's appointments and editorial decisions and yet I remained uncertain about his confidence in the *Telegraph*. We agreed that the design changes in the centre were unsuccessful and that the paper is looking grey and dull. Perhaps the fact that we couldn't ever get down to a coherent discussion of what's going on at the paper is because what's going on is itself muddled and inconsistent. The shape our conversation took was that I asked for his opinion on different matters and he gave brief and quick answers. Behind my questions I was probing as usual for some sort of information that would help me decide about my own future. There is no doubt that I've started veering about again, and I do not feel that at the moment the *Telegraph* is a happy place.

Martin too is trying to decide whether to stay or go. *The Times* and the *Independent* have made overtures to him. He feels sure he could walk into another job tomorrow – but doesn't know whether he wants to or not.

He showed me a memo from Max inviting him to join a weekly lunch party that the *Telegraph* is going to hold. Sometimes it is intended to ask a few guests along, and Martin was requested to put forward names of interesting people to include. As he handed the paper to me he said, 'This made me feel encouraged and wanted.'

I read the note. 'Suggest my name,' I said, feeling quite sad not to have received an invitation of my own. Martin at once said very nicely that of course he would.

I asked him directly whether he felt any loyalty to the *Telegraph* and if so did it make the decision to stay or leave more difficult. He said he did of course feel loyalty to it, and affection, but not so much that he couldn't easily leave.

He described a conversation he'd had with Conrad Black at a lunch earlier in the week. Black is an historian and so is Martin. Black's hero is Napoleon, and somehow Martin found himself pointing out a serious error in something Black said about the great man. 'I don't know what came over me – I had a feeling I just didn't care. I said to him, "That isn't quite right, because as you will remember in the Treaty of . . . blah-blah-blah". People round the table were listening open-mouthed.'

'How did Black react?'

'Perfectly OK – no problem. But I had this feeling of no longer caring what I said – to anyone.'

'Quite right, too. Why should you care?'

Martin picked out Graham Paterson as a strong figure on the *Sunday Telegraph*. He likened him to a charging bull who simply went for what he wanted, and '. . . he'll get it until someone builds a brick wall in front of him.'

I tried asking for his opinions on the *Independent* but he replied quite correctly he had no opinions because at the moment there was nothing to go on.

Later in the day Richard Ingrams rang to ask me to do a drawing for the *Eye* and we talked a bit about the *Telegraph*. He had no particular views, just some light-hearted stories about Perry that Alexander Chancellor had told him. He sounded like everyone sounds these days – wanting the paper to do well but not feeling reassured by things so far.

The next phone call I got was from Andreas Whittam Smith.

A: I was wondering if we could meet – perhaps for lunch – and talk.
ME: I'd like that very much.
A: I understand very well what your position is. I think I am very well informed, but I don't want things to just end. I'd like to . . . er . . .
ME: Er . . . sort of settle things.
A: Yes, settle it.
ME: So would I.
A: Can you make next Tuesday?
ME: Yes, fine.

A: Is the Garrick all right? Not too public?
ME: No, of course not – what the hell.
A: Yeah, what the hell. OK then, Tuesday 1.00.

While I was still thinking about this Morrison came in for a chat. Just as with Martin it was impossible to get from him anything but a general feeling that he is uneasy about the future of the paper. I asked, for example, what Andrew Knight was up to these days and Morrison said that the management was desperately trying to come to terms with the unions about redundancy payments when we go over to direct input in the autumn. I could not follow all the technicalities of this but the impression is that behind the struggling editorial front of the *Telegraph* there lies a beleaguered and desperate management hanging on by their eyebrows.

Each department of the paper is independently budgeted and every few weeks up pops an alarming figure on a computer telling the departmental heads that they are nearly in the red. Max has been spending like a sailor – not just on commissioning articles but on rebuilding and partitioning office space, new equipment and new staff.

Morrison told me that leader writer conferences are improving a bit, getting more chatty, particularly now that Bill Deedes attends them.

I was genuinely amazed. '*Bill* attends leader writer conferences? 'Good God!'

I really ought to go to a few of these sessions. I cannot but believe it's a mistake for Bill to go. It is essential for Max to develop an interest in politics and to begin to create a coherent *Telegraph* line on things. This is simply impossible with Bill around. For a start, where Bill does have a reasonably clear view over, say, South Africa or Northern Ireland, Max disagrees with it, and elsewhere Bill is notoriously changeable in his views, which of course leads him into difficulties.

The whole thing is daft. Retiring bosses should always keep away for a bit to allow the new boss to find his or her way.

Morrison didn't appear to find anything strange about it – but he rarely gives much away. I couldn't even find out from him what his own job is. It is almost as if in spite of everything, in spite of Andrew Knight and Conrad Black, and the change of editor, and the hirings and firings, the *Telegraph* is just steaming on in its majestic, aimless way. The fact that it is holed below the water line, has lost its rudder and that its engines have rusted up, hasn't made any difference.

Except perhaps that it is settling lower in the water now.

I asked Morrison to get me an invitation to Max's lunches. He was surprised I hadn't already been asked and said Max probably just forgot. He also said Max would probably feel that if I was suffering from a sense of isolation I should start attending the morning conference.

I felt irritated by Morrison saying that; the mornings are the only time I have for doing things other than *Telegraph* work, and I won't give them up.

Monday 28 April

Morrison came to my office today to ask about something or other and, still puzzling over the question of Bill at the leader writer conferences, I put it to him straight.

'Don't you think it's a peculiar arrangement for an ex-editor to become a leader writer?'

Morrison gave a particular smile that he does at such moments. Roughly translated it means, you've hit the nail on the head, and it would be wrong of me to comment, but I'm going to anyway. He perched on the edge of my desk. 'I think Max panicked when he saw the appalling standard of writing that the leader writers he inherited were producing.'

'So why not recruit some good ones?'

'He did – he recruited Bill.'

'But while Bill is a marvellous writer his political views are not Max's – where they can be defined at all.'

Morrison's smile broadened. 'Of course that is a problem. Today for instance, Bill wanted to write on South Africa but Max said, "I'd rather you did that under your own name." Max has a rather brisk way with him. He doesn't find it difficult to speak his mind.'

'What an awkward arrangement.'

'It isn't really. What Max wants is to appoint a main leader writer to be a sort of guru and set the style. He hasn't found him yet and Bill is standing in until he does.'

Morrison told me that he'd raised with Max the question of my being invited to his lunches. He then stopped speaking, leaving me with the uneasy feeling that Max had not been very interested in this suggestion.

'And?' I said.

'He said – er – yes, well – I told him you'd like to come.'

'But what was his reaction?'

'As I said, he said he'd, er, that he would see what he – he didn't really . . .'

'Morrison,' I said, looking him in the eye and feeling distinctly irritated, 'what did Max actually say?'

'Yes – he got the message.'

I gave up.

I met Bill waiting for a lift.

He assumed his chatting posture, one hand thrust deep into a trouser pocket, the other holding some papers high up, pressed over his heart.

His whole body bends like a longbow, his head sinks into his shoulders and his tummy pushes forward as his back arches.

'Working hard?' he asked pleasantly, grinning at the floor.

'Everyone is working hard, Bill. These are difficult days.'

'Ah, shoulder to the wheel; stand by; all hands on deck; save the company,' he said, remaining upright by an extraordinary feat of balance. 'That's the ticket.'

'That's right,' I said.

'Working *too* hard,' he said mysteriously, moving towards his lift and vanishing.

As usual he left me with an agreeable sensation that nothing matters very much and hardly anything matters at all; or, as whoever it was said, 'The situation is critical but not serious.'

What a survivor Bill is! How beautifully he is now placed to modestly accept a great dollop of credit if the paper succeeds, and, if the new regime flops, equally modestly to say he'd stood by and done what he could. I can't help liking him more for it.

Earlier in the day I was in the art room looking at the day's crop of pictures and talking to Bernard. 'Ah!' he said, 'there's our front page picture.' He picked up a photograph of a pretty young woman walking down a street.

'Who is she?'

'Doesn't matter,' he said, with mock urgency. 'She's young, she's good looking and she's a she. Max says every day, "We've got to get pictures of young attractive girls into the paper" – so that young people will buy it,' he added by way of explanation, flicking his eyes upwards to indicate scepticism. He put the photograph to one side with a decisive thump, and I laughed.

Tuesday 29 April

I shouldn't have laughed. The picture appeared large on today's front page. The girl is the daughter of an aristocrat and the caption explained that she had been snapped on her way to work. Oh dear, oh dear, oh dear! On the front page of *The Times* there was a photograph of the interior of the nuclear power station in Chernobyl.

I went to the Garrick at 1.00 to meet Andreas. In the foyer I met Eric Shorter the critic, and Desmond Albrow, from the *Sunday Telegraph*. I asked Eric how he found things at the *Telegraph* these days. My question stimulated an outburst of anxious shrill remarks about 'Oh my God . . . I mean, who knows? Isn't it just panic stations everywhere? One spends one's life on one's knees, literally praying for survival – I mean to say . . .'

Desmond listened, huge and still like a giant bullfrog. He said, 'I never see you these days. Come and have a drink.' He gestured upstairs.

'I'm waiting for someone; he's due any second, but thanks awfully.' Somehow I felt I shouldn't say who I was meeting.

The two *Telegraph* men walked upstairs. They looked so English and Establishment, comfortably mounting the broad staircase of their club in search of large gins.

The next man to walk past me was Perry. He touched my shoulder and also at once invited me for a drink. Once more I explained why I would not join him.

'Right-o, but if he doesn't arrive soon or you get tired of hanging about, I'll be in the bar.' His perfect manners, his relaxed charm and completely open friendliness made me wish I could accompany him, but the prospect of Andreas joining us inhibited me. I watched him too climb the stairs. A few moments later I saw him greeting Rhodes Boyson MP with whom he was obviously lunching. Alongside Perry's elegant figure, Boyson's parody of a Victorian villain was even more successful than usual. The scene was like a borzoi meeting a pug dog.

By twenty past one I was getting extremely bored and left the club to go and buy a *Standard* to read about the Russian nuclear disaster at Chernobyl. I returned and read until Andreas arrived some minutes later having had great trouble finding a cab.

We went upstairs to the bar where it seemed to me every second person was from the *Telegraph* and I was glad when we left fairly soon for our table.

As soon as we sat down Andreas began to talk about the *Independent*. I approved of the businesslike way he got down to why we were lunching and I listened with some interest to his description of how the last few months had been a struggle to get the money together. He said he'd found it very hard work and mentioned, with a pang of remembered pain, that he'd had to face some pretty hostile questions during these sessions with hard-bitten City men who were anxious about the wisdom of investing in a new paper. As he talked on I became convinced that to him, at least at one level, I was just another sceptic who had to be persuaded. His voice was low, almost monotonous, and his gaze had a birdlike fixed quality, sometimes straight ahead and down, sometimes shooting intense sideways glances at me.

I began to see a new side of him. I remembered Tony's description of him suddenly breaking into emotional recriminations over Tony's doubts about the *Independent*'s success. I also remembered someone describing Andreas as a bully and trouble maker. But I recalled James's words of praise for him, and Matthew's and Stephen's obvious affection and respect.

This apparently irreconcilable mixture of impressions resolved itself almost at once.

I saw Andreas as far less stable than I had thought him to be. I realised he was under great strain, and at times there was something almost frantic about the way he simply went on talking through a question I tried to interpose. But behind the compulsive talking and hard sell, there was something else. He was thinking and talking like an editor. The bit I'd always missed in conversations about the *Independent* fell into place.

His mind raced off into an account of how he'd try to deal with the Chernobyl disaster. Almost to himself he said he'd like to look at the possibility of hiring time on a satellite to take pictures of the damaged plant. A moment later he misheard something I'd said and his reply indicated how much he is missing being a working journalist.

The madder I thought he was, the more I warmed to him, and the more respect I had for him. If I'm right and he is mad, then he's made like General Wolfe and should bite some other editors.

He asked, with a kind of tense brightness, 'What are they saying about us at the *Telegraph*? Are we forgotten, or remembered as traitors?'

I replied that neither statement was true. They are remembered, and are considered as dangerous but honourable rivals.

He said anxiously, 'We told Don Berry all about our design and production ideas when we were negotiating with him. I hope he won't use that information against us. He is an honourable man, isn't he?'

I thought Andreas could forget that worry, and that Don was trustworthy and straight. I couldn't actually see how Don could make damaging use of anything he'd learnt, anyway.

'What would I find different if I walked into the *Telegraph* today?' he asked.

I tried to describe the differences between Bill's open but vague style of editing and Max's urgent and decisive mode. The former continually wandering aimlessly downhill, the latter plunging off cliffs. I said whilst Bill's door had been literally always open (true, you could never be too sure that what he was telling you was permanent or even particularly accurate, but he gave you the feeling that you were involved), Max's door was always closed, and not infrequently locked. The snapshot of Bill I carry in my head is of him tilted back in his chair with one foot on his desk; smoke is curling from his cigarette, his tie loosened and he is grinning. Max is caught hurrying down the corridor with his jacket off and a large cigar in his hand. He is in the act of calling over his shoulder to an unseen colleague, 'I'll report back to you later!'

There are many changes that flow from this fundamental difference, and the conversation deteriorated for a while into a comical gossip session during which Andreas laughed out loud, very loud, several times, and expressed great surprise at the news that Bill is now a regular leader writer.

Returning to business, he asked me what my attitude to the *Independent* was; whether I would definitely never join or whether he could still hope I might.

I tried to describe my feelings, but the truth is I'm so confused I found it very difficult. I said I didn't know who he'd recruit and therefore I was unsure what kind of paper I'd be joining and also was unsure whether the paper would survive. Andreas reacted extremely sympathetically to this somewhat bleak description of my uncertainties. He said I was right to be wary but he felt absolutely certain their editorial line-up would be very, very good. As for the survival of the paper, he said it was assured by the quality and resources of the management and the investors. 'If after a couple of years the paper is floundering, they'd get rid of me, and quite right too.' He masochistically emphasised this possibility. 'They would send for me and say, "Well, we've listened to your ideas and they are no good, they are not working, off you go." And I'd be replaced by someone they had more confidence in. But there's no way they'll close the paper.'

I thought of the sinking *Today* and he seemed to read my mind.

'It's not like *Today*. They are financed quite differently.' He spoke encouragingly about the people he was going to recruit, especially from *The Times*. He said he had three heads of departments in his sights. Queues of *Sunday Times* men meet each other coming in and out of the *Independent* offices. Andreas said he and his colleagues have made lists of contenders for each job and in every case they have first of all approached the man or woman they think is best. No matter how happy or established each journalist is in their present job, the *Independent* has made them an offer.

While he spoke I was to a certain extent won over to the idea that the *Independent* may be a very good paper.

When he spoke about my possibly joining the paper he was very soft-sell and nice about it. 'We really want you.' I entirely believed him. He said he was the world's worst negotiator, meaning that I could screw them down to a very good contract. To illustrate his own shortcomings as a negotiator he told about him wanting to offer a certain amount for a library (a cuttings library, I think) that was for sale and his business manager getting it eventually for a fraction of what he'd had in mind. 'I just haven't the nerve to say to people, I'll offer you half.'

The story was one of those that we all tell now and then in an ostensibly self-deprecating mode, but actually to illustrate how likeable, generous, unworldly and rather terrific one is.

In the end he said I could leave everything as late as I liked, right up until 1 September. That would give me a month or so to work out my time at the *Telegraph*. We agreed to be in touch before then.

Wednesday 30 April

This morning as the family was dressing and drinking tea and starting the day, I said casually to Caroline, 'Do you think I can publish my Fleet Street journal and keep my friends?' She answered that some passages would have to be toned down because people could be hurt. And she also thought that some colleagues should not be identified as the source of certain quotes because friendships other than mine would be badly affected, if not ruined.

While we idly discussed these things both my sons vehemently joined in, saying that if anyone was going to be hurt by something I'd written it should definitely not be published. Alexander was particularly strident on this point. He has just been made editor of a highly satirical magazine at his school and I teased him, saying 'Are you going to be careful not to upset any of your schoolmasters with the jokes you make at their expense or the unflattering cartoons you draw of them?'

'That's quite different,' he said. I think he's right.

MAY

THE THINKER after Rodin

2 May, *Daily Telegraph*

Thursday 1 May

I had a chat with Max today when I took in my cartoon. He got me an invitation to the leader writers' lunch.

He told me that he expected to lose one or two people to the *Independent* but that *The Times* was more vulnerable to them than we were. He even seemed to say that he and Charles Wilson had some sort of agreement not to poach from each other, but I may have misheard that. I told him that *The Times* had been after me and that I thought there was an unprecedented battle going on in the newspaper industry to steal good people from each other. I said I'd heard Murdoch people, particularly *Sunday Times* staff, were flocking to the *Independent*. Max said we'd got enough *Sunday Times* chaps and anyway he had no more jobs to offer. The *Telegraph* hasn't the space to find room for any more star feature writers. I thought to myself, well, you've got to find something to go opposite the leader page.

As if I'd spoken aloud, Max said, 'I'm not going to turn this into a features paper.'

He also said that there had been an attempt yesterday to get my cartoon on the front page but he'd stopped that. 'We've got it established on the leader page now and we can't change that.' Once more I feel the boring rigidity of the new *Telegraph*. High tech means everything becomes more difficult.

I asked Don later whether this decision means I'll never go on the front page again. Cautiously he said that was not necessarily the case, but I got the feeling he was misleading me. The work required to move my cartoon, which means of course filling up a huge hole on the leader page as well as re-jigging the front, means it will probably never happen.

I sat for a while in Sue Davy's office and listened to her talk with humorous despair about the way things are done nowadays. She is worked off her feet, and by a boss who does not have Bill's easy charm.

Bill was floating about in and out of her office while we talked. 'How's he getting on?' I asked.

'He's so wonderful,' she said. 'He works so hard. Of course it would have been impossible for him to sit at home . . . he couldn't have done nothing.'

'But he wouldn't have had to do nothing. People must have been dying to get him to work for them.'

'Oh, he had hundreds of offers, the *Guardian* for vast sums of money, but he wanted to give his services to the *Telegraph*.'

Bill came in. He gave Sue an envelope to post and carefully explained that it was *Telegraph* business. He was not using *Telegraph* stamps for a private letter. I remembered what I had written about him a couple of days ago and felt awful. Here he was, honest to the point of postage

". . . What can you want to do now?" said the old lady, gaining courage. "I wants to make your flesh creep," replied the boy. (Pickwick Papers)

11 May, *Sunday Telegraph*

stamps and giving up huge salaries to help out the old *Telegraph*. What a suspicious, mean-minded little shower I was.

Back in my office Charles Moore rang. Still feeling ashamed of myself I began to tell Charles about Bill working for Max.

'Isn't it wonderful?' said Charles. 'He's got what he always wanted: power and influence and absolutely no responsibility. He is a genius. The greatest survivor around.' Laughing out loud, Charles began a brilliant imitation of Bill. 'When he first left the *Telegraph* Bill used to say to me, "Musht recognise when it'sh time to go – mushn't outshtay your welcome – new broom – clean shweep – give the new chaps a chance to iron out the black sheep", and so on. Then his tack began to change and I'd hear, "Can't abandon the old place – needed on the bridge – musht do my bit – Max may be wallowing a bit, a shtitch in time may shave, to the pumpsh – ".'

We giggled away about Bill and I swung back to thinking perhaps I had not been so unfair to him after all.

I looked at some Manchester editions of the *Telegraph* today. Printed on the new machinery, they look tremendously good. The paper doesn't look anything like so dull and grey when it's properly printed.

Monday 5 May
Some days ago Don Berry asked me to do a drawing to illustrate a feature he had planned about cricket; then in Saturday's paper there was a long article about cricket illustrated by someone else.

At first I felt irritated that my drawing had not been used, then puzzled because the article was a completely different treatment of the

127

subject from the one Don had originally described to me. Obviously my drawing would not have been appropriate.

When I saw Don today I said to him, 'Was Saturday's piece on cricket the one you asked me to illustrate?'

'Oh no,' he said, after a moment's thought. 'No, no, that was quite a different article.'

I then saw him realise that I was piqued at seeing another artist's drawing in my place. He quickly reassured me. 'Oh no, the article you've illustrated will be published soon. I just had to separate the two.'

'I see,' I said. 'I just wondered.'

'But it was a totally different piece,' said Don. 'Your one is about Gower and the recent tour.'

'I noticed that. I thought you must have changed your mind.'

'What do you mean?'

'I thought that you'd kept the theme of cricket, but changed the treatment.'

Don laughed. 'Oh, no! We're not that disorganised.'

'That's not disorganised, that's being flexible,' I said, smiling.

'I'll remember that,' said Don as he moved away. 'Next time someone calls me disorganised – flexible, I'm being flexible.'

I had started this exchange quite ready to let Don know that I was not pleased to be asked to do a drawing that was then not used. He picked up on my irritation and replied in such a way as to mollify me. According to the complicated rules of the game he was quite within his rights to become irritated with me in turn, on the grounds that I had wrongly accused him of mucking me about. He didn't take up that option but he did very mildly chide me with the phrase '. . . we're not that disorganised.' Once again I could have been annoyed; I hadn't accused him of being disorganised. That's his anxiety, not mine, but like him I tried to turn his gentle counter-attack into a joke. He accepted my acceptance of the rebuke by laughing at my joke.

Such confrontations happen over and over again every day in large organisations such as newspapers. Not everyone deals with them as well as Don.

Tuesday 6 May
'How long have you known Max?' enquired Bernard. I was looking through some photographs near his desk in the art room. He was speaking in a quiet, intimate voice that promised revelations and he inclined his head away from the busy room as if to exclude the rest of his colleagues.

'I actually met him for the first time many, many years ago – but we've never been anything like close friends.'

128

'Does he have any sense of humour?' said Bernard in a let's-stop-beating-about-the-bush tone.

'Blimey, I don't know. In a way he doesn't. He has a loud laugh, but that is usually employed to demonstrate his independence and lack of concern. You know: laughing to show he is not upset or doesn't care about something. But that's not a sense of humour.'

'No.'

'He can be light-hearted and wry and humorously self-deprecating. But come to think of it I've never heard him make a joke. Why do you ask?'

'Well, maybe he just doesn't like me.'

'What do you mean?'

'Take today for example. He's been on and on at me for days. "We must have pictures of young people, good-looking girls." You know, liven up the paper. So today I go in and I say, before he says anything, "Max, I've got a wonderful picture of an exceptionally pretty girl for you today. Everyone has agreed she's a little smasher – she's young and right up to the minute – she's five years old and has just won the Pears Soap competition." '

He flicked a photograph of a pretty child across to me and I smiled. 'He didn't laugh, then?'

'Not a bit. Real frozen. He didn't seem to like it a bit. It must be me.'

I suddenly remembered making a crack to Max about him being a radical and him giving me a similar dead reaction. 'I don't think it's you,' I said. 'He did that to me the other day and I really think he likes me well enough. Certainly I've no reason to think he dislikes me. He just doesn't appreciate that sort of silly joke.'

'Silly fellow,' said Bernard, half smiling at the photo of the little girl. He adopted an exaggeratedly pained voice. 'I always like to make things go. You know – a bit of a swing; a quip here, a sally there . . .' He gathered up his photographs and shook his head.

Charles Moore gave me a piece to do a *Spectator* cover drawing for. It's a spirited attack on *Private Eye* and Richard Ingrams. Its peg is a nasty, lying story the *Eye* published about a friend of Charles's, but he uses this example to denounce Ingrams, the *Eye* and its style, methods and dishonesty. We talked around ideas; it's going to be a difficult one to do.

I told him I was having lunch at *Private Eye* tomorrow. He said he'd been invited to lunch recently but had told Ingrams he'd rather wait until the libel case arising from the attack on his friend had been settled.

Wednesday 7 May

I went to the *Eye* lunch today. My feelings about the journal are hopelessly mixed. Years ago I admired it enormously. I was proud to

129

work for it and valued the – albeit somewhat slight – friendship I formed with Ingrams and his colleagues, and wished it was closer.

This affectionate and nostalgic side of my feelings for *Private Eye* co-exists now with a distaste for much of what it publishes, particularly its inclination enviously and indiscriminately to go for quite harmless, innocent people, who have merely been unlucky enough to catch the attention of a giggling, spiteful *Eye* contact.

Like journalistic skinheads, hunting in a pack and looking for trouble, their great strength lies in the fact that they are not in the least bit inhibited by the idea that someone may get hurt. Confronted by evidence that they have harmed an innocent person, they appear genuinely puzzled. Brows furrowed, mouths drooping open in an effort of concentration, they try hard to understand and always reach for one of two excuses: 'But it was only a joke,' (translated into skinhead: 'We was just 'avin' a bit o' fun'), or 'Yes, well, he deserved it anyway – he's such a fool' (translation: ' 'E was arskin' for it – fuckin' nigger/fairy/bastard etc.').

Separated from the pack, *Private Eye* people are just like anyone else; together they are weird. They even have a strange noise they all make together; it's a forced cackling laugh (translation: 'Here we go, here we go, here we go . . .').

I had a ridiculous fantasy on my way to the lunch at the Coach and Horses, on my motor bike through pouring rain, that I would arrive dripping wet in all my protective clothing and Norman Baker the proprietor of the pub would say, 'Fuck off! You can't come and drip here', and I'd be able to flounce out and thus avoid the turmoil *Private Eye* puts me in. I've even got a drawing in the current *Eye*. I'm not just ambivalent, I'm downright split.

Jeff Bernard was at the bar talking to some friends and looking, in his own words, like a ghost. I said hello to him.

'Going up for a scintillating, witty, high-powered lunch?'

'That's right.'

I knew hardly any of the dozen or so people at the lunch. I spoke to Peter Cook, Richard, Andrew Osmond and the new editor, Ian Hislop. The conversation ranged over Mrs Simpson's letters to the Duke of Windsor; then about Prince Charles and Laurens van der Post. Christopher Booker was mocked as a loony and it was agreed that it was only a matter of time before Chris became a close friend of the Prince. There followed an extraordinarily silly conversation about Jung, who has inspired Laurens van der Post, I believe. Down the table I could hear the *Private Eye* cackle as the libel case Charles has written about was discussed.

'. . . The two beds had been pushed together. Never said *one* bed . . .' Giggle-giggle.

I fell over backwards to be nice about everyone I mentioned: no unkind gossip about the *Telegraph* was going to come from me. I listened with some interest to myself describing Max's excellent qualities. I did tell Richard that Bill is now chief leader writer, but presented this as Sue had told it to me, with Bill nobly turning down more lucrative jobs to do his bit for the old firm.

I looked across the table at Andrew, Peter and Richard, at their middle-aged faces, and thought how old we were all getting. I tried to recall the feelings I'd had about *Private Eye* when it first appeared, how I'd longed for them to notice me. I would have burst with pride if they'd asked me to do something for them. But if I cannot hate them as Peter Kellner does, I cannot love them as I once did. On the other hand, it's very hard not to become one of the pack when you are in it. Richard is simply not hateful to sit and chat to. He looks battered and melancholy most of the time, but laughs readily and warmly. Only rarely does he slip into mirthless giggle.

In the evening Caroline and I had dinner with John O'Sullivan and a friend called Philippa. In spite of the fact that Philippa tried not to show it she must have got pretty bored with the endless talk about the *Telegraph* and various journalists she'd never met. At least Caroline knew more of the background.

John and I reminisced about the old days. He laughed nostalgically as he recalled those happy times. 'Frank [Johnson] and I used to say to each other, "This can't last. Here we are having a marvellous time, earning tons of money, on huge expenses, able to travel more or less wherever we want, with engaging and pleasant colleagues; bugger-all to do; loads of free time – how long can it go on?" '

Even subtracting a part of these cheerful memories to account for sentimental exaggeration, those days remain and actually were special. I have not worked on any other national papers so I cannot compare the *Telegraph* with its rivals, but the paper always seemed to have a fundamentally tolerant and courteous way of proceeding.

For leader writers, special feature writers and the cartoonist it was like belonging to a club for eccentrics. *Telegraph* people were proud of the story that Lord Hartwell had suggested blind Peter Utley as TV critic, and relished in a friendly way the somewhat turbulent private lives of certain colleagues. I remember that it was only after one leader writer had sunk irrecoverably into paranoia and alcoholism, and had ceased to come into work at all for over six months, that anyone got round to suggesting they might have to stop paying him. The fact that Brian Harvey, the then features editor, had had another violent brawl with a colleague in the Kings & Keys was deplored but also enjoyed. And there was an extraordinarily talented lot of people working there.

'Looking back,' said John, 'it was like a wonderful play.'

131

It still is. A synthesis of French farce and Chekhov. I watch the acts and scenes unfolding every day. The extraordinary thing is the way the *Telegraph* style continues and what a hold it has on one's emotions. Even after Conrad Black and Andrew Knight and Max Hastings have come blasting in and done everything in their power to change and improve things, in many ways you could say the *Telegraph* is much the same. There's still a sense of no one having the faintest idea what's going on.

John said, 'Wonderful. Nothing seems to have changed.'

He allowed himself to admit that certain losses from *The Times* and *Sunday Times* were worrying. He felt Andreas was doing OK. He recalled feuding with Matthew at the *Telegraph* and though he was quite good-natured and funny about it there is little love lost between them.

Caroline told me later that John leaned towards her while I was talking to Philippa and said conspiratorially, 'Tell me, Caroline – do you think we're going to get your husband?' Caroline had answered extremely non-committally that I had been a bit scared off by Charles Wilson's hints that I might expect a degree of editorial interference if I worked at *The Times*. John was horrified and said he must speak to Charles about that. Caroline also said I'd obviously got on well personally with Wilson.

I wondered a little at John's political judgement when he said his two political heroes are Ronald Reagan and Mrs Thatcher. Then he said rather touchingly that his great admiration for Reagan might have had something to do with the fact that as a boy he'd been hugely impressed by Reagan in some movie. He'd written to him and eventually received a signed photograph which he had much prized.

'My mother gave it away,' he added sadly.

Friday 16 May

I've not written anything in this journal for some days because bugger-all has happened. Also I've been trying to write an article about the Slade School of Fine Art that has used up tons of my writing energy, leaving none for this.

The *Telegraph* continues to wallow on. Things are settling down. You tend to hear fewer jokes about chaos and summary dismissals. The general rigidity of the paper is ossifying; at least, I think it is.

There has been a great spate of petty thieving round the building: handbags, wallets, even jackets, vanish every day. Last week some ambitious robber carried away a brand new and very expensive photocopying machine from just outside Max's office. God knows how it was done; it's a huge piece of equipment. As part of the campaign against the thieves, a door has been installed on the second floor between the back of the building, where my office is, and the front. You can pass through this door from front to back but you cannot open it from my side. Therefore everyone who goes through wedges it open so that they can get back. This they do with newspapers wedged under it, or in the hinges, and security men come by from time to time and close it again. This process has gradually pushed the door out of wack, so now it won't close. It thuds mournfully against the jamb each time someone passes through. The security men fume, the workers are pleased as punch and the burglars presumably flit to and fro as they always did.

I spoke to Posy Simmonds today and asked whether the *Independent* has been after her. It turned out they hadn't but *The Times* has. We talked about swapping papers and she said one or two very helpful and sensible things. She has no problems herself, because she has a contract with the *Guardian* that she couldn't break even if she wanted. She said the only reason to change papers is if you have become bored and unhappy where you are. I am neither bored nor unhappy; I'm just afraid I may miss being part of something very good by not joining the *Independent*.

Posy then said that you are what you are partly because of where you've developed. She went on to say that it's easier for a journalist to move papers than for a cartoonist, because a cartoonist's work always looks very different in a different setting.

'Will Jak look any good in another paper?' she wondered, and added, 'I think you're so good in the *Telegraph*.'

I asked whether when she is approached by other papers she considers how her drawings will be presented and therefore look in that setting and she replied, 'Yes, at once; what I think of the paper and how they use drawings is of primary importance.'

Finally she said, 'I can't see any *reason* for you to change.'

I told her the only reason I could think of: not missing out on a good new venture. She understood that feeling but seemed to be saying, 'That's not a good reason to move.'

Today the first of Max's leader writers' lunches was scheduled, and when I got to the office I dropped in on Sue Davy to find out where and when we were expected. For the last few days I'd noticed that a new young secretary was sitting at the desk and I assumed that Sue was on holiday. Today as I walked down the corridor to her office an odd memory floated into my mind. Sometime in the last few days I'd seen Sue's husband apparently trying to fit an old bicycle into the boot of a car. At the time I'd thought, it's not going to fit, and wondered why he was persevering with such solemn doggedness. Now I thought to myself, but if Sue is on holiday, why was her husband doing this ridiculous chore at the *Telegraph*? Had something happened?

The new girl didn't know where the lunch was or what we were invited for. She looked in a diary in a flustered and haphazard way and then said, 'I don't know, I'm afraid.'

'Never mind,' I said. 'I'll find out somewhere.'

'Who are you?' she asked almost suspiciously, looking at me with a blank expression.

I told her, expecting the usual flattering spark of interest.

'Oh,' was all she said. 'I'm not certain who anyone is yet.'

'Have you taken over this job, or are you a temp?' I asked.

'No, I've taken over.' Still she spoke in a reserved, cut-off manner. No sign of friendliness or interest flickered over her strangely stony young face.

'Has Sue left, then?'

'I think she's working upstairs.'

'Where?'

'I'm not sure where her office is.'

With hindsight I think her behaviour was likely to have been caused by an awkwardness she felt about her position as a usurper. She must have known that Sue was an extremely popular and respected figure. Even so I was irritated by her grumpy and sullen manner.

I went down the passage to Peter Utley's room and found Sarah Compton Burnett. I asked her at once about Sue. Sarah told me that last Wednesday Sue had been informed that her services were no longer required and that she must be out by Friday.

'Whatever last dregs of respect I had for Max have gone now,' Sarah added. 'When Bill heard he made a fuss and a job was found for her as number two to Andrew Knight's secretary.'

'Christ!'

'If Bill hadn't been able to help she might just have been out.'

Peter came into the room and agreed that the whole episode was absolutely disgraceful.

'And it's so stupid,' I said. 'Sue must be so valuable to Max. I mean, if you are going to keep on Morrison because you feel you need a link with the old regime, why get rid of Sue?'

'Exactly. I've spoken to Stephen at the *Independent*. He says that all the main secretarial jobs have gone but there are plenty of perfectly good and interesting positions for Sue to choose from. She can't wait to leave this place now.'

I remembered Sue's great loyalty to the *Telegraph* and how often she's urged me not to defect. 'What went wrong between her and Max?'

Sarah's account was a classic story of how a close personal assistant cannot simply be handed on to a new chief. Sue and Max never even began to get on. She couldn't bear being shouted at and ordered around. She had remarked very sadly that there were no jokes now, no courtesies, no gossip. Morrison's secretary, Etty, who has sometimes worked for

Max, got on with him better. She is about the same age as Sue, I suppose, but is a brisk, straightforward Scot whereas Sue is a witty, feline southerner. Sarah said, 'There came a time when, if Max pushed Etty too far, she stood her ground and said, "No!" Max seems to have liked her for it. But Sue never could do that. She just felt miserable.'

I feel Max has behaved like a blundering oaf to treat her as he has, but it does not surprise me in the least that Sue managed to irritate him. She could have felt compelled by her devotion to Bill to express her antagonistic feelings, even if only with looks and pauses and smiles.

Peter said of Max, 'I think he is settling down.' But he went on to criticise him for his clumsy, rushing way of doing things.

'Jock had a word with him, and now the leader writers' conference takes half an hour or so instead of ten minutes.'

'Jock told him to take more time?'

'Yes, and to allow discussion to proceed. But the point is, Max hasn't got the faintest idea how to edit a paper.' The picture that Peter sketched in is the one you get from everyone who is close to Max. It is of hurried decisions, snap judgements and a fundamental and fatal absence of any guiding plan, coupled with a disastrously off-hand manner towards close colleagues. No one says they really dislike him, except possibly some secretaries or lowly journalists who have been bullied by him; but neither is he liked. He gives one the impression that his mind is on other, probably higher, things. No one admires this and no one seems in the least convinced by it. Most of my colleagues believe that Max has brought about one or two fairly good changes at the *Telegraph*, and a lot of fairly useless or bad ones, but they've been achieved on a monkeys-and-typewriters principle rather than as part of a coherent plan.

I reminded Peter that Max had once said he'd welcome criticism and that he knew he'd make mistakes. 'Perhaps someone should speak to him again. Tell him to take his time, talk more freely with his colleagues and stop whizzing round in panicky circles.'

'Perhaps they should.'

'I've sometimes thought I should,' I went on, 'but I'm so removed from him and the centre of things now I feel too out of touch. You'd be so much more magisterial . . .'

'I don't know that anything "magisterial" is required,' said Peter.

'I withdraw the term at once,' I said. 'I didn't even mean that, it came out wrong; I meant something like authoritative or weighty or convincing . . .' I babbled on with a Kinnock-like list of confusing adjectives.

'Hmm,' said Peter.

The lunch turned out to be on the fifth floor. The whole of the front of that floor was once a great and grand apartment where Lord Hartwell lived. It includes several large reception or dining-rooms. I was asked to one of Lord H's lunches many years ago, and otherwise have only visited this strange place on two other occasions. The first was when Lord Hartwell sent for me to ask me to change a caricature I'd done of Maurice Green (the then editor who was about to retire). I said that I couldn't do what he wanted because the drawing he held in his hand was my best shot, and I did not know how to improve it. This was nothing to do with being brave or standing up to the boss; I really was at a complete loss about how to do what he asked for. He looked mildly surprised and let the matter drop. He used my drawing anyway on the menu for Maurice Green's farewell lunch, and in his speech referred good-naturedly to my stubbornness.

The second time was at Colin Welch's farewell drinks. While Lord H was giving his speech Michael ffolkes was standing just in front of me – well, not so much standing as swaying. He was blind drunk and barely able to remain upright. Every now and then he said, 'Yes!' very loudly, or 'Absolutely right! Hear, hear!' Suddenly he staggered to his right and fell heavily against the squat figure of our legal correspondent, who in turn reeled against his neighbour. For a moment Lord H paused. In the heavy silence Michael was pushed angrily upright by the outraged legal man. 'It's all right,' said Michael at the top of his voice. 'I just fell over!'

The fifth floor was not as I remembered it. For one thing, it was now bustling with activity, doors opened and closed and voices echoed down the quiet passage. There were two lunches being held, one presumably a business affair. A waiter pointed out the room set aside for 'Mr Hastings'. A huge table was laid for twelve or fifteen people. There were drinks on a sideboard and nuts and snacks in bowls. It looked so grand I thought I must be in the wrong room, but Max came cruising in saying, 'Oh, hello, Nick.' He was with Morrison, Julian Critchley MP and Tony Jay. I was introduced and at once began talking to Tony whom I hadn't seen since 1964, when I'd worked for him at the BBC.

I heard Max saying to Critchley, 'Come down here. Have you seen this, have you been here before?' They went down to the end of the room where french windows give on to a garden with flowers, bushes and a lawn. It is laid out on a balcony and hangs over Fleet Street quite unseen from below, like an invention by Magritte.

More than ever before, I thought this was like the revolutionary junta taking over the old Imperial Palace. There should have been rifles with long bayonets stacked in the corridor, and Max should have been in uniform, with epaulettes and a pistol and rows of medals.

At lunch I was put on Max's left. On my left was Tony Jay. Opposite Tony was Jock Bruce Gardyne and on Max's right Julian Critchley. Further down the table sat Morrison, Godfrey, Andrew Hutchinson, a new leader writer called Simon, Nigel Dudley and another newcomer whom I gathered would be joining the *Telegraph* soon as a political writer.

Max barked a few questions to get the conversation going and Tony made a long speech about the economy that I found incomprehensible. I'm pretty sure it was intended to be incomprehensible but Jock appeared to be able to understand it, or at least he made one or two grunted interjections that made it sound as if he understood it. I think it is Tony Jay's kick to try to sound cleverer than everyone else around. He does this either by making elaborately convoluted statements that get too boring to follow or by being starkly pithy. Whenever he can he breaks into French. Sometimes these French spasms are quotes, which he identifies as such, but he speaks the names of the French authors with such exquisite French pronunciation that these too are more or less incomprehensible. It isn't the most engaging conversational mode I've come across.

He began to ask Jock questions about Whitehall and took notes for future episodes of *Yes, Prime Minister*. Jock was delighted to be able for once to be indiscreet and feel he was being useful at the same time.

Every now and then Jock and Critchley teased each other. Critchley has a very infectious laugh. His fat double chin shakes and his eyes crinkle up. He looks sleepy and confident and irresponsible. I liked listening to him. He was by far the cleverest man there and the wittiest. Even Jock laughed as Critchley contradicted and interrupted him.

After a while Critchley, Max and I began talking about the *Telegraph*. Everything Max said was bounced off circulation figures or possible reader reaction. For example, he said he'd told Mark Boxer that when he begins drawing for the *Telegraph* he must avoid making jokes about sex because readers won't like it. Several times he mentioned critical reader reaction to the new centre layout, or other features he'd tried.

Eventually I said to him, 'I'm not quite sure how to phrase this, but you've said nothing about your own views. You make guesses about what readers will or won't like but at what point do you feel free to indulge your own idiosyncratic whims?'

Max looked at me in some surprise and Critchley stared at me dully. I plunged on.

'What I mean is, shouldn't a newspaper reflect the character and tastes of the editor? I've always thought being made an editor would be like being given a wonderful and enormous toy. You could wind it up, point it in any direction you liked and off it would go . . .' Before their steady gaze I faltered and ran out of steam.

Max said, 'Well, there's no point in just plunging in and changing everything overnight and playing games. I mean, I've been bold, but

137

in little ways. I've done lots of little bold things. I think that's right, to change gradually.'

He hadn't quite grasped the point of my question but I let it pass. I felt I'd had a go. Down the table Godfrey and the others seemed to be having a pleasant lunch chatting to one another. I felt helpless and out of my depth. Critchley began an interesting conversation about the death of the right wing in the Tory party. Max instantly commissioned an article on the subject.

Framed on the walls were ancient *Telegraph* posters listing the main stories from issues of long ago. The pitch black ink had spread slightly into the yellowing paper. The words announced changes in the Tsar's health, the Queen's whereabouts, City and racing news. Through the french windows the surrealist garden hummed with bees under a blue sky.

Max was talking about the *Telegraph* again and the need to attract younger readers. 'Day after day I tell the picture desk, "We must have pictures of young people in the paper." '

'How are young people supposed to discover that there are photographs of young people in the paper?' I asked.

'What?' said Max.

'What I mean is, how do you persuade new readers to pick up a copy of the *Telegraph* in the first place? Are you going to have a publicity campaign, for example?'

'The trouble with previous *Telegraph* publicity campaigns,' said Max, 'is that they were not coordinated with any improvements designed to please new readers. We got new readers for a few days, but they found the paper as dull as they'd always thought it was, so they stopped buying it again.'

There was something wrong with this remark. It clashed with Andrew Knight's statement, made during his address to the staff months ago, that the *Telegraph* was the best paper in the world. I seem to remember him saying we had many absolutely peerless writers and we had earned the respect of discriminating readers the world over. How come new readers found us so dull? Presentation, perhaps?

In Max's mind the views that the *Telegraph* is both very good and very dull appear to co-exist. The first makes him terrified of change, the second terrified of not changing. Result: indecision.

It's obviously sensible to have some idea of one's readers in mind; on the other hand, it's hopeless to try to cater to the tastes of a *Telegraph* reader. Seeing there are over a million of them you are bound to get it wrong, and anyway it's not interesting to try to give people what they want. You should give them what *you* like.

Max said, 'We're still losing readers.' He made a familiar downward gesture with his hand like a plane diving. 'We'll go on losing readers until the autumn. Then we go over to the new printing machinery and we'll have sorted out all the design problems and we'll have a massive publicity campaign.'

Why do martial images come to mind all the time? Max was like a World War I Field Marshal describing an autumn offensive.

After work I went to a wine bar near Ludgate Circus where Sebastian Faulks was having a farewell drink. He's off to the *Independent* to be their literary editor.

I joined Oliver Pritchett and Robin Gedye and a number of other *Telegraph* hacks at the crowded bar. The talk was very comic and all about the *Telegraph* and Max and defectors. Charles Nevin reached over between us to get some glasses of beer and Robin said we must watch our tongues because an editor's nark had joined us. Charles laughed and said he was off duty.

Because Charles works in the same open-plan office as Don Berry, and because Max confers each morning with Don, Charles sees more of the editor than the rest of us. He said, 'You can pick up quite a lot about what's going on just by keeping your eyes open. For instance, Don leaves his diary open on his desk so I can read the lists of Murdoch men and women he's having lunch with each day. There are thousands of them.'

'What do Don and Max talk about?'

'Oh, everything. Articles, staff, reader reactions . . . you know.'

'And you just listen.'

'Yes, I'm so lowly, I don't think they even realise I'm there.'

'They know you're safe,' said Robin. 'I think you report to them about what's going on.'

Charles turned to me. 'What do you think of our new editor?' He mimed holding a microphone towards me.

'Oh, I think he's absolutely terrific,' I said.

'Right-o,' he said and switched off his imaginary tape recorder. 'Carry on.'

He took his beer away.

Oliver mused on the extraordinary state of the newspaper industry. 'It's a very odd time for us,' he said. 'I realised the other day that I could throw up my job at the *Sunday Telegraph*, I could walk into the *Sunday Times* and say, "Can I have a job?" and they'd say, "Yes." '

'They would,' agreed Robin. 'There are suddenly thousands of jobs.'

I asked whether they thought the staff losses from the Murdoch papers, specially the *Sunday Times*, would bother the management there. On the whole Oliver and Robin thought not much.

Then I murmured something about not wanting myself to work in Wapping.

Robin suddenly burst out, 'You're living in a fool's paradise if you think we can avoid Wapping.' The joky, bantering tone of the conversation had altered completely. 'We're heading straight for that ourselves, aren't we?'

'Are we? I thought our management had come to terms, or was trying to come to terms, with our unions and – '

'Yes, trying to come to terms – but they won't. We're going to have the lot – pickets, police, Wapping – right here!'

He was angry and sounded upset. Oliver pulled a face and said, 'Oh, Christ,' then added that he was unaware until that moment that that was to be our fate.

Charles rejoined us and the banter about stool-pigeons began again. We talked flippantly about Max but behind the light-hearted anecdotes there was anxiety about what was going on.

Oliver invited Charles to join him and Robin and several others in starting a restaurant and a country pub that was their fantasy raft in case of catastrophe. They began to suggest absurd names for the pub that were all plays on names of type faces. Someone suggested 'Max's Head'.

Saturday 17 May
James gave a marvellous lunch party to celebrate the publishing by *Granta* of his long account of his visit to the Philippines at the time of the fall of Marcos. I have begun reading it and it is very, very good. What he does superbly well is to reveal everything through descriptions of apparently peripheral and unimportant events, and to throw in the lateral, almost unrelated thoughts that crossed his mind at the time. The effect is to convey with tremendous clarity a sense of sharing an experience; but then his writing is so honest and his descriptive powers are enormous.

We drove up to Oxford to the party and found Andreas and Stephen were both there. I met and liked Andreas's wife.

I said to Stephen, 'Everything's going very well for you,' meaning the recruiting. He replied with uncharacteristic confidence, even self-satisfaction. The paper is now beginning to look like a winner. From being a small embattled blob on the edge, it's becoming a magnetic and glittering star near the centre. Yet in direct proportion to its growing power I feel less drawn to it.

I'm not quite sure why this should be. Perhaps in the company of so many stars I would never be as close to the decision-makers as in my fantasy I would have been. Perhaps part of the thrill of joining the *Independent* was the huge and dangerous risk involved. But it can't really be that, because it was the risk that kept me at the *Telegraph*.

Whatever it is, I feel more and more like an old *Telegraph* hack the more I become aware of *Independent* confidence.

I asked Tony Howard, who was also there, what he thought. My heart sank at his answer.

'Lately I begin to think that maybe I'd been a bit hasty, and given you the wrong advice,' he said.

'Oh, Christ.'

'But some of their appointments have been disastrous,' he added cheerfully.

We talked a little about the *Telegraph*. I told him about Sue Davy's dismissal. His attitude was that the way it was done may have been insensitive and reprehensible but he had sympathy for Max in that situation. Inheriting a secretary who has given her loyalty so completely to your predecessor is a hopeless situation and has to be ended, even though there are tears before bedtime.

Tuesday 20 May
The last two days have been very difficult at work. My brain is sluggish and I am tired. Since the new layout at the *Telegraph* I have been waiting for the day when I fail to get a cartoon done and I have to go along to Don and tell him he has got a hole on the page to fill. I've discussed this possibility with him and he's completely reassuring. We agreed that it's not necessary to have a stand-by picture every day, but if I could let him know by 4.30 when things are going badly he'll get someone to start looking at photos.

Yesterday was the first time we went on to this yellow alert. I told him I was struggling a bit, and he reacted more than very well; he was perfect. First of all he didn't catch my mood of restless gloom. He made light of the problem of searching out an illustration *should* it become necessary. Then he agreed with me that the news was difficult to make anything of. We moved across his office to the TV and he mucked about with the remote control to get the news headlines and latest news-flashes to see if that produced a subject, or even an idea.

Somehow he included Charles Nevin and Margot Norman from features in our conversation and soon we were pursuing an idea based on the news from South Africa. I could feel myself relaxing as my colleagues tried to help and Don continued to go through the TV stations, occasionally producing ludicrous scenes from children's TV of failed actors and actresses gong through their routines with ever more desperate and forced gaiety. What a life, prancing about in an airless TV studio, playfully entertaining a camera that stares at you unamused from the surrounding dark. No wonder they look mad. Suppose it crosses their minds, as they caper about, that millions of small and innocent children are sitting frozen and silent, watching images of their actions on TV screens. How do children's TV teams deal with their guilt? If I knew that each working day my task was to

141

stuff intellectual kapok into the developing minds of small children, and that all my powers should be bent towards keeping children passively watching a machine, I'd begin to feel I should blow my brains out rather than theirs.

Ten minutes after leaving Don's office I had started on a cartoon. It was not great, but it was perfectly respectable.

Today at 4.30 I was back in Don's office telling him to stand by again.

'You just like scaring me,' he said and we went through a similar routine. It finished the same way too, with my doing a cartoon.

It's a curious thing that some people are helpful with ideas and some aren't. It is nothing whatever to do with the cleverness or expert knowledge of those whose help you seek, nor is it to do with how much they want to help. The cleverest people can be the least helpful. Matthew Symonds, for instance, would always reel off facts and opinions if I sought his aid, but all that did was muddle my mind further. Stephen Glover would tend to look troubled and say anxiously, 'I'm afraid I'm not being much help.' James usually starts making jokes about completely unrelated things and seems to be saying, don't bother me. Godfrey Barker is a bit better. He'll respond to my ideas and try to think of cartoons himself, although he makes the common mistake of over-complicating things: 'Why don't you show Mrs Thatcher as an auctioneer selling off a number of lovely antiques, while Heseltine and some of his cronies are changing the labels on a batch of rather dubious looking . . .' John Thompson was very good, always helpful, as was Peter Paterson in my earliest days. Tony Howard is fairly good but he tends to see why things won't work or don't quite fully express the truth. John Burgess and Bernard Foyster are two of the very best, and now Don is in that category as well. Colin Wheeler, who sometimes draws his cartoons in my office, is not bad, but he likes to suggest wildly inappropriate cartoons in extremely poor taste and then pretend to be surprised when I say, don't be silly.

'Why don't you have Kinnock riding bareback on Mrs Thatcher, you know, like in a turn-of-the-century whorehouse? She should be in net stockings and things, and Whitelaw could be bursting in and . . .'

'Oh, Colin, for Chrissake!'

'You mean it would outrage Col Blah-Blah, Staines?'

'It outrages me, let alone Col Blah-Blah.'

'Mm – I sometimes think there must be something wrong with my sense of humour.'

I've read more of James's report from the Philippines. It gets better and better. I rang him and told him how good I thought it was and tried to tell him why. You have to be quite careful how you tell people what it is about their work you admire. You may describe something they have not intended, or even done; and you may like the very thing they most hate. At one point I compared James's deceptively simple and straightforward style with Redmond O'Hanlon's self-conscious and preening way of writing. He said, 'What Redmond doesn't realise is that sometimes your material is so good all you have to do is get it down.'

This is a somewhat misleading remark because it makes something that is complicated and subtle appear simple. Many people will pass by good material unable to recognise it until an artist comes alone and points it out. Others will dimly see that the material is interesting and promising but believe it needs dressing up and developing. And even if you do realise how good your material is, 'just getting it down' is immensely difficult.

I once tried to do some silhouette portraits of my children and a few friends. I traced shadows of their profiles and reduced these drawings with a pantogram. I thought this would be a purely technical matter quite devoid of artistic and creative endeavour; but it wasn't. Trying to be even that simple and uncomplicated involved masses of decisions and judgements. Attempting to write simply is something like that.

'All you have to do is get it down', indeed.

Thursday 22 May
I found myself this afternoon hanging around at the picture desk looking at the day's crop of news photographs.

I'd come to hand in my cartoon, and for me work was over. The rejected photographs are put into a bin divided into two parts, one for home pictures, one for foreign. I like to check them over and I often take some to use as references. I keep them in an untidy heap in a drawer: shots of empty railway stations, garages, the outside of coal mines, lines of police in riot gear, endless portraits of politicians. Usually when I look for one to actually use, I get bored going through the heap and finish up going down to the picture library for my reference anyway. But I add to my collection nevertheless. Some of the politicians have long since departed, others now look much older and greyer than my pictures, but I rarely throw them out.

Today I didn't find anything useful but I chatted with Charles Clover. As usual these days, we discussed Max and the new *Telegraph*. Charles is a feature writer. Like everyone else, he thinks the whole place is in chaos and that no one, Max included, appears to have much idea what's going on. But Max has been exceptionally nice to Charles, admiring his work and generally encouraging him and now promoting him to TV critic with apparently a roving commission to cover films sometimes.

Charles saw, as I had done, that the upheavals in the *Telegraph* could

143

be turned to advantage. At the moment he is poised to become considerably more important on the paper than he has been and he was studying the ground carefully. He was critical of Max, but only up to a point, and obviously feels he owed him a lot.

I said that I thought being a TV critic was a non-job because TV isn't any one thing. TV is news and documentary, plays, games, bullshit, pap, books, old films, more pap and bullshit, talks, music (pop and classical) and so on: the list is endless. Being appointed TV critic is a bit like being given a personal column. It can only be used to show off and muck about, as Clive James showed so successfully, and to a certain extent Julian Barnes too. TV can't be criticised in the same way that plays and films or books can.

Charles listened without saying much. I urged him to talk to Tony Jay and Jeremy Isaacs if they'd see him, because they are both men who have worked for years in the medium and are dedicated to it, in love with it perhaps. I thought they might give him a framework within which to regard TV. His own intelligence would provide the necessary scepticism and contempt. I'm a bit nutty about TV. I think it is a corrupting thing and has already done appalling damage to mankind. In Manchester I once saw a Pakistani woman with five or six small children sitting in a row in a darkened room watching TV on a fine late summer's day. The woman didn't even speak English. It was one of the saddest sights I've ever seen.

Friday 23 May
After work I called on Don Berry to tell him I was going to take Monday off. As I left I passed the open door of Godfrey's room. He was writing a memo and had a glass of white wine by his side. This had come from Don's office and it was not clear to me whether it signalled an occasion of some kind or whether they always drank wine on a Friday evening.

I interrupted Godfrey's work and sat on the edge of his desk to chat. He introduced me to Victoria Mather, recently appointed film critic, who was at her desk a few feet away. She was talking on the phone brightly about someone's marriage ('. . . is she the one who married that other man – you know the one . . .').

While Godfrey and I talked several people came and went. Each one talked to him as arts editor. Someone came in to discuss some expenses: 'I had to stay up in London in order to be in early this morning – I was, er, wondering if it would be in order to put the hotel on expenses?' Godfrey lolled in his chair, a poacher turned gamekeeper who likes to keep his hand in at poaching all the same.

'I'll turn a blind eye to that,' he said, smiling at the very modest request.

Victoria left with good wishes for a pleasant weekend in the Isle of Wight. She in turn hoped Godfrey would enjoy his holiday in Cyprus.

I asked him how things were going. His main anxiety was that he felt Max had created a mood of terror in the building. No one knew quite what is expected of them, only that Max is frequently not pleased with their efforts. There are whole offices full of people who fear for their jobs. He mentioned Sue, saying she had been quite unable to stand the strain and had quit. I said I'd heard she'd been pushed and he at once altered his version and agreed she'd been sacked rather than resigned. The point being, either way Max was impossible.

He discussed at some length a leader we'd published on the question of sanctions against South Africa following their anti-terrorist raids on several neighbouring states. In Godfrey's view it was the worst leader ever published in the *Telegraph*. He has a comical way of being simultaneously scandalised and amused. He is constantly playing two roles. The first is responsible and conservative and authoritarian, the second is delinquent, sly and self-interested. The latter is constantly giggling at the pomposity of the former.

'I've never read such an incoherent load of balderdash. I met Bill in the lift and I said, "Bill, who wrote that leader?" and he said, "It'sh better I don't shay who wrote it." It turned out of course *he* had written it, but Max amended it. Bill had waffled on about building bridges, need for understanding and so on, and in came Max with "The system is vile." Eh? one asked oneself. Moments later, same thing again: South African scum must be wiped from the face of the earth. When Peter saw it he went to Max and said, "After reading that leader I found it impossible to say whether the *Telegraph* was in favour of sanctions or against them." Max laughed his head off. "Exactly the impression I was trying to achieve." I mean, really. This is madness.' Godfrey frowned and grinned.

He assumed that Black must be fed up at the wobbly political line that is emerging from the new *Telegraph*. Reaction to the Libyan bombing was bad enough, and now drenching wetness over South Africa.

Godfrey puzzled over Max's editorship. 'The curious thing is how much he cares about reader reaction. We've had a letter from someone high up in the world of the arts deploring our criticism of a certain production – '

'Who?'

'I can't possibly say: too dangerous, too political. The point is, Max is really taking it seriously. I mean, in the old days we'd have angry letters from all sort of people – Cabinet ministers, lords of the realm. Bill would laugh and write back telling them to get stuffed. But Max keeps calling meetings to plan how to react to this preposterous old fool.'

I suggested that what lies behind his anxiety is simply lack of conviction. He has no views on anything, except perhaps whether or not some incident makes a good news story. Therefore, when as editor he has to defend a point of view he is lost because he's never thought about it. He has no way of telling whether the colleague or the irate reader is correct. This is true of arts features, articles and leaders.

'All he can do is say that he doesn't like something. He has no capacity to criticise constructively. He can't say *why* he doesn't like something or how it could be improved. For example, he has taken against two critics in this department and . . .'

'Who?' I said. 'What's the point of gossiping without names?'

Godfrey snapped into his Establishment mode and looked shocked. 'I won't tell you,' he said self-righteously. 'Anyway, he's taken against them and cannon balls come bowling down this corridor every day, but that's all. He has no idea what he wants; all he can do is wield the stick.' He went on to describe the awful fate of Sean Day Lewis. In Godfrey's view, Sean is not writing too well at the moment and his spirit is quite crushed by having various tasks taken from him and given to others. He has been told to make suggestions about what he might do on the paper. 'I thought he should put in for books editor, but he seems to have lost all confidence in himself.'

'Books editor? Does that mean David Holloway is leaving the job?'

'He's broken his back,' said Godfrey, as if saying he'd got a heavy cold. 'He fell over on board a ship and – well, he didn't actually break his back, he's in a lot of pain and, er . . .'

'But does this mean he's leaving? This is awful; poor chap. When did it happen?'

'Recently.' Godfrey can be very vague.

His point was that Sean is a casualty of Max's clumsy way with colleagues. 'It's no way to treat a man who's been here for twenty-five years. And no fun at all for a chap who is fifty-four years old . . .'

'Does anyone say anything to Max about the effect he's having on morale around here?' I asked.

'Josie does: his new secretary. One should be very careful what one says to her.'

'You mean, it all goes straight to Max?'

'Yes. Nothing wrong with that, but people complain to her or let her know what they think and she mentions it to the boss.'

'How the hell do you know that?'

'He told me!'

Godfrey drained his glass of wine, and back in his naughty-boy role he said he must get on because he was now an hour and a half late for an appointment.

Throughout our conversation, Godfrey had invariably referred to Max as 'Bomber Command'.

Tuesday 27 May
Robin Gedye burst into my office holding a tell-tale notebook in his hand. When they are collecting money, there's a special way someone carries a notebook and speaks while apparently checking a list.

He said, grinning cheerfully, 'Can I put you down for a contribution to John Miller's farewell? He's had enough of this mad-house.'

'What do you mean?'

'He's got fed up with the way everything is done around here – resigned.'

'Christ. What's he going to do?'

'Dunno. Write books maybe.'

I gave him a fiver. Robin was conveying the feeling that the continual crumbling of the old order and the consequent spread of alarm and despondency filled him with a kind of black glee. There was a triumphant note in his voice and he kept his boyish grin firmly in place.

After he'd gone I asked Bernard what he'd heard about John's end. Apparently John had been offered the job of deputy foreign editor at the same time as Nigel Wade was confirmed as permanent foreign editor. For some reason this had been too much for him.

At that moment we saw Max further down the corridor and I hurried after him to present my cartoon. He'd vanished again when I got to his room, but reappeared suddenly behind me.

'Hi, Nick, how are things?'

I sat opposite him and asked him the same question.

It was like putting on a record. He went into his speech about declining circulation, angry readers' letters, desperate economic crisis and general despair. He mentioned Mark Boxer's imminent arrival and said again that he'd warned him off jokes about homosexuals and sex.

I interrupted to say that when I'd arrived on the paper I'd never done a political cartoon in my life and I'd always been grateful for the freedom I had been given while I found my feet, and how I had been protected from adverse readers' reactions.

Max seemed to think that was a different case. He described the debilitating effect of receiving scores of letters each day from depressed and scandalised *Telegraph* readers. 'I begin to wonder who we are producing this paper for. Are they all purple-faced floggers and hangers?'

147

'Only loonies write angry letters. Ordinary people don't bother. How often do you write letters to editors?'

Max smiled. 'I said to Charlie Wintour the other day, "When does editing become fun?" He replied, "When you go into profit." '

I asked him whether *any* of it was fun at the moment.

'If I last a year and things have settled down a bit, maybe it will become fun. It's fun recruiting good people, but it's no fun firing people.' He went off into an extraordinary account of how two old Washington correspondents are being brought home and younger men being sent out. I gathered this was partly to save money and partly the hope that younger men would perk the bureau up. Max seems to have a thing about age.

'Do you know what the average age is of our staff photographers?'

'No.'

'Fifty-two!'

I thought his amazed intonation was a little tactless, seeing he was speaking to a fifty-year-old.

'Good gracious,' I said, sounding as shocked as I thought appropriate. I couldn't see why these grizzled veterans shouldn't do just as well as younger men, but let it pass.

'I'm sending Martin Ivens to Washington.'

'Wow! How wonderful for him.'

'I think he's the brightest young man around here,' said Max. There was an enquiry about my own assessment of Martin in his tone.

'He's terrific, very bright, first class,' I said.

Max sprawled in his chair, his huge body unanimated. He looked defeated.

'Are you so isolated?' I asked. 'Don't you feel supported by the management and your colleagues? After all, you didn't start any decline; you inherited a paper in serious trouble.'

'Yes, but when things are running so badly . . . I mean, we've got to get through a bad patch – but it's no fun when day after day . . . The management are OK so far. Some colleagues are a delight to work for . . .'

At this moment Josie called out that Andrew Knight was on the phone so I took my cartoon and went down to Don's office with it. I'd hoped he'd say something about my Slade article but he just smiled at the cartoon.

I chatted with Mike Green who was working at his desk.

'Why did John Miller resign?' I asked.

'Because he's a fool. Rule Number One, never resign,' he said.

Max charged into the room, by now reactivated. He briskly set about organising Margot Norman and Paul Cox (the artist) to be sent to cover the Derby.

'Get them passes,' he snapped.

Margot said, 'I'll look out my third best hat.'

'They'll have to work fast to get their stuff in in time. You can phone yours, Margot. Better get a DR for Cox.' He marched out.

'What's a DR?' I asked Mike.

'Dispatch Rider. Weren't you ever in the army?'

'I thought people said "messenger boy" or "biker".'

'Can't call anyone "boy" these days.'

There is something about the way we talk about Max and the post-Black *Daily Telegraph* that is not pleasant. 'Disagreeable' would be too strong a word, but there is a degree of bitterness that was not there in the old days. Of course, we always slagged off the way things were run and laughed at crass appointments, but apart from a few months towards the end of Bill's editorship we were jeering and joking from within. There was affection for the mad old *Telegraph*, as well as exasperation and anger. In that way it used to be more like a family.

Wednesday 28 May

Sarah Jewell, who works in the foreign room, has applied for a job at the *Independent*. I offered to put in a good word for her and she came to see me. We talked mostly about the *Telegraph*, and I got a slant on the state of affairs that I found depressing and I'm afraid convincing.

She saw Max's arrival as a revolutionary takeover. In her department, the revolutionaries first of all shot Ricky Marsh, the then foreign editor, and replaced him with the bulky Nigel Wade who set about completing the work. It is now almost done. The two older men from Washington, Shears and Beeston, are indeed being retired and Frank Taylor and Martin are taking over, as I learnt yesterday. John Dudman, Ricky's deputy, has been axed for a similar reason – that is, he is too old. He's sixty-odd, I think. The Peking office is being closed and one opened in Tokyo. Stringers all over the world are being shed and Nigel is going to rely more on agency material.

This shake-up has meant the destruction of the old system that was once, so I've always believed, the pride of the *Daily Telegraph*. Furthermore, it has been done with a maximum of insensitivity. Dudman and Wade, who have to share an office for the next few days until John leaves, literally do not speak to each other. Sarah said the atmosphere in the foreign department is agonising. Dudman thinks Wade is a clod, and Wade thinks Dudman an old fool.

'But he's obviously not,' I said.

'Course he's not,' said Sarah. 'He and Ricky made the foreign department.' She added that she knew changes and upheavals meant ill-feeling and casualties but, given that, what was happening at the *Telegraph* was appalling.

She said the way Sue Davy had been treated was typical of the new order's house style. And all this in the hope that a newspaper would emerge that would not only appeal to yuppies but also keep the old *Telegraph* readers. 'It's nonsense. It can't be done.'

What struck me most about this was that it was evidence of the enormous amount of anguish, anger, fear and depression that is swilling about the place these days.

In order to ring the *Independent* on Sarah's behalf I went to find Sue Davy to get their telephone number. She was in a small office outside Andrew Knight's door. She was wearing earphones and typing and didn't hear me come in. In fact I gave her quite a start.

'I'm sorry to give you a jump.'

'Oh! You did.'

'Well – I miss you; I'm very, very sorry you've moved and I've heard all about it and I'm shocked.'

'Oh, how nice. Am I really missed? I feel forgotten.'

'No, no, you are remembered.'

'Oh, good.'

Just as I was explaining that I wanted the *Independent*'s telephone number the door opened and Andrew Knight came through. I was leaning over Sue's desk resting my arms on a VDU. Andrew smiled and walked into his office making a friendly greeting as he passed. Sue and I had started guiltily as he appeared and we both laughed as the door closed behind him. We started guiltily all over again as the door was immediately reopened and Andrew said jokily, 'What are you doing here, Nick? You look as if you are mending our machines.'

I thought to myself that's a good trick, disappearing and instantly appearing again. I began to splutter something about wanting to ask Sue something when she said, 'Nick is looking for a telephone number and I have it here in a book', and she began to rummage about in such a way that Andrew couldn't go on, so he vanished again.

I got the number and explained to Sue why I wanted it. She rather touchingly asked me to remind them of her plight if I wouldn't mind. She said sadly, 'I had hoped to hear from them by now.'

I promised I would.

When I rang the *Independent* I spoke to Linda, who has now stopped being Andreas's secretary and has a more senior position, in charge of publicity, I think, and general PR.

I gave her my messages on behalf of Sarah and Sue and then asked how things were going. She said everything was pretty chaotic and that she sometimes thought they'd never get it all straightened out, but she was laughing ruefully and not sounding at all disheartened.

I said I wanted to see Stephen when he got back from a short holiday. I plan to say to him that I was fed up at the *Telegraph* and wanted to get down to brass tacks: what will they offer, how would my coming-over be arranged?

I met Martin in the corridor and congratulated him on his new appointment. He snorted and said something rather indistinct. When I asked what he meant, he said, 'Got a minute? Let's go to your room and talk.'

He told me he was in a quandary. Max had offered him Washington and then New York, and Andreas has offered him the job of defence correspondent. He wants to go to the States, but doesn't terribly want to stay on the *Telegraph*. He wants the defence job, but thinks there may be too many good contenders for all future promotions on the *Independent*. He suggested to Stephen that he went to Washington for the *Telegraph* for a few months, just to have done it, and then came across to defence at the *Independent*.

'You cheeky bastard,' I said.

'Anyway, Stephen said, "No: either you're with us or you're against us." '

Martin said he just cannot make up his mind. He feels that he needs the experience of doing a top foreign job. That is, he has reached an age and a point in his career when that's what he should do, but defence correspondent is a really big job too and would certainly include quite a bit of travelling.

'I double my congratulations,' I said. 'This is just the sort of problem one wants to have *all* the time. Do you know, somewhere in your heart, which job you'll take?'

'No, not at all. I can't tell.'

'Well, let me know. If you go to the *Independent* that will affect my decision. I'd be more likely to go myself.'

'OK.'

If anything, Martin is less depressed by what's going on at the *Telegraph* than I am, but there's not much in it. He's not too impressed.

I discovered today that I can open the stupid bloody security door, the one that prevents me from getting from my room to the main building, with a piece of cardboard. It is possible to insert a strip between the door and the jamb and, by pressing it against the catch and gently jiggling the door to and fro, you can spring the door open. I've shown lots of people how to do it and have left several suitable pieces of cardboard on a little ledge near the door.

It gives me enormous satisfaction each time I open the door. Until the first time the door suddenly opened I'd never really believed burglars and detectives could open locked doors with bits of plastic.

Several people have called out to me in the corridor, 'Hey! It works!', which pleases me very much.

151

Friday 30 May

There was another leader writers' lunch today. The guests this time were Gillian Reynolds and a pretty lady from the Treasury. I didn't speak to either of them.

I did chat for a while pre-lunch to Ed Pearce, who told me he thought the *Telegraph* vastly improved by everything that's happened. His strange pudgy face glowed as he praised Max, and his eyes closed. His voice dropped lower and lower. '. . . It's a really interesting paper at last. All the things I've wanted to see happen . . . end of that sickening upper-class swinishness . . .' He looked like an oriental guru going into an ecstatic trance.

At lunch itself I sat next to Peter Utley but most of the time he talked to Bill. We did briefly discuss the *Independent* and he said he was afraid it might become like a boring *Financial Times*: too much talk and opinion. He also thought it would become an SDP rag. He thought Stephen was worried about an SDP tendency, he (Stephen) being a Tory and antagonistic to a certain wetness about SDP attitudes to certain social matters.

I couldn't see the point of the lunch at all. The table is so big that there's no hope of having a subject generally discussed and, while it's pleasant enough to have lunch with one's colleagues, that could be done out and about. I said how do you do to the guests, but that's all.

Going through the security door this afternoon I found Ronnie from the picture desk talking to Mr Hughes, the ex-policeman security chief. Ronnie looked guilty as hell and was obviously hiding something. I thought they might be having a row about jamming the door open so I stopped to listen. Mr Hughes once started to tick me off when he caught me at it, until I began shouting at him about how bloody idiotic the door was. Now, however, he and Ronnie weren't quarrelling; they were getting on in quite a friendly way. When Mr Hughes waddled away down the stairs, Ronnie began laughing.

'Did he catch you propping the door open?'

'No, he was just having a chat,' he said. 'What I was doing was measuring this up.' He produced a piece of cardboard that he proceeded to cut into a suitable shape to open the door. 'We're having a metal one made downstairs,' he said.

'Did Mr Hughes see what you were doing?'

'No,' said Ronnie still laughing. 'I dunno what he thought I *was* doing, though.'

Later in the day I saw Ronnie and John Burgess outside the door fooling about and giggling like schoolboys. They had a beautifully shaped and smoothed strip of zinc.

It worked brilliantly.

We looked about for somewhere to hide the door opener and found a perfect place above the entrance to a nearby lift.

JUNE

"South Africa will not crawl before anyone" (President Botha)

15 June, *Sunday Telegraph*

Monday 2 June

I passed Sue Davy in the corridor as we both headed for the lifts. She seemed unsure quite where she was going and said something as I approached.

'What was that?' I asked.

'I'm just muttering to myself. Like an old witch,' she said. We rode up in the lift together. 'The easy-going, slack times are over, aren't they? That's what we've got to realise. The nice, old easy-going times.'

She was behaving in a spaced-out, rather weird way. I said, 'Come and see me soon in my room and tell me about your new job.'

'Yes, I will; I'll come creeping along and we'll have a proper talk.' The lift stopped and she got out.

John O'Sullivan rang me this afternoon. He doesn't muck about any more. 'Look, we're still after you. What's going on? How are you feeling about the *Telegraph*?'

I told him.

He said he'd spoken to Charles Wilson and raised the question of cartoonists' freedom to express whatever views they liked. Wilson said I'd misunderstood him. He wouldn't dream of censoring or editing Peter Brookes or any other cartoonist.

Later Andreas rang and said he'd heard I'd like to meet.

'Yes. I'd like it to be a formal discussion.'

'You mean you want me to put on a suit?'

'Put on a suit, comb your hair and we'll talk about terms, and conditions, and timing.'

'OK, fine. I'll look forward to it.' We're meeting at noon this Thursday.

Mad Adrian Berry came bursting into my room, eyes popping. He is the science correspondent on the *Daily Telegraph*. He has a strange manner. He looks manically intense and vacant at the same time. 'Can you imagine the whole world bursting, like an egg hit by a hammer?'

'Yes,' I replied cautiously.

'Bursting! Exploding! Dreadful! And sort of imploding at the same time.'

'Uh huh, I can imagine all that.'

'Could you do me a drawing of it? Two columns wide. Looking really terrible.' He waved his hands in the air. 'Exploding and imploding, sort of . . .'

'OK.'

'It's all to do with a thing called – I've forgotten what. It's about the size of a channel ferry and travels at about one third the speed of light.' He struck his left fist into his right palm. 'The whole world just disintegrating.' From his beaming smile and burning eyes you'd think he could hardly wait.

156

'OK,' I said. 'Two columns.'

'Can they change the size of your drawings?'

'Yes – as large or small as you like. But the proportions always remain the same, of course. If I draw it rectangular that's how it will appear.'

'It's the columns. The straight columns. One day perhaps they'll invent a newspaper with wavy columns.' His hands waved in the air again, this time describing wiggly lines. He dashed from my room.

I took an anti-Reagan cartoon to Max.

'Oh Christ,' he said. 'If you knew what stick I was getting about our line on Reagan.'

'Who from?'

'Oh – er . . .'

'Well, don't take any notice. Reagan is behaving like an asshole.'

He handed back my drawing. 'That's fine, that's OK.'

'Who has been giving you stick?'

He smiled. 'Let's just say it was not a quiet weekend,' he said.

Wednesday 4 June

Max let me know today, in the middle of talking about something else, that he has to argue 'upstairs' that the cartoon must be allowed to diverge from the views expressed in the leaders. My main reaction was to be pleased because it means my cartoons must be expressing a point of view. Next to being incomprehensible I most fear being bland. Max also manages to make me feel sorry for him. He laughs ruefully with forced loudness at his own plight as he wriggles between angry readers and anxious management, and is watched by wary colleagues.

Thursday 5 June

If I join the *Independent* I'll look back and say, this is the day I made the decision.

I got to the *Independent* offices a little early. Before I went upstairs a security man asked me to sign in and I checked back through the last few days to see who else had been here recently, hoping to find a surprising name. All those I read were unfamiliar, but then many were indecipherable. I wondered whether these scrawls indicated the arrival of individuals who did not want Nosy Parkers to know they'd been here; probably not.

Upstairs the whole place had been transformed since my last visit. It was looking real and occupied.

In the main large open-plan office there were perhaps a dozen people, some at desks, some moving about with papers in their hands. The atmosphere was pleasant, busy but also calm, and not particularly solemn. There was a low murmur of voices. A small boy, about five or six years old, was scurrying about looking at piles of newpapers and crawling under tables. I was absolutely enchanted with the view from the plate glass windows to the left. I was on the second floor and could look down on Bunhill Fields Cemetery. Between the old gravestones the grass was freshly cut. A pink chestnut tree was in full blossom just outside the window, and the other trees had shaken out their new leaves. The sun was shining and people were strolling on the paved walks.

At the far end of the room, through glass partitions, were two further rooms. In one Andreas and Matthew were talking to two men; in the other was Stephen, listening to a man who had his back to me. I recognised Linda. She smiled and said hello.

When Andreas and Matthew emerged I went over to them and Andreas suggested he and I sat down and talked. He said he'd booked a table for lunch later. He paused for a moment to look through some notes on his desk and I said to Matthew that Sue Davy had sent a message to say she was anxious to hear of any work the *Independent* might be able to offer her. Matthew's only response was to say vaguely that there might be one or two suitable positions. I felt irritated. Sue is an old friend and you should find things you can do for old friends. Andreas beckoned me back into the glassed-off room he'd originally been in and we sat down. A girl brought coffee.

He began by going through a list of recruits. Some I'd heard of, some were unknown to me, and all were named with brief accompanying statements about how excellent they were. Many came from *The Times* and the *Sunday Times*.

I said, 'Christ, what are they going to have left by the time you've finished?'

'Not a lot.'

There were bits of information in the midst of this preliminary chat that interested me. Tony Allan Mills had resisted the *Telegraph*'s overtures and has agreed to go to Andreas to be South African correspondent, I think. There was no mention of Martin Ivens.

Stephen came in. He said to Andreas that he'd got a young man who was perfect for the post of Australian stringer. He was leaving for Australia tomorrow and we could get him if we moved now, but that he could slip away into arrangements with certain Aussie papers if no offer were made. Andreas asked in a calm and good-natured way what was so special about the young man and listened to Stephen's somewhat urgent answer. Then he smiled and said, 'In the City there is a well-known saying: if you are absolutely certain that cocoa is going to increase in value tenfold in the next few days, don't go out and buy shares in cocoa, go and lie down in a darkened room until the feeling passes.'

Stephen laughed and glanced at me in mock exasperation as if to say, what can you do with him?

158

Andreas went on to persuade Stephen not to do anything for the moment.

I liked the laid-back way Andreas behaved over this minor incident. It was very pleasant to see how the two of them could work so smoothly together.

After twenty minutes or so Andreas stood up and said he was hungry. He called Matthew, who was coming with us. As we got ready to leave Stephen said he'd come too. On the way out I was introduced to a secretary called Melanie and I took the opportunity to put in a word for Sarah Jewell.

We walked through the cemetery. The air was full of the sweet smell of cut grass. The sun was surprisingly warm each time we stepped out of the shadow of the lovely spreading trees. The ancient tombstones looked like peaceful and sturdy monuments to endurance and continuity rather than markers for the dusty dead.

All through lunch we talked about my joining. Sometimes the subject under discussion was how Max was doing at the *Telegraph*, or why Eddy Shah was in trouble, and so on; but the point was always the same: no other paper was worth working on.

Andreas said, referring back to the *Telegraph*, that Shears and Beeston had been offered one year's salary and £5,000 when they'd been retired from their foreign desk jobs. Matthew said, 'That's penury.'

I said I couldn't believe it.

'It's true,' said Matthew. 'The fact is it's disgraceful, but they simply haven't got the dough to pay more.'

While we talked and ate, *Independent* staff men kept coming into the restaurant. I was introduced to most of them. Matthew said two or three times in a genuinely anxious voice, 'The sooner we open a staff canteen the better. This place is costing us a fortune.'

Stephen said very little. What was happening was that all three of them were saying one way or another, 'Come on, join us.' Stephen was saying it quietly. Andreas was saying it by laying out before me how much he wanted me to join, and the excitement and adventure the new paper could offer. Matthew was doing the same, but adding his own touch by trying to spread alarm and despondency about the *Telegraph*. All three were successful. I could feel myself slipping my moorings from the *Telegraph* as the minutes passed.

Andreas asked whether I had time to come back to the office to see their newest dummies, and to see the room that was set aside for the cartoonist. It was getting late and I was beginning to worry about starting work on my cartoon, but I agreed to take a quick look. Back at the office Andreas led me to another open-plan room and began looking on a desk for the dummies. When Stephen and Matthew came in he

159

called out, 'Which is Nicholas's room. Whoops! That betrays my bargaining position.'

The room was off the open-plan office we were standing in, and looked down on Bunhill Cemetery. I thought to myself, I cannot resist this view, and felt the last few connections binding me to the *Telegraph* twanging like guitar strings under the pull of what Andreas was offering.

'It's lovely,' I said. 'How much does this view cost?'

'It's worth about £10,000 a year,' said Andreas.

'It's cheap,' I said.

We talked about the dummies a bit. I had a few doubts but didn't particularly labour them. It looked a bit too like the *Financial Times* for my taste. There seemed some very block-like headings and too many graphs and logos, but the centre spread was almost indistinguishable from the *Telegraph*. Where my cartoon was to go they had pasted a drawing by Wally Fawkes.

Before I left, Andreas said, 'I'd like twenty-four hours to think over all that we've said, then make you an offer.'

'Fine,' I said. I rode back to the *Telegraph* in a confused and excited mood.

Andreas didn't wait twenty-four hours. He telephoned at about 5.30.

'Hi – can you speak?'

'Yes.'

'I don't need twenty-four hours. I'll offer £42,500 and all the other things we've agreed. I'll put it all in writing as soon as you accept.'

I thanked him and said it sounded quite acceptable but *I'd* now need twenty-four hours to talk to Caroline and think.

He said, 'Of course.'

The thought occurred to me while I was at the *Independent* that simply because there were now offices and secretaries and a rudimentary staff I was taking the paper much more seriously. It had become real to me and at the same time my respect for Andreas, Matthew and Stephen also rose. It became dramatically clear how very difficult it must have been to keep believing in the project while in one way there was no evidence at all of its existence. And all that time they had been surrounded by disbelievers like me who most of the time thought the whole thing was a delusion or mirage.

While I was talking to Andreas before lunch, Matthew had come in and said, 'This is an historic moment, Andreas, you ought to come and look. There are two huge pantechnicons outside. The computers have arrived!'

Actually we didn't look at them till later, but Matthew's excitement was catching. Everything was taking off. As we walked to the restaurant someone, I think it was Andreas, said as we passed the gigantic lorries,

160

'It's extraordinary, we've done all this in such a short time. From a standing start to all this in less than a year.'

'And we've done it without a penny to start with; from just nothing,' said Matthew. I was impressed, and full of admiration for all they had endured.

James has gone away to Israel for a fortnight with his Aunt E. Before he went he said to me, 'Look, join the *Independent*. It's all part of my master plan. I want you to be in London to look after things here while I'm away in the Far East looking after the foreign side of the paper.'

I laughed when he said that, and replied that Caroline once said she thought I was wheeler-dealing in the *Telegraph* and *Independent* because I wanted to become the most powerful man in Fleet Street.

'No, I am,' said James.

I felt the usual need to speak to Tony Howard and Charles Moore and couldn't get hold of either of them.

When I took my cartoon to Max he groaned when he saw it was about Mrs Thatcher. 'Oh God, I've got to go to Number Ten tonight.'

I remembered there was a dinner in honour of Bill at the Thatchers' that evening. Max went through the guest list wondering and laughing at the funny mixture of people. Willie Whitelaw, Morrison Halcrow, Keith Joseph, Charles Moore, Conrad Black and so on.

I said it didn't matter about my cartoon because she wouldn't see it till the next day anyway.

'No,' said Max. 'But if only you could be nasty about the Labour Party sometimes.'

'Has Black been on at you again?'

'Whenever you see an enormous old Rolls hanging about out there' – he pointed down into Fleet Street – 'you know he is around.'

When I got home I rang Stephen – not, as I explained, to say anything particular, but just because our meeting had been very important, critical probably, and I wanted to talk about it.

He was as usual very nice and oddly reassuring. He seemed to understand my jangled mood very well, and talking to him calmed me down.

'Look, just say what you want; you'll get it,' he said.

We talked about Andreas and Matthew. He steered a delicate line between listening to, even agreeing with, some of my doubts about them and praising them for their good qualities. 'One mustn't be romantic about Andreas: he has his weaknesses, but he's a kind of genius.' He said Matthew was extremely good at getting things done. Someone would discover that no one had arranged for any desks for the secretaries or something like that, and Matthew would shoot out and fix it up and come darting back as if asking for the next task.

I couldn't sleep when I went to bed and was so restless I feared I'd

161

wake Caroline. I tried listening to my little radio with the headphones, but that didn't soothe me. At two o'clock I went downstairs and drank hot milk and read for hours.

Friday 6 June
Martin and I talked again, leaning against the wall round the stairwell outside the lifts on the third floor. Every now and then, because we were talking about the *Independent* and whether or not to join it, we dropped our voices or even stopped as someone went by. This happened particularly if we were repeating an offer Andreas had made, or quoting something Max had said, or some such thing that would make it obvious what we were talking about. As a matter of fact it was obvious anyway because McManus went by and said, 'What are you two plotting?' Once Martin actually signalled me to stop talking while some bloke went by. I looked at the man and back to Martin. He said, 'He is a notorious nark; he used to be Peter Eastwood's ears.'

Soon after that Oliver Pritchett wandered by, vague as ever, looking around like an untidy owl. 'Shhh!' I said loudly to Martin. 'Look out: *shhh!*' I indicated Oliver. Martin stopped talking and started ostentatiously looking around as if doing nothing.

Oliver smiled. 'Yes, look out,' he said. 'Take care because I am the *man.*'

'*The* management spy?'

'That's me,' said Oliver and went on downstairs.

Alexander Chancellor told me that Bill's dinner has been a bit awkward. Perry had told him. Bill himself had not spoken very well and Mrs Thatcher's speech, written by Perry himself, had bored everyone stiff, including its author. In fact everyone had been so bored with it that Perry had started to call out 'Hear, hear!' at frequent intervals in a pathetic attempt to get the thing going, without success.

Saturday 7 June
All day I churned over Andreas's offer and wondered what to do.

Sitting at the kitchen table, Caroline said, 'If you tell Max you're going, he's going to ask why. What are you going to say?'

'I'll try to tell him, I suppose.'

'Why *are* you going?'

'Actually, I've been rather surprised to find just what my motive is. When I first began thinking about joining the *Independent* my main worry was that it would fold within a year or eighteen months. But that worry didn't last. After one particular conversation with Charles I became more worried that it would be a dull, self-satisfied, small-circulation paper that no one I knew read. That worry also faded. Now my main anxiety is about my future on the *Telegraph*. I've heard such

162

frightening stories of people being prematurely retired with no money. I'm almost more concerned about my pension than anything else.'

'If you say that to Max he'll say, "I'll raise and guarantee your pension." '

'I also feel increasingly isolated from my colleagues and the general life on the paper . . .'

'I'm only trying to be the devil's advocate, but if you say that, he'll say well, come to the conferences; join us; drop in whenever you like and have a chat; you like Don, don't you . . . and so on.'

'The reason I want to go is because I find I am, after all, a member of the *ancien régime*. With all its faults and built-in obsolescence I understood it, and gave it my loyalty. I even liked what was absurd about it. It had made me, and I was indebted to it. Now I look around and see strangers making decisions I don't like. The mixture of revolutionary change and panic is disagreeable. If all the casualties had been suffered in the service of a new *Telegraph* that I believed in, I could stomach everything. But the politically wishy-washy, yuppie, carefully packaged mess that has been substituted for the daft old *Telegraph* has no attraction for me. For a moment when Max took over I thought it would have . . .'

'That's the real reason. Max will not have an answer to that. You've fallen out of love with it.'

'He will have an answer. He will say, give us time, of course we haven't got it right yet.'

'But that *is* the reason you want to go.'

'Yes, I think it is. Although there is another whole side to it. I want to be with friends again and I feel I'd find them at the *Independent*. Funnily enough, I think my future might be more secure at the *Independent* than at the *Telegraph*. I'd get more money. The share option might pay off. Another thing is, if I don't make a change now I think I never will. I face the prospect of working out my entire cartoonist's life in one newspaper. I feel the need for a change almost for its own sake.'

'I suppose Max could argue you're getting plenty of change at the *Telegraph*.'

'Perhaps the main reason is that I can't turn down the opportunity to work in that *Independent* office looking over such a view.'

'I want to see that office.'

'One of the main problems about leaving is how the hell do I tell Max? I get the heebie-jeebies each time I think of framing the words and seeing the irritation and disappointment in his face. And how do I empty my room? There is junk in there that has taken twenty years to accumulate.'

The other day when I said to Stephen that clearing my room was a problem he murmured sympathetically and said, 'But don't worry. I'll

163

help you. You can borrow my car. We'll go and do it one weekend.' He has a knack of making things seem possible.

This evening we had a dinner party. Our guests were Charles and Caroline Moore, John and Cynthia Thompson, Richard Hollis and Posy Simmonds and Stephen and Liesel Hearst.

It was a pretty good evening. Perhaps just too many people. I don't know the perfect number for a dinner party. It may be eight rather than ten. Charles was very funny about Bill's dinner at Downing Street. At one stage of the evening the lights were dimmed in the drawing-room so that the company could watch the Guards beating the retreat or flashing their colours or whatever they do. Everyone stood spellbound. But Conrad Black's act is apparently to be the one who knows everything, and he completely ruined the spectacle with an interminable monologue about the history of the uniforms and the origins of the ritual before them. Charles gave his spluttering laugh. 'And it was so boring and pointless.'

I spoke to Stephen Hearst about leaving the *Telegraph*. He asked difficult and challenging questions and made me feel uncertain. Later I had a conversation with John about it. To my surprise everything he said made me feel I should go to the *Independent* if the terms of the deal are to my advantage. I had expected him to try to push me into staying. He did the opposite.

When we discussed my pension rights at the *Telegraph* he said in his careful and precise way, 'I think you should go to Andreas and say, "Can you buy me a pension to compensate me for the one I'm turning my back on if I join you?" And I think he'll say yes.'

'Crumbs! Do you really?'

'Look, they want you. Your bargaining position is never going to be stronger. If you can secure your future in this way, I can't see an argument for staying.'

I expressed some surprise that he should speak so bluntly. I was trying to get him to say something about what he thought about the new *Telegraph*, but he remained silent on that theme.

He said, 'If you go it will be a heavy blow to the *Telegraph*, but that is no longer my concern.'

I never found out whether he had tuned in to my feelings and had decided to support what I was going to do anyway; or whether his more or less telling me to move indicated a loss of faith in the *Telegraph*'s future. I incline to think there was a strong element of the latter, but I could not be sure. Some months ago he told me stick around at the *Telegraph* and see how things turned out before coming to any decision about quitting. He made no such cautious remarks this evening.

I felt his words and advice were very helpful. My mind was clearer after we had spoken. I almost wanted to jump on my bike and zoom around to Andreas's house and say, 'Buy me a pension and I'll join your lot.'

I had no chance to speak to Charles about it all, but Caroline Moore listened to me talking to Posy and Richard about the *Independent*. They were both very helpful too, and I thought what they said pushed me towards Andreas.

Caroline looked down her beautiful nose and smiled a tight mischievous smile. 'You have to consider carefully the effect on your life of appearing daily alongside innumerable leaders by Matthew.' She sent this dart over the top of something that Posy was saying to me, so I chose not to reply to her and merely acknowledged with raised eyebrows that I had heard her.

Sunday 8 June
Restless still and wanting things settled, I rang Andreas and asked if I could come and see him later today. We arranged to meet at 6.00 at his house.

By the time I arrived I had my opening lines in my head and my negotiating strategy, such as it was, properly rehearsed in my mind.

We sat down in his very comfortable sitting-room. Some people have grown-up houses. Their rooms are neat and tidy. There are clear places to sit down and there is space to leave your coat. That's the sort of house Andreas has. By 'grown-up' I do not mean inhabited by adults (Andreas has two children, I think); I mean not like our house, which has clutter everywhere. No surface exists at home which does not have old newspapers, open books, toys, shoes and cups on it. It doesn't seem to matter how much Caroline and I tidy it up, it remains cluttered.

Andreas and I made small talk for a minute or two and just as I drew a breath to launch into my speech he said, 'About pensions . . .' and he explained carefully and simply what I could expect probably from the *Telegraph* and what I could expect from the *Independent*. While the *Telegraph*'s pension would be bigger because I had worked there so long, the *Independent* included what could be a very lucrative share option scheme. Andreas explained this to me.

When he had finished I began my speech. I began by saying that he once described himself to me as the world's worst negotiator. 'Well,' I said, 'you've met your match.'

I then said in effect I would like to be compensated for the difference between what the *Telegraph* would give me at 65 and what the *Independent* would provide. 'Couldn't you,' I asked, 'simply buy me a pension of that amount?'

I could see the idea taking hold of him, and he at once said that this could be a neat solution. He'd need to ask his finance director about it and there might be other ways round it because there could be tax problems about what amounted to a 'golden hello'.

For a while we discussed his first offer of raising my salary so that the extra could go straight into a personal pension fund. I said that was OK but what if the *Independent* floundered? I'd be back where I started. I wanted (though I did not use this expression) Barry Humphries' cash in the claw. He saw what I meant.

'If,' I said, 'you could find a way of buying me a pension outright I'd accept the rest of your terms.'

'That's very good to hear – and it makes it easier for me to go to my directors if I can tell them that.'

He said one problem was that he had taken endless pains to be fair to all his recruits and to treat them all the same, as far as possible. Obviously they could not buy everyone a pension like this. It would, if they bought me one, create an anomaly. But while that was regrettable there might be no way round it.

He even suggested that they buy a number of original cartoons from me, from my vast collection of twenty years' work. That way he could tell his people they were making a sensible investment and I could use the money to buy myself the pension. So in a friendly and cooperative way we kicked all these ideas around for an hour or so. By the time I left I felt it was all over bar a few technical arrangements. Emotionally I had left the *Telegraph*.

When I got back home and told Caroline she opened a half bottle of champagne as a half-way celebration or marker of the importance of this day. As Andreas had said, leaving the *Telegraph* for him and his colleagues, and for me too, was probably the biggest and most difficult professional decision any of us would ever make.

Thursday 12 June

Had lunch with Tony Howard. He is the spokesman for staying put and not taking risks. He mocks the chances of the *Independent*'s survival. He laughed out loud when I told him Andreas's share option scheme and at once told me of an acquaintance of his who has £100,000 tied up in the doomed *Today*. He has carefully worked out reasons why the *Independent* simply cannot make it. He can prove it to himself by references to the destiny of similar ventures and his knowledge and instinct about newspaper readers. But then Tony is a bit like that. It does not mean his advice is bad but he is not above spoiling things a bit. I always remember him telling me that I had been given the Cartoonist of the Year award by the Granada TV programme *What the Papers Say*. He had been part of the group that had made the award. 'Oh, I had to fight for you, I can tell you. Uphill all the way. Managed to do a deal in the end; got so-and-so to vote for you on condition that

I voted for his man. But what's-it remained a problem. "We're not giving it to him!" was his response . . .' and so on. I've never felt that I won that award, but that Tony wangled it for me.

He didn't muck about. He said bluntly, 'If I was you I wouldn't go. It's too risky.' He did also say that they looked more credible than they once did, and they do seem to have recruited a reasonably good team of journalists. Finally his attitude was that it was perfectly clear I had already made up my mind and therefore the sooner I told Max the better. He also rubbed my nose in the fact that Max was going to take it very hard.

Having said all that, he was also sympathetic to the idea of my simply wanting a change. Indeed, he even felt in an abstract way that he thought change would be good for me. It is also true that, when pushed, he quickly agreed that he could be quite wrong, and that it was possible that the *Independent* would be a success. It had a better chance than *Today*, and anyway even the *Telegraph* was not absolutely secure. He understood entirely my gloom about the disagreeable atmosphere at the *Telegraph*, and how I might long for respite from its collapsing morale, sinking circulation and frequent rounds of staff cuts and changes.

He also believed that Max might not last much beyond December. He based this view on Max's poor showing so far, and on what he thinks about the hard-headedness of Black and Knight.

Because I'd heard Alexander Chancellor was not too happy at the *Sunday Telegraph* I asked whether he'd heard the same and he said he had. He even said Alexander had spoken to Andreas again recently. In Tony's view Alexander still minds not having got the editorship of the *Sunday Telegraph* and realises he enjoyed editing the *Spectator* more than he enjoys being Perry's Number Two. Tony added that Charles Moore is now everyone's golden-haired boy because the *Spectator* is so good, but that this is truly Alexander's success and Charles merely inherited it.

When assuring me that Max would take my defection hard, he told me that Max had recently revealed how difficult it had been to get the *Telegraph* management to give me the pay rise I eventually got. According to Tony, Max had said the management thought I was lying about the offers I'd received from the *Independent* and the *Observer*. Consequently they argued it was unnecessary to give me more money.

I was stung by this and said to Tony, somewhat angrily, 'Did he really say that, that they thought I was lying?'

Tony looked a little nervous. 'Yes, he did, but don't use that story against Max.'

'It's not a story against Max. It's a story *for* Max. It's a story against

167

the management. Well, they'll find out whether I was lying, won't they?'

Tony continued to look nervous.

We also enjoyed the usual gossip. He'd heard that Bill had accepted a life peerage and that Tiny Rowland was going to buy *Today*. He said Charles would not be made editor of the *Telegraph* if Max went. Tony's tip for that job was Paul Johnson! He joked about young Graham Paterson whom he'd met recently and who was saying what a splendid and wonderful fellow Conrad Black was. Tony had got irritated and looked at the chubby lad and said, 'I remember you coming to see me bright-eyed and bushy-tailed and idealistic only six years ago. You have descended into decadence quicker than any man I've ever known.'

'It was seven years ago,' Graham had replied cheerfully.

I left the lunch feeling rotten.

Just before we got up to go, Richard Ingrams came downstairs into the restaurant followed by the tiny, grinning and oddly sinister figure of the new editor of *Private Eye*, Ian Hislop. Richard looked immensely tall and mournful, although he gave us his tight downward-turned smile as he passed our table. They stopped and talked for a moment before moving on, Richard in the lead: Don Quixote and his Psycho Panza.

I remember one other story Tony told me. The regular Saturday lunches that Hartwell always used to hold for the senior editorial staff of the *Sunday Telegraph* are still held, but only George Evans goes now. Perry or Alexander may look in briefly, but that's all. When George Evans goes at the end of this month there will be no one left for Lord H to have lunch with.

I am reading Kapusinski's book about the end of Haile Selassie. The similarity is striking.

I spoke to a girl from our pension office at the *Telegraph*. She explained to me that, if I left, the pension I'd earned so far is kept for me until I am 65. There are all sorts of additional aspects of this but basically it means that I cannot, do not need to, ask Andreas to buy me a pension. I rang Andreas and told him. Quick as a flash he said, 'Right, in that case let us meet and work out a deal. We now know enough. Can I come and see you at 9.00-ish this evening?'

He did come round, and with bits of paper and a little calculator worked out a deal. I was overcome with fatigue and was drinking white wine and fizzy water and couldn't really follow it all that well. I trusted him, anyway. Caroline came home after Andreas had been there only a few minutes and I think she could understand Andreas's plan more easily than I could. My mind was going into neutral to avoid having to make the final step.

Several times Andreas worked out sums a second or third time. 'I am obsessional about figures. I must get them right,' he said, prodding away at the slim calculator in his hand. It was clear negotiations were over. This was it.

'Do you agree, then?' said Andreas.

'Yes, I think I do. I am still uncertain about how to tell Max and there are other practical matters of that kind I must clarify to myself.'

Andreas looked beseechingly at Caroline. 'Has he agreed? What did he say?'

'He's agreed,' said Caroline. 'He'll take a little longer to make the final act. That's how he proceeds.'

'Good,' said Andreas. They both looked at me, Caroline indulgently, Andreas kindly, as if regarding someone who was going down with flu.

Caroline got out a large box of chocolates we'd been given; each chocolate is filled with a soft centre made from real cream. They are too rich for me; I can never manage more than one bite. Andreas ate about six or seven over the next few minutes. He said he was addicted to chocolates and seriously discussed with Caroline which of the ones in front of him were the best.

Both chose chocolate after chocolate and made appreciative noises, 'Mm – oh – oo – delicious . . . mm . . .' and laughed at their own greed.

Andreas was very good. He was sympathetic. He understood very well how hard it was to leave. He listened to Caroline suggesting a column about psychology. He said, 'I always love it when people say "our economic writer" – you are suggesting "our psychological writer".' She showed him some examples of what she meant and he asked if he could take them away. His response was alert and quick.

He listened equally attentively when I made a long rambling speech on the use of colour in the *Independent*. I believe it should be sparingly used, especially on the front page. The masthead must be in black. To try to persuade him I dragged in examples of the restrained use of colour in Corot's paintings, or the restrained use of movement in Jonathan Miller's crowd scenes in his ENO production of *Otello*. 'Restraint is all,' I said. He said they would try out everything and see what looked best.

Friday 13 June
Since seeing Andreas on Sunday my mind has been in turmoil. Yesterday should have helped, but hasn't. I swing wildly from a sense of elation at the prospect of leaving the shadowy *Telegraph* and joining the vigorous *Independent*; and back to gloomy anxiety that I'm throwing up security for a silly dream.

Before doing anything today I telephoned one of my closest friends Michael Irwin in Canterbury. It was about 8.15 and Stella was just rushing the children off to school but Michael and I talked even though

I could guess I was holding up his day. I explained how near I was to leaving the *Telegraph* and tried to give him the arguments for and against. He listened with his usual close attention, which makes one avoid all flim-flam. Even so he cannot help putting in jokes and comic asides from time to time. When I'd finished he spoke clearly and confidently. He said, 'Go.' One phrase he used stuck in my mind: 'There is a dynamic about going, but no dynamic about staying.'

He understood and expressed very well the restlessness I feel and how people of our age can benefit from a change at this moment in their careers. He says he watches his colleagues at Kent University and notices there are those who one by one give up all expectation or desire for change. They settle down. These men and women depress him.

Michael's robust and clear statements gave me enormous reassurance. He is one of the three or four people whose support is essential in any major decision I have to make.

I said, 'At the end of all this part of the process there remains one of the most dreadful bits of the whole business. I've got to go and explain it all to Max. I've got to go into his room and confront him; but what am I going to say?'

There was a little pause. 'Goodbye?' suggested Michael.

On my way down to work I called in to see Charles at the *Spectator*. I want his approval but don't need it like I need Michael's. When I explained how far things had got his attitude was relaxed. He did not seem to pick up or react to the seriousness of my mood.

'When Max hears this he's going to get up,' said Charles, rising to his feet and standing on tiptoe, 'and he's going to reach over his desk and pick you up.' He mimed this act, holding an imaginary figure by the throat, and began raining punches at its head.

'Oh God, is he really?'

'Yes, he is. He is not going to be pleased.'

Charles made no comment on the wisdom of joining the *Independent* or leaving the *Telegraph*. Either could turn out to be the best decision; on balance I guess he favoured staying put. His only serious advice was, 'When you go and see Max be absolutely sure that your mind is made up. He will try everything to make you stay, but if you waver and *do* stay then your life will be impossible.'

'What do you mean?'

'They'll think you are a wet and weak and untrustworthy and generally hopeless.'

While we were talking, he took a phone call. It was from a man who had agreed to join the *Spectator*, but was now under strong pressure from Max to go to the *Telegraph* instead. Charles said to me when he'd rung off that if the unfortunate caller broke his word he (Charles) would not be pleased. 'I'll make sure he never does *that* to anyone again. I'll make sure people know he is not to be trusted. His reputation will be of a man who'll let you down.'

He was speaking with unusual coldness. There was something vindictive about his words that I thought was disagreeable. My sympathies were entirely with the poor bewildered lad who didn't know what to do, being dragged in opposite directions by these two bullies.

I said something of that kind and was made aware that my position as a waverer was similar to that of the unknown young journalist on the phone.

Work was difficult. My mind would not connect with the news and my hand felt wobbly and weak. I could hardly draw. My mood had swung away from the peaceful confidence inspired by Michael. I was troubled again. I managed a cartoon in the end and driving home I saw Lennie Hoffmann in his garden; he lives right round the corner from me. We drank beer and I told him the story so far.

I said, 'I am very surprised indeed by how disturbed I am by this period of indecision.'

He replied, 'Why are you surprised? The fact is that in our lives we make very few decisions. Perhaps three or four major ones in all. Usually we allow things to take their course, adjusting small issues here and there. This is different. Of course it's difficult.'

Gill drew a parallel with Lennie's changing last year from being a barrister to being a judge.

'Yes, but I took a greater drop in salary,' said Lennie.

At dinner in the evening at a friend's house I met a young TV writer/producer. He is an economist and we discussed the *Independent*. He said he had the feeling it was going to be a great sucess; he's thinking of trying for a job on it. As I moaned on in my usual way he interrupted me. 'Go!' he called down the table, with awful finality.

My two children have strong views about my leaving the *Telegraph*. Both are against it. Alexander is straightforward about the risk involved. Theo worried about the risk, but he also said, 'I don't think you should leave the *Telegraph*. I'm angry with you.'

'Why?'

'Because they have done so much for you, and right now they need you badly.'

This did not make the decision any easier.

Saturday 14 June
A beautiful hot day. I went to William Shawcross's fortieth birthday party at Friston Place. I took my motor bike because Caroline was at a conference.

As I drove towards Fleet Street to cross Blackfriars Bridge I felt sick and weak. I told myself it was nerves and to do with this mid-profession

171

crisis. Once past the bridge I told myself I'd be OK. Look, I said to myself, calm down. If you don't feel better soon you can always go home. And, just as I'd argued, the deeper I got into South London the better I felt and by the time I was going through open countryside I felt fine.

The party was wonderful. A huge lunch out on the lawn. People were drinking Pimms under shady trees. Later a steel band plinkety-plonked and there was dancing.

I even felt OK on the ride back.

Sunday 15 June
I wrote short letters of resignation to Max and Perry.

I tried to write a letter to Bill about his getting a peerage and I tried to write to Willie to thank him for the party, but I was so restless and fretful that I couldn't. I mowed the lawn. I tried to help Theo with homework. I tried to read the papers. I was jumpy and nervous.

Rachel Miller dropped in at about 6.00 and she and Caroline and I drank half a bottle of champagne.

For the last two days the weather has been perfect.

John Thompson rang me to ask me to lunch next Tuesday and we talked. I told him I'd written the letter of resignation. I said I had been influenced by his not trying to get me to stay on the *Telegraph*. He laughed and said that was just because he no longer worked there and he felt it wasn't his business to persuade me one way or another. He still remained silent on whether or not I should go. He merely said there was a risk that the *Independent* might fold. I said everyone assured me that even if that happened I'd find a job.

He laughed again and said he was sure that was true.

It's funny which people make you feel good and which bad. I felt better after talking to him. He makes the world seem real. He is like one of those footballers who slows a game down for a while in order for his team to regroup.

By bedtime, I was still so restless Caroline gave me a sleeping pill and at last I felt a warm, melting sensation of relaxation steal over me.

Monday 16 June
I had to get down to work today, and the practical need to concentrate helped. The only trouble was I had to ring Tim Garton Ash and when I told him I'd decided to go his voice dropped about five tones and he said, 'Really? Oh – well – good luck.' It was as if I'd said I was going to try to swim the Channel or ski down Mount Everest. He said, 'You are very brave.' My heart sank. He was not making me feel good at all. 'I don't want to sound like a wet blanket. I don't know any more about it than you do . . .' But the damage was done.

172

When I tried to get him to say more, he reasonably enough referred to our last conversation about the *Independent*, when I had been sceptical about its chances of success.

He said, 'I was very influenced by what you said then.'

I spoke to Charles about a *Spectator* drawing but didn't mention the *Independent*.

I went into Fleet Street early and did the drawing for Charles there. I rang for a DR to come and get them and settled down to *Telegraph* work. But first I sealed my letters of resignation to Max and Perry.

I finished the cartoon quite early, before 5.00, and took it along to Max. He was not in his office and I had a brief chat with Josie, his secretary. For some reason today she was friendly and smiling. She said that she thought my cartoons were very good. 'They're so – political.' She also admitted to being a paid-up member of the SDP and said cheerfully that I should keep up the good work. I don't know exactly how these shyly-stated remarks hung together, but the overall effect was unmistakable. She was being very nice.

Max was in Don's room, so I took the cartoon down there. Busy as usual, carrying his inevitable bits of paper and looming like a great tree, Max passed the cartoon at once.

'Very good; brilliant form,' he said.

Don't be friendly, I prayed silently; be brusque and pompous.

'What time do you usually get in to work?' he asked.

'Oh, I dunno. It varies; usually around lunch time.'

'It's just that I am very conscious of your being somewhat isolated here. I don't know what I can do about it, can't really see how to change the [leader writers'] conference but . . . um . . .'

'Never mind about that. I appreciate your mentioning it but . . . er . . . I have lots of things to do in the mornings and . . . don't know how to change my routine, either . . .'

He was leaning on a filing cabinet and looking at me in a good-natured and concerned way. The wild thought crossed my mind, 'They know: he and Josie are making it as hard for me as possible.' The stupid thought made me feel even worse.

'Thanks, anyway,' I said, and took my cartoon through to the subs to tell them it was 'landscape shape with a caption'.

The features sub, Peter, who was dealing with the cartoon, told me how useful it was that I came to see them each night. Recently a cartoon came back from process without a caption and he'd noticed because I'd mentioned it earlier. 'I might have just let it through, otherwise.' He looked at me, pleased to be able to tell me that my cartoons were watched over carefully.

'How could they make such a mistake?' he said. 'When I told them

173

they'd left off the caption they said, 'Well, you can set it,' and I said, 'No, I can't. The style is, Nick writes the caption.'

Oh God, I begged, let someone say something nasty.

Peter looked at the cartoon and grinned. 'Jolly good,' he said.

Back in my room I went through the ritual of tidying it up. My room gets very messy during the day: pencil sharpenings, scrumpled newspapers, discarded roughs, empty plastic cups and splashed ink over the floor. Once years ago I found a crude cartoon resting on the upturned waste paper basket. A stick figure marked 'Cartoonist' was shown sitting in a chair throwing numerous bits of paper at an empty bin. As the rubbish piled up on the floor the figure was saying, 'Missed . . . missed . . . missed . . .' The drawing was signed 'Cleaners'. I left them a drawing that night that showed me apologising to them and clearing up.

When my room was straight, all I had to do was leave and drop off my letters on the way out. I lingered. I knew I was on the brink, but I still needed something before I jumped.

I rang Caroline.

We caught up with the day's news. Both our boys are doing exams, Alexander his O levels, Theo end-of-term exams. Theo is taking it harder than Alexander. I asked how he'd got on. Caroline said he was in a state of shock so she was not asking. Instead she was feeding him water melon until he felt like talking. Alexander had got on OK.

'What stage are you at?' she asked.

'I've finished.'

'Oh great: well, come on home.'

I explained that before I left I had to hand in my letters and something was stopping me. 'I feel such an important decision should be done with confidence and I still feel confused. I can't understand it. It's as if I'm going for the negative reason that I'm fed up here.'

Caroline thought for a moment. Then she said, 'I think that you're dealing into this moment something from other similar or related incidents in your life. Perhaps leaving home for the first time, even leaving your first marriage. It's as if you feel you're doing something wrong and are having to deal with feelings of guilt. But you have nothing to feel guilty about. You're doing nothing wrong.'

I thought about her idea for a while and said, 'There may be something in that; I don't know. But I don't think I feel guilty exactly. For reasons that I am not responsible for, my quitting the *Telegraph* delivers a much harder blow to them than most resignations would. It's not my fault, but there are so few political cartoonists that they're going to find it very hard to replace me. I fear that is true anyway. That is why I feel so awkward about leaving. I really don't want to hurt them but I'm afraid they will see it that way. It makes me feel trapped. But the prospect of staying here depresses me. It would be like giving up, in a way. I would settle back and serve out my time without pleasure or excitement or challenge.'

Caroline made sympathetic noises of agreement.

I went on. 'I was talking to someone or other about it the other day, they said, "Oh how difficult! But now, if you don't go, it will be as if you were chickening out." '

Caroline laughed.

I said, 'It's what it feels like. But in the confusion and fog there is one thing that glitters: that is the prospect of a new paper, new colleagues, a new start.'

I cannot remember quite how she phrased it, but Caroline recognised that, however rambling my expression of it, the reason why I was going, and must go, was here. Staying at the *Telegraph* was prematurely to accept old age. Leaving was accepting a risk, having a go, advancing. The choice was actually not between the *Telegraph* and the *Independent* or Andreas and Max. It was between stagnation and action.

As she talked I felt my uncertainty fade away.

I said, 'Right, that's it.'

'Are you coming home now?'

'Yes. You are very good.' I meant that she had given me what I had been looking for, that she was very clever. I added one more thought. 'It could make quite a difference to your life, you know. When we talk about risk, there really is a risk. You may have to start taking a great many private patients.'

Caroline reminded me of a time when some years ago she had said that as we had slipped into financial security she sometimes missed the struggle of our earlier days. 'You thought I was mad, but I meant it,' she said. 'And I look forward to the uncertainty, if that doesn't sound too crazy.'

I said again, 'Well, there is a risk, and it is real.'

She went into another personality, an early American pioneer woman. 'Ah mean t' stand by mah man! Ah'll face th' future, fair 'n' square; if Ah have to take on more patients Ah'll do it . . .' This ridiculous act reeled off into utter nonsense and we hung up.

As I left my room I met Morrison coming through the security door.

'How can I prop it open so that I can get back?' he said.

'You don't have to prop it open, you just open it.'

'What?'

'I'll show you how but I must ask you not to tell anyone because the security men wouldn't like it if they found out.'

'What are you talking about?'

'I'm facing you with a moral dilemma; are you prepared irresponsibly to keep a secret in order to gain advantageous information?'

175

'I'm always facing moral dilemmas,' he said meaninglessly.

I showed him where the 'key' was hidden and how it worked. He laughed and looked almost embarrassed.

'Don't tell anyone,' I said.

I didn't care whether he told anyone or not; after all, I was off.

As I left the building I gave the two letters in to the reception desk to be delivered. Walking across Fleet Street to my bike I felt better than I had for days.

At about 8.00 I rang Andreas because I knew he'd be anxious to hear and I wanted him to be able to stop worrying. Valerie answered the phone and said Andreas was out and would not be back until 10.00 or 10.30. I asked her to tell him that I had resigned from the *Telegraph* but there was no need to call back. I'd be at home tomorrow morning.

At about 9.30 Matthew rang to say they had received my message and were absolutely delighted. The warmth and relief in his voice was unmistakable.

We arranged to have lunch on Thursday. He also told me in deadly secrecy ('Don't tell Stephen I told you') that Alexander Chancellor was negotiating with them to become Washington bureau chief. I was extremely interested in this news and found at once that I hoped desperately that Alexander did join the *Independent*. He is a very, very good journalist and it would put me in good company among *Telegraph* defectors.

Later in the evening both Andreas and Stephen also rang. Both of them were obviously tremendously pleased. I felt embraced by my new colleagues.

Tuesday 17 June

It is 11.15. I have spent the morning sitting in the garden writing up this journal. About thirty-five minutes ago I walked down the road to take a break and do a little shopping. Outside the newsagent I met my son Alexander who was also taking a break from revision. He said, 'Max Hastings just rang you. He wants to speak to you urgently.'

Once again I took myself by surprise. My confidence gave way to butterflies in the stomach, and dread of this confrontation overwhelmed me.

Alexander and I walked back up the road together. He was chattering away about a holiday job he wants to get. As we reached the house the phone was ringing. It was Max.

I had run the last few yards because I could hear the telephone and was annoyed to find myself panting slightly. This promised to be difficult enough anyway without having to gasp for breath at the same time. However, as soon as Max's rueful and conciliatory voice came down the line I felt OK. First I reassured him my decision was not a criticism of him or the new *Telegraph*. I tried to explain that I had arrived at this point because of a constellation of events of which the passing of the old order and imposition of the new was important but not decisive. I mentioned my need for a change.

He was understanding and tried to be firm, but every now and then he took a deep breath and said, 'Oh gosh!' He tried to make me name a price but I said *The Times* had already offered more money than the *Independent* had. I told him how much and he said, 'We'd pay more.' He said Jak got close to £100,000 a year on the *Standard* and was worth it. He said, 'We'll set you up for life.'

I heard myself replying that I was not going for money and this was not a bargaining manoeuvre. Max at once said he knew that, but he was desperate. My leaving the *Telegraph* was a shattering blow and it was worth anything to keep me. He sounded desperately unhappy and at a loss. 'I'd rather you went to *The Times* than to the *Independent*.'

I tried to be as cool as possible and not to give in to this injured and gentle approach. Max switched to a different mode. It would be misleading to say he got tough but there was a note of anger in his voice nevertheless. He indicated that he thought my behaviour was, not to mince words, dishonourable. I had accepted his generous terms and that amounted to a gentleman's agreement to stay. I was letting down the side just when I was most needed. Perhaps it is not surprising, but as soon as he began to sound shirty I relaxed. An onslaught I can take; it's tears that undo me.

He didn't go on in this mode very long and anyway it was no more than a touch of it. Back in his cajoling manner, he said, 'You must do what you think best, of course, but I don't think it is unreasonable for me to ask that you postpone your departure at least until the end of the year.'

Not unreasonable to ask, I thought, but unrealistic.

I pointed out that there was a flaw in this proposal. If the *Telegraph* was going to have an autumn re-launch campaign, it is not wise to make my temporary presence an important part of that campaign. And anyway, I went on, the *Independent* would also be launching itself at that time, and they would not want me unless I was there at the beginning. He said that was nonsense, they'd want me any time they could get me, but of course he understood the point.

At some juncture our conversation began to go in circles and we ended it. I get the impression that Max had not thought out any tactics to try to make me change my mind. And I also thought he had no cards. The only time I'd wavered was when he said he'd set me up for life. The wonderful fantasy of being rich flickered across my mind. No more worries about repairing the roof, rebuilding the kitchen, securing the education of the children. In a flash I saw my brand-new powerful

177

motor bike, Caroline's new consulting room, the children's secure future . . .

But even that fantasy was spoiled by the image of Andreas's disappointment and rage; and doubts about my own weakness if I copped out like that. I also knew that it was only a fantasy.

A long way behind everything I said lay an attitude formed by rumours of how the *Telegraph* had treated many people in the last few months. Whether it was relevant and justified or not, hovering in the back of my mind was the thought that the man I was talking to had been pretty ruthless himself lately. He had had to harden his heart and deal out much more devastating blows that the one I'd caught him with. In the immensely complicated tangle of my emotions, I reached now and then for that thought to find some sort of dubious comfort.

As he hung up Max said, 'See you later.'

Before I left to meet John Thompson for lunch, Don Berry rang. He said Max had told him the devastating news and he was consequently devastated. He asked if we could talk and I said, yes, but not now on the phone. We agreed to meet later in the day.

Almost immediately after this call James rang. Slowly he said, 'I hear you've resigned from the *Telegraph*.'

'Yeah, I have.'

'Good.'

I gave him a quick account of how things had happened and added that now there were two things I wanted to say to him. The first was an idea Tim Garton Ash had suggested to me which I thought promising. It was to have a European page in the *Independent* as well as home and foreign pages. I'm not sure why this appeals to me but it does. There is nothing in the world duller than the EEC or more incomprehensible, but Europe is not dull and I like the idea of it being talked about as an identifiable whole. I feel European.

The second matter was much more important – perhaps 'crucial' was not too strong a word. 'We must make absolutely certain that when the *Independent* is published the masthead is in black.' James was silent. So I went on. 'They are going to use colour on the front – a spot down the page – a weather map or something. Well, that's OK. But it's essential that the masthead is in black because . . .'

'Because otherwise it won't look like a newspaper,' said James.

'That's right.' I was so relieved he agreed. 'I look down the rows of papers in our newsagent and I see the black and white pages; then there is the coloured *Today* and it just looks daft.'

I said to James that written into my contract was the promise that I could travel abroad for the *Independent*. 'We could go together to, say, Korea. You write and I draw. How about it?'

James slowly said, 'Mmm.'

'If the idea appeals to you . . .' I suddenly thought of James liking to travel alone, making his contacts and following his nose.

'Oh yes, it appeals to me,' he said, and we left it like that.

John Thompson had asked me to meet him at one. I enjoyed our lunch together. He listened to my story in his usual wise and calm way. I told him everything I could remember, even throwing in Tony's story that the *Telegraph* management had been sceptical about the original offer from the *Independent*. John said he doubted that. 'You hear so many rumours,' he murmured.

Finally he said that me leaving the *Telegraph* troubled him deeply. He thought my future was made less secure while the damage to the *Telegraph* was severe. 'A long-established cartoonist is almost like the paper's masthead. You going to the *Independent*, along with one or two other good *Telegraph* men, means that the *Independent* can say, "Look, here is the new *Telegraph*, complete with all the best features of the old, but improved and redesigned and terrific." '

There is a confusion in this formulation, one that I constantly find. If the *Independent* were a real threat to the *Telegraph* then it would survive, and if it survived how was my future insecure?

We joked about the old *Telegraph* and about the extraordinary character of Bill Deedes. He told me that Bill once informed Jock about the appointment of some chap to the staff and went on about what a fine and useful man he was. Jock had commented, 'Mind you, if it was announced that a certain Mr A. Hitler had joined us Bill would go around saying, "First-class fellow, absolutely brilliant, solid gold . . ." '

Perhaps aware that he was not at any point pressing me to stay, as opposed to merely pointing out dangers, John said, 'Don't go around telling people I urged you to join the *Independent*!'

I promised I wouldn't.

His final word to me was on the subject of money. 'If they make you an offer you can't refuse, don't refuse it!'

At work I talked to Don for a short while. He was, as I expected, both understanding and sympathetic. His main message was that he was terribly disappointed to hear I was going. 'What I want to say to you is, don't be afraid to change your mind.'

He said that Max had told only him, Nigel and Andrew Hutchinson. Later, back in my room, to my surprise John O'Sullivan rang.

'I hear you are going to the *Independent*.'

'Yes. How did you hear that?'

'As a matter of fact, my editor told me. He berated me for my poor intelligence work.' John wanted to head me off and get me to *The Times*. I declined an invitation to drink champagne at his club.

'I've got too many people to see here. My announcement has put the cat among the pigeons.'

179

'I bet it has,' said John.

When I saw Max he said, 'Take a pew!' I think that is one of the silliest expressions in the English language. Our conversation was a rerun of our earlier exchange.

He threw in more pressure of the stay-longer kind. He told me he'd stayed an extra five months after giving his notice to the *Standard*. He even used Bill as an example of stalwart loyalty and devotion to duty.

'He has decided to do everything he can to help us through.' This did not impress me. Bill can't bear doing nothing, and I'm sure he thoroughly enjoys his extraordinary position at the *Telegraph*.

Max looked at me through his large spectacles, a lock of hair falling over his forehead. He unwrapped a cigar. He appeared agitated and unhappy, and I think was really trying to control quite strong feelings. He kept saying, 'Of course, it's your life, and you are free to do what you like', or 'It's up to you, I know that'. Charles always says of Max that he is nicest when he's being most natural, which, paradoxically, is when he is being rather abrasive, even disagreeable. The point being that Max is an eccentric and people who understand that are prepared to put up with it and recognise that he is also warm hearted and not vindictive. But when Max tries to be considerate and restrained he suddenly seems false, and when he's striving to be nice he's at his least attractive.

Before I left his office he made a statement about how bleak the prospects at the *Telegraph* were. He also said he believed the paper would survive, otherwise he'd quit, but the next few months were critical. Union problems loomed over the switch to new printing machines and technological problems did too. He expected terrible hiccups before it all began to run smoothly. The editorial changes were not complete, and the shape and direction of the paper still needed a lot of work. Circulation continued to fall.

'I give us till Christmas,' he said. It was not clear quite what he meant.

'Do you mean if the fortunes of the paper have not turned round by Christmas, Black will sell it, or what?'

'Well, if it's not on track by then something pretty drastic will have to happen.'

We ended with him urging me to put off my departure at least until New Year; but the dreams of great wealth were not referred to again.

Heigh-ho, as John O'Sullivan says.

Wednesday 18 June
No more pressure from anyone today. Max said when I handed him my cartoon, 'I wish you'd do some lousy cartoons.'

Charles rang this evening. We had a long chat. The one thing that stood out was that he said that last night at a dinner Andrew Knight criticised Max's editing for the first time. He was speaking only to Charles at the time but he said that Monday's leader on South Africa was pathetic, just not good enough. Charles took this as an ominous sign because Andrew always speaks well of people and usually goes in for exaggerated flattery.

Thursday 19 June
John O'Sullivan telephoned this morning to make one last-ditch attempt to get me to *The Times*.

I said, 'No.'

He said, 'Heigh-ho!'

Lunch with Matthew and Stephen. I didn't see Andreas but left him a postcard of a Corot showing the typical splash of red that the artist always included in some detail to lift the surrounding green.

Stephen, anxious as usual, asked why I wanted to see Andreas. 'Is it to discuss some problem that has come up?'

'No. I just want to leave him this card. There are no problems.'

'Just as well,' said Matthew with jesting menace. 'Or you would have a very unpleasant lunch.'

I felt the usual burst of irritation with him.

Much of our talk at lunch was about the *Telegraph* and its new look and political direction. Stephen wanted to know ('if you feel you can say . . .') how Max took the news of my departure. I told them as accurately as I could everything that had happened.

It is difficult not to dramatise and improve the story, or make it comical; in fact it's impossible. Several times I felt compelled to say, 'I'm making this sound funnier than it was; actually it was rather painful.'

When I asked them who told the *The Times* I was leaving the *Telegraph*, Stephen and Matthew replied in unison, 'Ed Steen probably.'

When I arrived at the *Independent* office before lunch Steen had come over, shaken hands and said, 'Welcome aboard.' He didn't mean to, but he sounded almost as I had joined him rather than the newspaper. He too asked me how Max had responded and when I said he had been dismayed Ed said angrily, 'Well, I'm not sorry for him.

Stephen said the *Observer* was doing a big piece about them this weekend and a photographer was coming round later that day. I said, 'It'll be Jane Bown. You lucky devils: it's one of my few ambitions to be photographed by her.' I have this ambition partly because she is a genius, and partly because her work is a record of our times and it would be nice to be part of that record.

As I arrived home this evening Caroline told me Alexander Chancellor was on the phone. Stephen had told me that he and Alexander had

181

joked the night before about the irony of Alexander being asked to try to get me to stay while negotiating with the *Independent* himself. I wanted to ask Alexander about his plans but Stephen made me promise I wouldn't let on I knew anything about them.

Alexander was ringing to suggest I stayed on the *Sunday Telegraph* when I went to the *Independent*. He suggested even more money and said the two papers were not in competition. The money was attractive but the idea a non-starter, I thought. We agreed to discuss it later after I'd spoken to Andreas.

The whole idea came to nothing.

Friday 20 June
I had a letter from Bill today thanking me for a drawing I'd sent him when his peerage was announced. It ended by saying, 'I was greatly saddened to hear of your decision, but I quite understand it. Yrs ever, Bill.'

Michael Hogg put his head round his office door as I walked by.

'I hear you are leaving us,' he said, leaning exhausted against the wall. 'You lucky devil.'

Morrison came in to chat. I thought he'd want to ask me why I wanted to leave, but instead he already had theories about that. He began by saying: 'Max hasn't talked to me about your decision but Andrew Hutchinson has. He said, "Why does he want to leave? We've given him more money, he's got the most prominent slot in the paper, his cartoons are printed larger than they ever have been before, what does he want?" I told him that you were worried about falling intellectual standards at the *Telegraph*.'

This information gave me quite a turn. I've never said a word about intellectual standards, and I don't think it's a phrase or formulation I would ever use. I do believe that some editorial changes have been mistaken, but that's not the same thing at all.

I told Morrison that he was misrepresenting me and tried to draw a distinction between my actual criticism of the paper and his version of my attitude. Even as I spoke I realised I was not getting across. Everything I said he simply pigeon-holed under 'Intellectual standards (falling)'.

Morrison is like a man sitting on a liferaft after a shipwreck. He is glad to be on it and does not feel like trying to swim to any nearby island. But he feels extremely fed up that the shipwreck occurred in the first place, and wonders about the seamanship of his fellow survivors. He also worries about their cannibalistic tendencies, should they fail to reach land fairly soon.

Sunday 22 June
The *Observer* piece by Michael Davie was very sympathetic and made me look forward eagerly to the *Independent*. He said I had been 'poached' from the *Telegraph*. The phrase made me sound too passive; like an egg. Caroline said it was a good word. 'They knew they wanted you from the beginning. They hunted you down and got you.'

Monday 23 June
Clive Barrow stopped me in the corridor at work and said he was sorry I was going and went on to say the *Independent* was doomed unless they realised one crucial mistake they had made in their plans: they wrongly believed that you could put a paper together with sub-editors.

'They think you wallop it all on to a computer screen, hit the right button and some extraterrestrial power produces the perfect headlines and cuts the whole thing to size. It won't. They will have to employ subs.'

'If that is obvious to you, why isn't it obvious to them?'

'It is, to some of them. That's why they asked me along to take a look. It's Andreas who will not see the problem.'

'They will presumably find that out during the month that they are producing dummies.'

'Yes, they will, but then they will have to rush to get subs. They haven't made the error Shah made in recruiting journalists from provincial papers who are not absolutely first class. They've got very good writers indeed, but they will have to look for subs from provincial papers in order to get them in time, and they will not be good enough.'

Clive spoke as usual with calm confidence.

Sue Davy came to see me and I urged her to ring Stephen and press him to give her a job. She is obviously very anxious to leave the *Telegraph*, but afraid of being a nuisance to the *Independent* editors if she keeps bothering them.

'You haven't kept bothering them. I've bothered them a little on your behalf.'

Our roles have altered completely. As Bill's beloved secretary she was powerful and could, and often did, help me. Now she has no power base and I can help her; or want to.

I tried to warn her that her age was counting against her because they all, particularly Matthew, were anxious about whether she could stand the pace that would be set in the early days. As tactfully as I could I said I'd heard them discussing someone else in these terms. I could see Sue getting the message and tactfully not laughing at my transparent ploy.

I said, 'Ring Stephen, tell him you want to be offered a job. You feel your years and experience would be extremely useful to them. If the work is going to be difficult and taxing ask to be told that, and say you will decide whether or not you feel you can do it or want to do it.' I tried to give her confidence by truthfully reporting that Stephen particularly had a high regard for her abilities, and that they all reckoned her a valuable colleague. I felt foolish talking to her like this. She knows far more about newspapers and how they are run than I'll ever begin to know.

We talked also about Max and Bill and she readily conceded that her relationship with Max could never have survived her regrets about Bill leaving. She is very wise and although she criticised Max she did it more in gentle mockery than with bitterness. She simply mourns the passing of the old days.

She bustled out of my room, gathering up her bags and papers and, half joking, said she was going to telephone Stephen at once while my words were still in her head. She left muttering, '. . . valuable colleague . . ., years of experience . . . can decide for myself . . .', pretending to be a child rehearsing its lessons before an exam.

Andreas asked me to lunch on 4 July.

John O'Sullivan rang to say he wanted to add to *The Times*' offer that they'd give a three-year contract with a three-month get out for me. He added that if I went to the *Independent* then '*The Times*'d have to do something' – meaning hire another cartoonist whose presence would destroy all overtures to me.

Tuesday 24 June

Max called me into his office this afternoon. He closed the door leading to Josie's ante-room and said he just wanted to say one 'pre-emptive' thing. It turned out to be a request. 'Should the *Independent* fail and you find yourself looking for another place, I suppose you might think that the last place you'd want to go to is the *Telegraph*. Going backwards, as it were, to somewhere you thought you'd said goodbye to. But I hope some vestigial loyalty to the *Telegraph* would mean you would come and see us first. What I want to ask is that you undertake not to go anywhere else without letting us make you an offer first. It would be more than flesh and blood could stand to wake up one morning and find you'd gone to *The Times*.'

I gave this undertaking very readily. After all, it bound me only to listen to their terms. In fact, I found it rather comforting to know they'd have me back. He said that Charlie Wilson had said to him that my going to the *Independent* is a considerable threat to *The Times* but that's another matter. I wonder why he said that to Max. Or if he did. It sounds so barmy.

Max read me the findings of a survey showing where *Telegraph* readers were going. Most to *The Times* and the *Mail*.

I called on Peter Utley whom I saw sitting alone in his office. He invited me to have lunch with him next week. He made no secret of the fact that he is thoroughly fed up with the *Telegraph* and cannot wait to go. But he was in the middle of composing a leader and when Sarah, his secretary, came back I left. I came away with the clear impression that he was going to *The Times*.

I asked Bernard about Clive Barrow's doubts over the *Independent*'s plans to do without subs. Bernard thought I must have heard wrong. You couldn't, in his opinion, plan a paper without subs. He was very complimentary about Clive. 'Best night editor we ever had.' Bernard said Clive had one fault: he didn't give a sod for his bosses. 'He used to say, "When I'm night editor *I* decide what goes in the paper." It didn't matter who had said anything else. If Eastwood said, "Put this in", he'd just spike it if he didn't like it. That's why they had to get rid of him.'

Wednesday 25 June

Sarah, Peter's secretary, and I met in Fleet Street as I walked out to buy some coffee. I said, 'Peter seems extremely fed up with the *Telegraph*.' She went off into a strongly worded attack on everything that has happened since Max took over. She is still hopping mad about the treatment Sue Davy received. She was scorching in her criticism of Bill. 'He's come out in his true colours. He's writing nonsense. Max says write this and Bill trots off and writes it.'

She confirmed that Peter was definitely leaving but to my great surprise said that he couldn't finally make up his mind between *The Times* and the *Independent*. She said, 'If he goes to *The Times* I'll try to get a job on the *Independent*. She related horror stories about the violence at Wapping and said two journalists had been attacked miles from work. One had been in the tube and got punched by a 'printer' who said, 'We know you. We never forget a face.'

According to Sarah, Max is 'terrified' of losing Peter and keeps sending him memos congratulating him on leaders. 'But Max doesn't realise. The real reason Peter can't get on with him is because Max is not a gentleman.'

She was so serious, even passionate, that I didn't laugh. Instead I asked what being a gentleman meant in this context.

'Max just had no idea what's done and what's not done. No idea at all. He doesn't know how to behave.' This was said with such finality and firmness that I could not pursue this interesting view of Max any further.

When I took my cartoon in to Max. Josie told me he'd already gone home. She asked to look at the cartoon and smiled.

'Brilliant,' she said kindly.

'Thank you.'

'Do you ever sell your cartoons?'

'Yes.'

'How much for?'

'Depends on the cartoon, and who's buying. Why?'

'How much is this one?'

'Do you want it?'

'Yes.'

'Why? I mean, why *this* one?'

'I like it. I like it's simplicity.'

'It costs a bottle of whisky.'

'OK. Done. What sort of whisky?'

'Bourbon.'

'I'll hold you to it.'

I took the cartoon along to Don Berry because Andrew Hutchinson was also out. Mike Green told me Don too had gone home.

'He's ill.'

'What's wrong with him?'

'Exhaustion, I think. He's here twelve hours a day, working flat out. I keep telling him to take a break. Now he has.'

'I've thought Don seemed a bit flat lately. Is it exhaustion or disappointment about the way things are going?'

I saw Penny Jackson from features who, I heard from Stephen, is going to the *Independent*. She told me she'd been on the *Telegraph* for seven years and was anxious to leave.

'It's rotten here. No one knows what's going on. Everything happens late and in a rush. You don't know who you are working for, there are dozens of people who seem to be in charge. It's hopeless.'

Thursday 26 June

Matthew rang this evening and, speaking in a low steady voice, the one he uses when he can scarcely control his elation, said, 'I thought you'd like to know Alexander Chancellor has joined us.'

I was glad; but I felt a pang for the old *Telegraph* too. If Ferdie Mount were now to stop writing his political column I think the paper would roll over, put its face to the wall and die.

For some reason or other, Alexander is the *Independent* recruit who gives me most confidence. It's not just that he is such an outstanding journalist. His confidence in the paper increases mine to a dispro-portionate degree.

Friday 27 June

Charles telephoned me this afternoon to tell me what illustration he wanted for next week's *Spectator*. But first he said, 'There's a strong rumour going round that there has been another big defector to the *Independent*. Do you know who it is?'

'Yes, I do.'

'Who?'

'You've got three guesses, but I'll give you a clue; he came from the *Telegraph* stable.'

'Colin Welch.'

'No. Anyway, I mean from the present stable. He's come from the *Daily*, the *Sunday* or the *Magazine*.'

'Lord Hartwell!' After a few jokes about other unlikely recruits he said 'Alexander.'

'Yes.'

'So he finally went.'

'It will be a heavy blow to the *Telegraph*. But I had heard that he wasn't happy.'

'He never is.'

'Really?'

'I'm not surprised, though. He was telling me the other night that he was pretty fed up.'

'Did he say why?'

'Yes, but I couldn't really understand what about.'

'Who did you hear the rumour from?'

'I met Andreas and he said they'd landed a big one but he couldn't say who. So I rang Stephen and he wouldn't say either. So then I rang the biggest tittle-tattle I know.'

'Don't say that, I am completely discreet. And you have promised not to tell.' (I had sworn him to secrecy before I told him.)

'Don't worry, I won't.'

'The reason is that Perry wants to have chosen his successor before it goes public.'

After work I went to El Vino for a farewell drink with Ian Waller who has just quit as the *Sunday Telegraph*'s political editor. I spent most of the time talking to Martin Ivens. He is going to Washington for the *Telegraph* for three months and then he's having a spell in New York. After that he's not sure. Both *The Times* and the *Independent* may have something for him but there is nothing on offer at the moment. If it came to a straight choice he'd go to the *Independent*. I imagine he'll do well in the States and finish up working there for much longer than three months.

He told me a good bit of silly gossip. In this week's *Private Eye* there is a story about a group of women all of whom are said to have been to bed with Max Hastings, and who meet him for lunch and discuss his rating as a lover. This garbage so agitated Andrew Knight that he sent for Max and gave him a lecture about this sort of publicity being bad

187

for the *Telegraph*. I laughed and said, 'That can't be true.' But Martin insisted that it was. He said Andrew has a thing about *Private Eye* and takes it seriously.

'Nobody takes *Private Eye* seriously.'

'Knight does.'

Charles, who was also at Ian's farewell, confirmed that Andrew minds very much what *Private Eye* says. Charles even reported that Knight keeps a file of *Private Eye* stories.

If the account of Max being ticked off is true I hope he told Andrew to get stuffed. It's bad enough to be sniggered at by *Private Eye* without having your colleagues taking it all seriously.

Over the last few days many of my colleagues at the *Telegraph* have come up to me in the corridors to say how sorry they are that I am leaving. They say the same thing; that it is a pity and a loss to the paper. All of them have been extremely sympathetic when I have explained, as well as I could, why I want to go.

Bernard Foyster was the first to speak to me. 'What's this I hear? I told them it couldn't possibly be true. You're not leaving, are you?'

Only Desmond Albrow, from *Sunday Telegraph* features, struck a slightly different note. I passed him coming through the doors onto the third floor corridor. 'You sod!' he said.

'You sod?' I replied slightly nettled. 'Most people say they are sorry.'

'Yes; you sod. I *am* sorry you are leaving. I wish you weren't. It's a great loss. You sod.'

There was a kind of heavy rueful humour behind his words but a touch of genuine anger as well.

Godfrey said my departure finally broke what remained of the old guard.

Each time I see Clive Barrow he grins and says, 'Changed your mind yet?' to which I reply, 'Are you still here?'

A great many of these exchanges are with people I've seen around for fifteen years or so, and have never spoken to before except to say 'Good morning' in the lift. Their kind words mean a lot to me and come as quite a surprise.

When I've finished a cartoon and handed it in I don't think about it any more. Often if someone says, 'Nice cartoon today', I have to rack my brains to recall it. In this way my work unravels behind me all the time. So it comes as a pleasant surprise to know that in the minds of my colleagues the cumulative effect of my cartoons is stored up, and even to an extent valued.

Monday 30 June

I've had the first volume of this journal typed out by Margaret, an ex-secretary of Caroline's. Today I went to pick it up, and she said that she felt I had been very hard on some of my fellow journalists. 'You say some rather awful things about them. It's not very nice. I mean, it's not just that you express yourself very frankly about them but you also write down the things they say about each other. They've spoken to you in confidence, haven't they?'

I said I knew what she was saying was true, but that I'd written down a spontaneous version of events in order to try to record the passing days in as uncontrived a way as possible. I also knew that later I would have the chance to take out anything too wounding or treacherous.

I had lunch with Peter Utley and Sarah Compton Burnett today. Throughout our conversation two things were very clear. One was that Peter has entirely lost any loyalty to, or respect and affection for, the *Telegraph* as it now is, and second is that he is leaving for *The Times* as soon as he has worked out his contract. He expressed no violent feelings against anyone and no bitterness at all, just a kind of regretful contempt.

He asked advice about one or two issues; first at what point should he announce his departure, and what sort of response might he expect from Max? He also wanted to know what I thought of Charles Wilson.

His attitude to the *Independent* was friendly but he didn't think they had anything to offer him at the moment. Being obituaries editor, which is what he will be at *The Times*, has not the same kudos on the *Independent* or the *Telegraph*. Most important, *The Times* have offered him a column as well, where he can write about his beloved Northern Ireland.

He said that when he first heard about the *Independent* he thought it was a manoeuvre intended to get Andreas the editorship of the *Telegraph*. It took him some time to realise it was what it purported to be.

After describing his discussions with Stephen and Andreas about joining the *Independent* he said, 'What I try to do, what I have decided to do, is to tell the truth. You ask me about the *Independent* or Max or anything, and what I tell you is the truth. It makes you feel good, telling the truth.'

'It's quite hard to know what it is,' I said.

'Yes, quite hard.'

'Oscar Wilde once said, "Being natural is a pose, and the most irritating pose I know of." Perhaps telling the truth is a pose as well.'

Peter laughed and said he thought it was, in a way.

We gossiped about colleagues. About Morrison he said, 'He nearly didn't survive. In fact, what saved him was a phone call Max received from Jock. Jock had heard that as soon as Max arrived Morrison had been told, very insensitively, that he was no longer features editor. Jock rang Max to say he thought it was deplorable to treat a man so brusquely. Max misunderstood and thought he was being criticised for demoting the guy at all and promptly reinstated him as editor of the leader page.' We talked about Bill and his responsibility for the collapse of the old *Telegraph*. Peter likes Bill but thinks him hopeless for all the usual reasons.

Peter has no confidence in the future of the *Telegraph*. 'It's very difficult to see what will happen to it or where it will end.'

I asked whether he thought Max would last much longer and he said he didn't know. He felt that Andrew Knight was probably more responsible for many of the staff changes and new looks than Max was. He sees Andrew as the only real power about the place and Max as a front man who has got a bit out of control over certain issues (notably the Libya bombing and South Africa). This would tie in with Caroline's theory that poor Max has been employed in the role of scapegoat, to be blamed should the paper fail.

Peter drank quite a bit at lunch, two large whiskies and most of a bottle of wine, and he became very merry and relaxed. At about three o'clock the car we'd ordered arrived. 'Let's keep it waiting a bit,' he cried and ordered more wine and coffee. When at last we got outside into the blazing sunshine – we've been having a wonderful heatwave – he complained cheerfully about the weather, saying he couldn't bear it.

Driving back to Fleet Street he ordered Sarah to organise a farewell party for me. 'Would you rather a large crowd downstairs at the Cheshire Cheese, or a smaller lunch at the Café Royal?'

'The Café Royal.'

He began making a guest list. I could only think of Bernard Foyster and John Burgess, and asked if I could have time to think about it and come back to this ticklish problem.

'Of course, dear boy, dear boy.'

Peter is a great man. It is his departure from the *Telegraph* that will be the actual end of the old days, not Bill's going or mine or anyone else's.

At about four o'clock, the time when I begin to panic slightly if I haven't got an idea for a cartoon, Morrison came in, saying he'd like to talk. He said later would do, but there was something in his manner that made me ask him to sit down and tell me what was on his mind.

He'd received a letter from Max. The gist of it seemed pretty clear. As he put it, 'They're trying to get rid of me.' The letter apparently said something like, 'If you are not happy perhaps you'd like to think about moving on . . .'

Morrison's attitude was what I've come to expect. There was no fight in him at all. Not even any anger, just helpless acceptance and deep distress that he tried to hide.

He said he was back to square one.

I've always been surprised that he survived the earliest purges and everyone has known that the arrangement with him and Don overlapping, with no clear boundaries between their respective territories, is unworkable. Part of me thinks Morrison should go; but however I judge him I think he is being treated in a disgraceful way and my first impulse was to express for him the anger he would not let himself feel.

I told him that if I were him I'd be livid to get a letter like that. 'You came to an agreement with them and you kept your side of the bargain. What are they playing at?'

In my mind I could hear Max saying the same sort of words to me. '. . . I thought when you accepted our new terms you had agreed to stay on.' I knew it was bullshit at the time. It's just another example of how not to be editor of a paper. He can't treat Morrison like a football and expect the rest of the staff to remain confident and loyal. Every single journalist on the paper will think, 'There but for the grace of God . . .' and begin to plan where to jump if it becomes necessary, or even possible.

My disapproval of Max seemed to give Morrison some heart but he continued to say hopeless things such as, 'Of course he's right, I've not been happy and they know it', or 'But I know as well that the present arrangement is no good'. I found I was getting as irritated with him as Max obviously does. Morrison is not stupid and he often says very sensible and constructive things, but he is never light-hearted. He is dour and lugubrious. He always produces in me the desire to speak irresponsibly and to behave like a fool. He makes me behave in a way that leaves me feeling uncomfortable, as if I've been lying.

He said he'd looked everywhere for another job and there was just nothing around and he asked whether I'd speak to Tony Howard to see whether there was anything at the *Observer*. A hopeless quest, that one, but I agreed to do it.

I suddenly thought of the *Sunday Telegraph* and decided to give him something. I said, 'I'm going to tell you a secret because it may help you, so long as you realise it must be kept a secret.'

He said, 'I've told you one or two.'

I couldn't remember any but I went on, 'Alexander is leaving the *Sunday Telegraph*. Therefore it would be a good time to apply to Perry. Alexander's departure is bound to shake things up there like anything.'

For a moment genuine interest and a certain alertness illuminated Morrison's face and he thanked me for the information. He was, also, obviously pretty surprised to hear the news, but he didn't say anything about it being another blow to the old *Telegraph*. Perhaps he is beyond caring too much about that.

He left after a bit, thanking me for being so kind. What a complicated fellow he is. I hadn't felt kind. I'd felt angry with Max, exasperated

191

with Morrison, sorry for both of them in a way and generally fed up with the whole mishandled miserable business.

JULY

"...I WISH YOU WOULDN'T KEEP APPEARING AND VANISHING SO SUDDENLY: YOU MAKE ONE QUITE GIDDY!"

3 July, *Daily Telegraph*

Tuesday 1 July

Max has gone on holiday for a week. When I'd finished my cartoon this evening I couldn't find anyone to show it to. Don is still away sick. Andrew Hutchinson was nowhere to be found.

I sat for a while in Max's office with Josie and Claudie Worsthorne who were watching Lendl play at Wimbledon.

Josie said Sarah Jewell has accepted a job at the *Independent*. I asked whether she knew of any other defections and she said she'd heard that Sue Davy was probably going. I was trying to find out whether she knew about Alexander.

She said that if she were Sue she'd leave. I asked what she meant and Josie said that her own arrival on the paper had been made terribly difficult by the dreadful way Sue had been treated.

'No one blamed you for that,' I said, remembering guiltily how irritated I'd been by the poor girl at first.

'Well, I had a rotten time,' she said. It had taken her a little while to find out what had gone on, and she still seemed bothered by it.

We talked about the attempts the *Telegraph* is making to appeal to younger readers. Josie, a perfect example of the sort of young person being courted, said nothing on earth would make her buy the *Telegraph*. It was boring, fuddy-duddy, dull, 'and I absolutely cannot stand Page 3!'

'What's wrong with Page 3?' asked Claudie.

'It's full of death, awful stories about people falling off mountains and things.'

Claudie laughed. 'The *Telegraph* has always loved stories like that. I used to cut them from the paper and send them to Colin Welch. You know, stories like "Cockerel slays farmer's wife by pecking varicose vein".' Claudie snorted with amusement and lit a cigarette, which surprised me because everyone has been worried and disturbed recently by the news that she has cancer. 'All they're doing,' she waved her hand to indicate Max's office, 'is losing the old readers.'

'They'll never get the young ones,' said Josie. 'I've tried to tell him so over and over, but he won't listen.'

Anne came in. She used to be John Thompson's secretary and is now Alexander's. She had copies of a memo from Perry announcing Alexander's departure.

Josie was clearly shocked. 'Max will go crazy,' she said.

Anne said, 'It's happened to me again. First I lost one boss, now I've lost another.'

I asked whether Alexander's replacement would take her on. She said, 'No, he's got a terrific secretary already.'

Thursday 3 July

Alexander Chancellor called on me at the office to offer 'fraternal greetings'.

We laughed at the absurd situation of his being asked by Max to do what he could to make me stay when he had already more or less agreed to go to the *Independent* himself. I told him that when he had rung me I already knew his position because Stephen has told me.

'It was awful,' he said. 'I felt more and more like an East German spy.'

He then asked me whether I'd seen the dummy that the *Independent* has produced. When I said I hadn't he described it to me.

He made three basic criticisms. The first was it is wrong to use colour on the front page. No matter how good the photo or the reproduction, it gives the paper the look of a cheap handout or advertising brochure. Second, the masthead is in the wrong typeface. It is too big and too black, giving an unattractive insistent quality to the look of the paper. Third, the news pages are laid out in such a way that they look like boxed-in bits of information from specialist pages in the *Financial Times*. He added a number of small criticisms, for instance the rules round the 'news in brief' spots have rounded instead of right-angled corners and the arts page is a mess.

He took these matters very seriously and said he'd been worried by Andreas saying, 'I think we've got it 70 per cent right.'

'Actually, it's more like 70 per cent wrong.'

'Did you tell him?' I asked.

'Well, no. I mean, I didn't want to hurt his feelings, sort of come in saying, "Christ, how awful." I mean, people have been sweating blood.'

'You should have told him.'

I said I was having lunch with Andreas the next day and I would tell him but he, Alexander, must as well. I thought everything Alexander said sounded convincing, and I was touched to hear the genuine concern and seriousness in his voice.

'It's very important that they get it right,' he said.

When he talked a little about why he was leaving to go to Washington for the *Independent* he said, among other things, that he was fed up with other people's problems. 'For years on the *Spectator* and now on the *Sunday* I seem to have spent my time listening to people complaining about everything under the sun. It's a very boring part of being an editor. It will be lovely to be miles away from head office.'

It is Alexander's way to speak in a self-deprecating roundabout manner and by trying to write a brief account of his views I misrepresent him. He puts across his point of view with charming casualness. It barely sounds like criticism when he says it, although when put down in a shortened version without the grins and spluttering laughter, and without the cigarette smoke and prowling to and fro, it is in fact quite tough.

Friday 4 July

While I waited for Andreas at the *Independent* I met Tom Sutcliffe. He said he was enjoying himself and found life on the paper very exciting. We were joined by Michael Sheridan, who has just come to be Rome correspondent. We went to Tom's office to look at the dummy. Several people have copies and they are kept carefully locked up away from other newspaper men.

Michael kept up a continual stream of clear and sensible criticisms. 'There are not enough stories on the front page – looks dull – empty . . . that's too big—why put a box there? . . . colour looks wrong . . .' and so on.

I too was disappointed by the dummy but saved up my comments for Andreas, except for trying out my intense dislike of a colour picture on the front page. Tom didn't agree with me. 'But it's a wonderful picture,' he said. It's quite a good picture. It shows some black children in a South African township sitting on a wall and looking at smoke rising from nearby burning houses.

'The excellence is neither here nor there, it's the colour that's wrong,' I said.

He shrugged. I couldn't tell what Michael thought.

A woman sitting on the other side of the desk we were standing at ended a phone call and smiled at me and said, 'Hello.' I saw it was Miriam Gross. 'Oh, hello,' I said and we shook hands. 'I'm sorry, I didn't recognise you.' She is Tom's associate arts editor. Stephen told me later she had insisted on the title 'associate' instead of the original 'assistant'. He also said he was a little worried about the difference in ages. Tom looks about twelve years old. She's been around the literary and arty world quite a bit longer. Stephen is aware that this difference in age and experience could produce difficulties. But today she looked happy and relaxed.

I went downstairs to find Andreas and he immediately took me off to look through a dummy. He said he felt it was 70 per cent there and did I agree? My answer was long and complicated but basically I said no.

My main criticism was that it looked so designed. I felt that somewhere there was the impulse to produce something different from the other three quality papers, but I felt Andreas should try to do the exact opposite. In other words, it should look as much as possible like what is best about the *Guardian, The Times* and the *Telegraph*.

'You've tried to take all their best people; go the whole hog, copy their best design ideas too.'

I said there was time enough to go in for idiosyncratic design ideas once they had established themselves as a serious classical newspaper. What will reassure potential readers more than anything else is old-fashioned traditional columns of print with headlines and black and white photographs.

'The more you look like *Today*, the less you will worry *The Times* and the *Telegraph*.'

I said that the reason news is laid out one way and features and comment another is because that's the best way that has been devised. It's the same reason that cars all look more or less the same these days. The same safe, roomy, most streamlined and economic design is arrived at by all the best designers. It is the solution. Clever-dick variations look like just that and they don't fool anyone.

'Furthermore,' I argued, 'even if you wanted the *Independent* to look exactly like, say, the *Guardian* you couldn't do it. You could not completely disguise your designer's style any more than you could completely change your handwriting. You will achieve an *Independent* style without falling over backwards to invent one.'

We were still talking about this by the time we were at a table in the restaurant. We had walked through lovely Bunhill Fields and we began lunch with a glass of champagne each.

Andreas was worried by the problem of designing a paper. He said, 'If you play me a piece of music I'll tell you after half a dozen bars roughly when it was written. Show me a room in an art gallery and I'll name most of the artists without looking at the labels, but I have a sort of blind spot about typography and newspapers. I don't feel confident about what's good and what's bad about newspaper design.'

He said that on Monday there was going to be a meeting of all the heads of departments about the dummy. They would all have consulted their staffs by then and he asked me if I'd like to come. I said yes and told him to ask Alexander as well.

'Your ace in the hole is your writing team. People move from one paper to another for all sorts of reasons but not because they long for a bit of flashy design.'

Andreas asked me about the *Telegraph*, as he usually does, and listened to my gloomy report without pleasure.

The idea that newspaper people behave to each other like back-biting show-biz hysterics is generally untrue. Once upon a time keen young news-hounds used to race for stories and devise cunning ways of scooping their rivals, but telephones and jet planes and TV and now computers have largely finished that 1920s derring-do. The only people I can actually recall expressing hopes that the *Independent* fails are John Miller, Peter Birkett and possibly Nigel Wade, but him only by report.

Andreas must be content to hear that things are not going well at the

Telegraph, but I don't think it gives him any pleasure. Apart from anything else, his whole concentration is on getting the *Independent* right, not crowing over his rival's difficulties. If the *Telegraph* is in trouble it simply means that's one front that can be left for the time being.

This is not to say newspapers don't watch each other with some alarm; and sometimes, for instance the *Mirror* and the *Sun*, they actually declare war on each other. But individual journalists are not in my experience nasty about each other, or driven by a desire to see each other fail. Such criticism that they make tends to be comical and sarcastic and can usually be laughed off. When James Fenton was theatre critic on the *Sunday Times* and wrote lively criticism of some of his fellow critics many journalists were quite thrown. That sort of thing just didn't, shouldn't, happen. It would be a good thing for journalists to be more roughly criticised. Poets and novelists, actors, directors, politicians and trade union leaders are criticised the whole time – often by journalists.

When my work has been criticised, however painful it is to have my limitations described, I think on balance the effect is good. It always makes me think I'll show the bastard,'and the only way to do that is by getting better.

The plan for a meeting of all the heads of departments bothered me a little. Too many people discussing a question of design is notoriously unproductive. An editor, an assistant editor and a designer/typographer is about all you need. But I couldn't say that to Andreas. He feels uncertain enough as it is.

As usual I enjoyed lunching with him and indeed visiting the *Independent*. The offices are beginning to look lived in. There are small accumulations of rubbish, Perrier bottles, cigarette packets, empty plastic cups and scattered piles of newspapers. Today scores of red filing cabinets were being delivered. Rows and rows of them like tin guardsmen stretched from the road, across the pavement, up the steps and into the foyer.

Stephen said, 'Matthew went mad and ordered two million filing cabinets. No one knows what to do with them.'

When I took my cartoon to Perry later, he smiled and said, 'So you persuaded Alexander to go with you.'

I put my hand on my heart and protested, 'I never ever said a word to him about it,' but Perry just smiled as if forgiving me for lying.

Saturday 5 July
This morning Theo, Alexander, Caroline and I went down to the *Telegraph* and began to clear out my stuff. At 10.00 Stephen came to help us.

Most of my cartoons were already packed into some thirty brown paper parcels and I wrapped up the last few packets while the rest were taken out to the cars. Some of the drawings done fifteen years ago or more were already yellowing with age. The politicians in them seemed to come from ancient history: Couve de Murville, Duncan Sandys, Bottomley, Cousins, Vic Feather, Dean Rusk. . . . There were cartoons of LBJ tangled up in the Vietnam war and the ridiculous figure of Jeremy Thorpe. I had thought it might be an emotional experience to turn out so much old rubbish but in fact it was just a rather boring job that seemed endless.

There were literally hundreds of little drawings on scraps of paper that I don't really know what to do with. Some are caricatures of colleagues, some are sketches of politicians done at party conferences, some scribbled notes and roughs for cartoons. It seems a pity in a way to chuck them out but where the hell am I to keep them?

By the time the cartoons were all packed up and put into the cars Stephen had to go, so we drove over to City Road. It was fun showing Caroline and the boys the office and my lovely room, which they admired very much.

The ragged heap of cartoons stacked against the wall and my battered cuttings books from 1966 to 1986 didn't look much to show for twenty years' work.

They were all impressed by the newsroom. The VDUs on the desks and their new keyboards blew Alexanders's mind. 'Cor!' he said, and asked Stephen how much each one cost.

'About £3000 I think,' said Steve. 'Vastly over-priced.'

Standing three-deep down the length of the room were the hundreds of red filing cabinets. 'Perhaps we can sell a few,' said Stephen.

Monday 7 July
I broke a rule yesterday – keep Saturday and Sunday for rest – and did my *Spectator* drawing in order to be free this morning to go to the discussion at the *Independent*.

I got there on time and sat next to Stephen. The meeting was in a glassed-in area at the end of the newsroom. Andreas sat at a central table alongside his secretary. Sarah Hogg was the only other woman, and a dozen or so men were seated in a semicircle round Andreas's table. A number of dummies lay scattered about. I was introduced to several people, but couldn't catch any names and never quite knew who they all were or what their jobs were.

The meeting began promptly, with Andreas spreading out his copy of the paper and inviting comments on the front page. I was disappointed that Alexander was not there, but Stephen had a neatly typed list of reactions from his foreign department staff. The conversation was brisk but my heart sank as I realised everyone was suggesting changes and adjustments to the existing dummy, not a radical new design.

I waited until I heard someone say, '. . . but if we are going for something different from all our rivals then that is what we must do.' The talk continued until Andreas said, 'Nick?' I said, 'I want to refer back to something that gentleman said, when he referred to the need to look different from our rivals. I believe that is a mistake. It leads to all kinds of design decisions being taken for the wrong reasons, which are consequently the wrong decisions. What we should be designing is a perfectly straightforward classical newspaper. If it comes out looking in part like *The Times* or the *Guardian*, far from that being something to be avoided it should be sought. Both of them are good-looking newspapers and all three of our main rivals have something in common. Their evolution has been similar. They have similar ways of differentiating between news and features and similar ways of making use of graphs and pictures. We should do the same. The methods they have developed are good and therefore they should not be avoided.' My heart was beating very fast and as I glanced round the room I saw the man who had spoken of the need to be different staring hard at me. Andreas was looking at me sideways, his head inclined and resting on his hand. Among the strangers in the room Sarah Hogg was the only one who reacted; she nodded her head slightly and looked quite friendly.

While I paused Alexander entered the room. He sat down in the corner opposite me and lit a cigarette. He was the only smoker there.

There was not much reaction to what I had said. Someone said something about not wanting just to 'look like the *Guardian*'. I said there was no such danger. 'We will develop an idiosyncratic style willy-nilly. What I am saying is that we must not make it our starting point that we *have* to look different.'

The meeting began at 10.30 and went on until almost 12.45. The mood was workmanlike, good natured and rather muted. Obviously no one thought the dummy was any good and parts of it were frankly declared to be disastrous. I joined in fairly frequently, mainly to say the use of graphics and graphs was poor. I criticised one drawing strongly, saying that the artist and the commissioning editor were making the wrong use of an illustration.

'It often happens that an artist tries to sum up the entire article wittily in one drawing. In this case Eddy Shah's economic difficulties, his predatory rivals and his possible saviour, Tiny Rowland. But that is not what the drawing is for. The drawing is to attract the readers' attention. It is to decorate the page. It is to amuse, delight or alert a reader. Above all it must be comprehensible at a glance. In this drawing you cannot tell whether Shah is bursting volcano-like upwards or drowning. You have to read many words all round him before you realise he is surrounded by newspapers. The action of the figure of

Rowland is ambiguous. Is he hurting or helping Shah? The drawing is too big for the page and for the article.'

I also attacked one particular graph. It showed a stylised map of Europe from which sprouted hieroglyphs representing nuclear reactors. It was printed almost right across the page and was absolutely incomprehensible. Alexander chipped in, 'I agree – I couldn't understand it at all. When I realised these things were reactors I found myself moronically counting them.'

I agreed with nothing anyone said except Alexander, and everything he said was simple, pertinent and convincing.

In the end Andreas pushed his copy a few inches away in a gesture of finality and said, 'This has been a very useful discussion – I'd now like two weeks alone in a Scottish hideout to think about it all.' Everyone smiled sympathetically. 'But can we agree that we are on the right track and have made a good start?'

At once Alexander began to speak. He said that he did not feel at all happy with the direction the paper was going. He said a *Times* reader who might be thinking of changing would simply be put off by this sort of paper. 'It doesn't look remotely like the sort of thing he's used to.' He made a devastating case against the decision we had been discussing. I listened to him with pleasure and considerable excitement. It was like a closing restatement of my opening remarks, only much more eloquent, and I looked hopefully at Andreas to see whether he was taking it in. He looked troubled.

When Alexander stopped speaking Andreas said rather defensively, 'But we *have* worked along the lines you have indicated.'

Alexander pressed on, 'Did your approach dictate this choice of typeface, these rounded boxes, this rather odd use of graphics, the size of these headlines?'

There was a kind of hiatus.

I said, 'Andreas, in answer to your question, "Are we on the right lines?" my answer is, no, we are not.'

The meeting ended shortly after this with a raggedy burst of muttered tension-reducing remarks and we all left the room. I found myself next to Andreas. He said, 'I'm rushing off to a lunch, I'm afraid. Thank you very much for coming.' I said I'd enjoyed it and found it extremely interesting.

Alexander called out would I like to go to lunch with him and Stephen and we walked through Bunhill Fields towards the Troquet restaurant. Stephen said, 'You two couldn't have done that better if you'd met for breakfast and rehearsed it.' Alexander laughed and said, 'We didn't.' I wondered whether to own up to the fact that we had talked together twice last week but I let it pass.

James Fenton and Nick Ashford joined us at lunch and the conversation ranged widely. Alexander and Stephen talked about going together to the States to set up the Washington office. James made jokes about how good the *Sunday Times* had suddenly become. This mystified everyone until I realised he meant how delighted and amused he is by the *ST* writing about the Peter Hall/Trevor Nunn scandal, where the two directors of the National Theatre were accused by some of making themselves rich by transferring NT productions.

We did talk about the dummy a bit. James made a penetrating statement about the over-designed newspapers that were difficult to read and irritating to look at. Stephen said, 'I thought you hadn't seen the dummy yet.'

'I haven't,' said James.

'Oh Christ,' said Stephen. 'But you wouldn't say it was a catastrophe, would you?' he asked, looking unhappily at me.

'Yes, I would,' I replied.

Nick said gently, 'Oh I wouldn't – I wouldn't say a catastrophe.'

'What would you say?' I asked.

'Well . . . um . . . er . . .' He fished about for the right word and finally said, 'Well, I wouldn't buy it.' Even Stephen laughed and I said, 'That *would* be a catastrophe.'

Tuesday 8 July

Last night I kept thinking about the meeting and I got more and more depressed. I remembered gloomily Charles Moore's original doubts about the paper and John Thompson's questioning of Andreas's experience as an editor.

At about 7.00 pm I rang Matthew and Stephen but they were both out. I tried the *Independent* but there was no reply. At 9.30 I tried Stephen again. He said that he had agreed with *some* of what Alexander and I had said. I felt bad. It did not make sense to agree with *some* of it. It was not divisible into parts. We were saying that the starting point and direction the *Independent* had decided on were fundamentally wrong.

I asked if there would be more dummies and when. He said the next would come along quite soon, perhaps in a couple of weeks, and would be a development from the existing one. I realised that by then Alexander would be in America, James would be heading off very soon for Manila and I'd be on the point of leaving for France. All three of us would be away while the final shape and look of the *Independent* was created.

By this morning I was so agitated that I woke at 6.30 composing a letter to Andreas. In it I urged him to go and read the words on the tombstones in Bunhill Fields, and to learn principles of layout from the beauty and simplicity of the letters and their perfect placing. I did not actually write the letter; instead I rang Alexander at 9.00 and said I was worried about the lack of response to what we had said yesterday and did he think we should follow-up our efforts?

He said we should, or perhaps we should just resign. I admitted that the thought had crossed my mind. In fact Caroline had said this morning that I could say, 'Change it all or I resign.'

'Well, shall we?' said Alexander.

'Oh, I don't think so. I don't think I could face Max and Perry again so soon.'

He laughed and said, 'OK.'

He then amazed me by suggesting that he should contact a designer friend of Stuart Read's and commission him to do a front page for the *Independent* along the lines we agree on. 'Then we'd have something to show Andreas,' he said. 'Would you come in on such a plan?'

I certainly would. The idea struck me as excellent. It was in fact the only thing to do and it at once revived my hopes. I said there were two things that worried me. The first was, would it be very expensive, and how would we pay him? Alexander said, 'Oh, I'll give him something – it won't cost much.'

The second and much more important problem was, shouldn't we tell Andreas in case he thought we were plotting against him in some way? Alexander's view was that to tell him would simply alarm him and confuse him at this stage. What we should do was have something to show him to set alongside the other effort. 'We need actually to have something in our hands; there is too much talk.'

I said, 'OK' and he rang off, saying he'd set it up and I must call him later at about 11.00.

In fact I didn't speak to Alexander again until mid-afternoon after I'd had lunch with Tony Howard. As we were ending our meal Roy Hattersley came over to the table. Tony told him I was going to the *Independent*. Roy looked interested and pleased and said he had a feeling the *Independent* was going to be a success.

'This old hack thinks differently,' I said, nodding to Tony.

Roy said, 'The only problem is with so many honest, decent, fair, straightforward, unmalicious journalists there, who is going to provide the fun?'

When Alexander came to my room at 4.00 he had already contacted the designer and proposed that we went ahead and saw him. I said I was still very anxious about appearing to go behind people's backs; I thought we ought to tell Andreas what we were doing and why. Alexander said, 'You're right,' and at once reached for the phone to ring the *Independent*. Andreas and Stephen were out. Matthew was somewhere around but we didn't speak to him.

The more I know Alexander the more I like him. He is extraordinarily easy to talk to – he listens to the spirit of what's being said and he entirely lacks any desire to puff up his own role or position. Over this particular business he is simply trying to do his best for the *Independent*. There is no latent challenge to anyone. His actions do not amount to professional manoeuvring for long-term advantage. He just thinks the dummy is bloody awful and must be made bloody good.

Later in the day he managed to get hold of Stephen, who thought our plan a good one and undertook to speak to Andreas. I felt quite happy about proceeding in these circumstances and Alexander fixed for us to meet the designer at 10.30 tomorrow morning.

The above account of the formulation of this plan is very shortened. It involved the usual jokes, asides, admissions and so on. But we are committed, unless Andreas says no, to preparing a re-designed *Independent* in about two days. Oh, Christ!

Wednesday 9 July

I rang Alexander at 8.30 to find out whether our meeting with the designer was on. He said he hadn't yet spoken to Stephen and therefore had not heard Andreas's reaction. In the background I could hear Susie, Alexander's wife, calling out something about a bath overflowing. I said I'd ring Stephen and Alexander said, 'OK. Thanks. And I'll go and finish cleaning my teeth.'

Stephen had already left the house. Celia said, 'He's gone to pick up a car.' I wondered how many company cars he had. He's driving a very cool Saab these days, which was 'on the house'.

I decided I'd ring Andreas myself. I paused, considering whether I should get Alexander to do it, but decided it didn't really make any difference. Andreas was at his best. Friendly, attentive and encouraging, but also a touch reserved as if he held to his own views but was prepared to listen. He told me to go ahead with the new design and that he'd not only look forward to seeing it, he'd pay for it. He said he had been influenced by all the talk at the meeting and found his ideas changing slightly.

I reported this to Alexander and then had to take Theo to buy some new school trousers, because today is Speech Day and his only trousers suddenly have three large holes in them and are filthy.

By the time I'd done that it was getting late and when I got to the designer's office Alexander was already there. They were sitting at a table with newspapers, including the *Independent* dummy, spread out before them.

As Alexander had by then begun to describe what we were looking for I gave the designer – Nick Thirkell – my version of it.

In my brief conversation with Andreas that morning he had listed three factors that had directed his thinking during the creation of the dummy.

1. People already know each morning what the news is because they saw it on TV the night before. Furthermore our readers are busy and in a hurry. Both these factors push us towards presenting the news in summary form and towards analysis.
2. We have new tech at our disposal and should therefore make use of it. (This really means colour.)
3. We are going for young readers and that means we give great emphasis to listing entertainment and cultural events.

He further added that to signpost the paper clearly, as if it were a foreign country, was also important. By that he meant page numbering and identifying pages at home, foreign, features, arts, etc. Finally Andreas had quoted Tom Sutcliffe, with approval, when he had said we should be after 'quality with a twist'.

I began by repeating these thoughts and then saying in my view they should all be ignored, on the grounds that they were either obvious or misleading. I maintained that the first step should be the creation of a good-looking, ordinary, quality newspaper. It should resemble in style our three main rivals. The presentation of news, the use of colour, efforts to attract different groups of reader should all fit into and be built from that basic classic design. I had in mind a loyal *Times* reader picking up the *Independent* out of curiosity. I would like him to feel at once that he is quite at home. He should be able to recognise at a glance whether he was on a news, a leader or an arts page. His concentration should not be disturbed by tarted up graphics clamouring for his attention. The use of photographs should be sparing, but where they were used they should be given generous space. Colour should be avoided unless it was a tiny spot here and there, perhaps a page number or a date, no more. (I would concede that the sports pages could use colour and after some months, should a particular event call for it, a front-page colour picture could be used as a surprise and a treat and a sort of promise of what is possible and in reserve.) This *Times* reader I had in mind was a conservative sort of person. He or she would accept gradual change, but was not inclined to pursue a new trend. The *Independent* would break new ground but it must lead its readers forward at a gentle, steady pace.

When both Alexander and I had finished speaking Nick said he agreed with everything that had been said and he shared our doubts about the dummy. He said he tremendously admired the present look of *The Times* and gave a potted history of its development over the last fifteen years.

'My problem is going to be how do I stop myself just copying it.'

Taking up this point he and Alexander began to compare *The Times* and the *Guardian* and they soon agreed that although in some ways *The*

205

Times had an almost perfect front page, the *Guardian*'s looked more 'friendly'. There was something appealing about its mixture of headlines and stories that went across the page and others that went down. The *Times* had a certain formal sterility in its very perfection.

After perhaps an hour and a half Nick pushed the papers away and said, 'OK. That's a perfect brief.' He said we'd meet again in a week's time and he'd show us what he'd done.

I suggested that perhaps Penny Jackson, who is joining the paper as a features assistant, might come to that meeting because she sympathised with our views and had more practical experience than any of us at actually putting pages together. They both agreed.

As we got up to go I noticed that Alexander was leaving his dummy copy of the *Independent* behind. 'That's terribly secret,' I said. 'I'm not sure we shouldn't take it.'

'But he'll need it,' said Alexander.

'I suppose so – but Andreas would faint dead away if he knew there was one just floating about.'

Nick picked up the paper, folded it and put it under the others on the table. 'Don't worry,' he said, 'I'll make sure no one sees it.'

Alexander and I walked out into Regent Street. He said he was going to the *Telegraph* and I offered him a lift on my bike. 'No, no,' he said. 'Anyway I haven't got a helmet.'

'I've brought a helmet.'

'But I'm a coward.'

'That's OK. It is frightening but it's also exhilarating.'

'Oh, Christ!'

We arrived at the bike, and I gave him the helmet.

Before he got on he said, 'Where do I put my feet? On those things?'

'Yeah.'

'Do I hold on to you?'

'You can if you like but you don't have to. Just sit there – and you don't have to lean or steer or anything.'

We set off. I tried terrifically hard not to wobble or jerk the gears. Now and then, down the empty Haymarket and getting away from traffic lights, I accelerated a bit, but mostly I drove very sedately.

As I dropped him safely outside the *Telegraph*, he called out, 'Absolutely terrific – I'll get one tomorrow!' Everyone enjoys going on motor bikes. Giving people rides is one of the pleasures of having one.

When I asked Penny if she'd like to come to our next meeting she said yes. But she also worried a little about protocol. She was afraid that her head of department at the *Independent* might not be pleased if she appeared too closely associated with the creation of a new design. I thought this was a serious and real objection and all ill feeling had to be avoided. So we left it open.

This week has shot by. Time always accelerated as a holiday approaches.

The farewell lunch for me that Peter proposed has been changed by Max to a dinner. The date chosen is 22 July. I asked Etty why evening instead of lunchtime. She replied that she thinks Max doesn't like lunches or, rather, long lunches. 'If he's been out to a lunch you'll see him walk back down that corridor at 2.30 sharp. Bill used to come back at 3.00. He'd only just make the conference at quarter past.'

I think I prefer dinner to lunch. It means it can drift on a bit and everyone will feel less pressured.

The only people I have asked to be invited are John Burgess, Bernard Foyster, Sue Davy, Charles Moore, Alexander Chancellor, John Thompson, Colin Welch and Caroline. Otherwise leader writers seem to be automatically asked, so are Bill and Max. It's an odd thing that after twenty years here there are so few people left whom I feel I must say goodbye to.

Caroline suggested that we give a drinks party at home one Saturday evening to *Telegraph* people and I immediately thought it an excellent idea. But when I began to make a list I realised that all the friends I have made at the *Telegraph* have already left. It seems silly to ask Peter Paterson or Matthew Symonds or Ian Waller to come to say goodbye to me when they are not there.

There are plenty of people I know and like whom I've got used to seeing around the office, but I don't feel I know them well enough to ask them to my house. For some reason the idea alarms me. I think they wouldn't come or would be horribly embarrassed.

There is one part of leaving the *Telegraph* that has been bothering me. I don't know quite how to do it but I feel I want to bid farewell, and acknowledge my debt of gratitude, to Lord Hartwell. While I lay awake last night unable to sleep I began to write him a letter in my head and an opening phrase occurred to me that I might be able to use.

I once heard a tale about the infant Mozart. He would get up at night to play scales and chords on the harpsichord, a habit that his father did not object to except that the child would then go back to bed leaving an unresolved chord hanging in the air. His father would be quite unable to sleep until he had got up, gone downstairs and struck the final notes. I could explain to Lord H that I feel a similar nagging need to resolve my departure by making some sort of contact with him. The difficulty is that, although he has been an important figure in my professional life and has shown me great generosity, he is an exceptionally remote and elusive man. I've spoken to him so rarely that there is almost no relationship between us. Writing to him without explanation might alarm and upset him. You always felt you were invading his privacy if you said good morning to him in the lift. The odd thing about it is that his withdrawn state is not unfriendly. On the contrary, it is rather appealing. He really is diffident and feels genuinely awkward. It sounds ridiculous but he always makes me want to put him at ease.

I have spoken to Stephen a couple of times during the week. He tells me that Matthew is coming round to the idea that the design of the *Independent* should be more conventional. Stephen always adds, 'I agree with much of what you say.' He means it well but it always makes my spirits sink.

Yesterday Virginia Hampton, a colleague of Stuart's in the *Sunday Telegraph* features department, told me she had resigned and applied for a position at the *Independent*. For some reason or other she had been speaking to Edward Steen about it and he asked which department she preferred. When she told him he said, 'Don't go there – that lot is full of the *Times* mafia. Come to the foreign room.' My first reaction to this was a jolt of irritation. But it also interested me and I began to wonder whether the large group which comprises the *Independent* is split into factions along lines formed by earlier loyalties. It is probably inevitable that something like this is happening, and it should not be encouraged by Ed Steen or anyone else.

Last night was the *Spectator* party. The usual crush. *Spectator* parties are so full of well-known faces that it's very difficult to talk to anyone because your attention is continually caught by passing celebrities.

I did talk for a moment to Sue Davy who has given up hope of a move to the *Independent*. I said, 'I hear you are going to Letters.' She looked very surprised and said, 'Yes – you keep your ears to the ground.' I had the sudden thought there are no secrets, no unknown moves.

Andrew Knight moved smoothly up to us, chin tucked in, slight smile, guarded manner. He makes an enormous effort to give an impression of emotional stillness. He is a Martian.

He expressed disapproval at my leaving the *Telegraph*. He is a black belt at disapproval. 'I thought we had secured you earlier on,' he murmured. I remembered rumours that Max had had to fight to get me a raise, and stories of the vast amounts of money Knight gets himself. I also remembered ex-colleagues who had hoped their positions had been secured. I bristled slightly and tried to smother the annoyance I felt. 'I'm sorry you are leaving,' he whispered with an eerie absence of sincerity. 'And sad, sad.'

I spoke to Peter Paterson. 'When are you actually leaving?' he said 'Christ, it's one in the slats for them. Is it true they offered you £100,000?'

'No,' I said. 'I just put it around they did.' I wondered quite what I said to whom about that. Not only are there no secrets but neither are there any reliable versions of what happened.

Today, as I was delivering a drawing to the features department of the *Sunday Telegraph*, Alexander called out to me.

'I've had a very disturbing phone call from Andreas,' he said.

'What about?'

'He said, "My mind is now clear about the design of the paper." Very worrying.'

'Did he say what he had in mind?'

'No. What do you think he meant?'

'I dunno. You spoke to him – what did you think he meant?'

'I've no idea. But how can he suddenly have made up his mind? Does it mean he has accepted our ideas, or settled for someone else's?'

'If he has settled for ours it's very clever of him, because until we see what Thirkell produces I'm not sure myself.'

Alexander laughed. 'Exactly. That's what's so worrying. While his mind was not made up we had a chance of directing it.'

Jeremy Deedes, Bill's son, who works for the *Daily Telegraph* on the management side, passed by and he made a jesting remark about us leaving for very uncertain careers, saying he didn't think the *Independent* could make it.

Alexander agreed that was a fair guess, and I chipped in, 'If they get the design right they'll make it.'

Jeremy lit a cigarette with the deftness of a heavy smoker. He drew a great lungful and tightened the corners of his mouth before exhaling, making a little grimace that a lot of smokers do. 'It's more complicated than that,' he remarked wisely. 'Fancy leaving after all this time.'

'Not like you,' I said. 'You leave after only a few weeks.' I was referring to him having left *Today* after only a short stay to go to the *Telegraph*. He laughed good-naturedly and said, 'I don't want them to be a colossal failure – just a small failure.'

'So that they can offer you a job to get them out of trouble,' said Alexander.

'Do you think they'll succeed?' asked Jeremy.

'I'm not going to them because I'm sure they'll succeed,' said Alexander, 'but they'll go on for a bit – perhaps a year or two.'

I thought he was being too pessimistic, and Jeremy repeated he was sure the *Independent* would fail and we'd be looking for work very soon.

'In that case,' I said, 'should my remarks about you leaving jobs after a very short time have given you any offence, I withdraw them at once.'

He laughed and prodded me lightly in the chest. He is physically very like Bill and has a lot of his father's friendly, slightly playful manner.

Saturday 12 July
I met Hugo Young, the *Guardian*'s political columnist, in the local delicatessen this morning and we talked for twenty minutes or so about the *Independent*. He said they should be aiming to replace *The Times* as a serious quality paper. *The Times* and the *Telegraph* have set off down-market to catch young readers and broaden their appeal. They are prepared to compete with the *Mail*. This leaves a gap at the very top. Hugo absolutely agreed that the design of the paper should be straightforward classical. No tricks. The more like *The Times* the better.

He said he had spoken frequently to Andrew Knight about the *Telegraph*. Andrew's great fear is that the *Independent* will take just enough readers from the *Telegraph* to kill it – but he thinks they won't take enough to survive themselves. This nightmare is not one I've heard described before.

Hugo thought I was absolutely right to go to the *Independent*. He said changing from the *Sunday Times* to the *Guardian* was the best thing he'd ever done. It gave him new excitement, interest and energy. He felt much better for it.

Sunday 13 July
Lying in bed this morning drinking tea and reading the *Observer*, I found my mind continually turning over the question of the design of the *Independent*. I was quite puzzled by the degree to which this interrupted my reading. Instead of scanning the lines of a story my eyes were studying the layout of the page. I was counting the photographs, not looking at them, and measuring the size of headlines, which remained unread.

I telephoned Matthew, driven by an impulse to give my thoughts words. The conversation was extremely interesting. It quickly became clear that the second dummy, due on Wednesday, was going to be very different from the first. All the changes that Matthew listed were steps towards the kind of design Alexander and I were arguing for. While this was encouraging I also felt there was a way to go yet.

Matthew said at one point, 'Don't think of yourself as part of a sect, separate from the rest of us. There is less dividing us than you seem to think.'

I thought this a sensible thing to say and he did it very straightforwardly. I assured him, 'I don't think of myself as part of a sect. After all, as soon as Alexander and I thought of producing a dummy front page of our own we asked Andreas whether it would be helpful. There was nothing secret about it. It's just that I find I feel surprisingly strongly about it all.'

I told Matthew I'd met Hugo and gave him a résumé of our conversation. I said something about Hugo's manner had made me think that he might just possibly be interested in an offer. Matthew said he thought Hugo was too contented at the *Guardian* and would feel far too loyal to them to consider a shift. I agreed readily but nevertheless thought it might be worth a try.

I went on to say I'd been surprised to hear from someone last week that Max had not been too impressed by the dummy. 'I thought the whole thing was frightfully secret. How the hell did he get hold of a copy?'

Matthew said he had heard the same thing and wanted to find the leak. Every copy had been numbered and everyone who had been given one had had to sign for it. Matthew said, 'I called in every copy. They were all accounted for except one. That was Alexander's. He told me it had been left with the other designer.'

'That's right,' I said. 'I saw him hand it over.'

'Do you think he showed it to Max before that?'

'I've no idea. Can't think why he should have done.' I asked why it was all so secret and did it matter much anyway.

'No, not much. I suppose if *The Times* saw how much space we've given to listings they might copy it and do it before we come out. That sort of thing. But I don't think it matters much.'

At first this chat made me feel better. I went out and bought the rest of the newspapers and made myself some coffee. Caroline was away for the weekend and I sat in the sitting-room reading. To my annoyance I still could not concentrate. Eventually I went upstairs and wrote a long letter to Andreas in which I tried to express my ideas about the *Independent* and, where possible, why I thought what I did.

When Caroline came home at about five o'clock I showed her the letter. She said I should definitely send it. My anxiety about giving it to Andreas was complicated. Partly I felt that he was already shifting in the way I wanted him to go so I mustn't do anything that might interrupt that process. I was afraid that my views might sound a little extreme, even eccentric. Another argument against sending the letter was that he might think I was over-reacting to his invitation to express my views. A paper's political cartoonist chatting and attending meetings was one thing; long rather intense letters was something else entirely. I feel anyway in an exhausted and manic state and do not trust my own judgement too much right now.

Unable to make up my mind I rang James Fenton to ask his advice. He said at once, 'Send the letter.'

'You haven't heard what it says yet.'

'That doesn't make any difference. I know you should send it anyway. He'll be pleased that you bothered even if it is a bit hysterical. By the way, is it?'

'I'm afraid it might be. I'm also afraid you're going to have to listen to me read it to you.'

'All right. But I'm telling you now – send it.'

I read him the letter and he said, 'See, I told you – send it.'

'Do you agree with it?'

There was a pause. Then he said, 'Yes.'

By this time I was in a complete turmoil, and thought, Oh, what the hell, I'll take it to him. I rode over to Andreas's house in Kensington and rang the bell. We went upstairs and I explained that I had brought him a letter and described how and why I came to write it.

He was very nice about it and went through a dummy that he had, showing me the changes that he proposed to make in the next one. I didn't stay very long and left hoping he wouldn't think I was as crazy as I felt I was.

Sunday 13 July 1986

Dear Andreas,

I have been sitting downstairs, drinking coffee and reading the Sunday papers, but my thoughts continually turned to the *Independent* and its design. Like a sleeper, visited by ideas of such startling clarity and originality that they seem to present solutions to the most perplexing problems, I reach for my pen to jot them down . . .

The motion of appealing to young readers is a mistake. 'The Young' in the sense of a group of potential readers, do not exist. There is no group contained within clear boundaries defined by tastes, attitudes, ambitions, interests and youth. For example, the young Matthew Symonds would have looked with mere amusement at a newspaper that tried to interest him because of his age. He wouldn't have bought it. The kind of reader you want is intelligent, full stop. His or her age is neither here nor there.

The very formulation of the idea of appealing to the young is not just dangerous, it is fatal. I won't labour the point. I'll just ask you to consider the self-inflicted wound the *Telegraph* has suffered by deciding that their only hope is to appeal to the young. The whole journal is awash with trivia and you do not need to be very old to notice it.

Incidentally, the generous space you have given to the listings in the *Independent* is a very good idea but not because it appeals to the young. I am 50 and it appeals to me. Sometimes visitors to London ask me what plays and exhibitions to go to, and I have to send one of my children to buy *Time Out*. The *Independent*'s listings pages would mean I had that information to hand. My teenage children would of course also make use of it for themselves. What I am trying to say is that you could have reached the idea that space should be given to listings without ever using the word 'young'.

I disagree with the assertion that because people have seen last night's TV news they do not want to read about it in the next morning's papers. To believe this is to misunderstand the different kinds of information that you get from TV and newspapers.

TV is a branch of showbiz. It belongs almost entirely to a world of titillation

212

and entertainment. News on TV always comes with moving (in both senses of the word) pictures, and these images interpose themselves between the viewer and matter being reported in such a way as to inhibit thought. You come away from a TV news bulletin with pictures in your mind. I am haunted by the faces of the spectators at the shuttle disaster, by the pathetically ordinary aspect of the bombed streets of Tripoli, by the desolation of the streets of Soweto. But it is through newspapers that the significance of the news is mainly conveyed. I do not mean through journalists' comments, I mean through written news. I can think for myself about the rights and wrongs of the Libyan bombings once I have been given the facts to go on. I am extremely interested in comment but my first need is a comprehensive account of what happened. Radio is always superior to TV as a medium for reporting for similar reasons. TV can be more entertaining and more exciting. And, most seductively, it requires infinitely less effort from its audience. But as a rival to newspapers TV is just not in the same class and can be ignored. Indeed, it should be ignored because if you try to take it on on its own ground it will beat the shit out of you.

My wide and deep researches into the question of colour on the front page show that it would be an extremely serious error and probably lethal. There is no doubt at all that colour on the front page brings to mind advertising brochures, small-time local papers, cheap magazines and *Today*. I cannot think of any other single decision that is more likely to put off the kind of reader you need than putting coloured pictures on the front.

I have already explained to you the Corot principle: the tiny touch of colour that brings a whole picture to life. This principle could be applied by deciding, once the *Independent*'s black and white Page 1 is established, to produce suddenly a lovely coloured picture because of the coming together of a certain constellation of events. You might then use a coloured picture of (say) the Pope in billowing red robes visiting the Kremlin, or astronauts stepping in wonder on to a distant planet, or when at last the time comes and we do actually gaze upon the face of Agamemnon. But then sharply back to black and white after you've shown what you can do.

I think newspapers will all be in colour one day. Time enough for that; don't hurry.

Even in the period since the *Independent* was conceived, newspapers have changed. A circulation war has broken out between *The Times* and the *Telegraph*, and the *Guardian* is keeping a careful eye on what they are up to. Murdoch has boasted he will double the circulation of *The Times*. Andrew Knight's reaction to that was, 'If Murdoch says he'll do something he usually does it.' *The Times* is no longer the distinguished establishment newspaper it used to be. It's a good-looking, rather abrasive modern newspaper that is more likely to get ambitious *Daily Mail* readers than anything else. The *Telegraph* is desperately diving down-market as well. *Times*-like, it goes over to sexy women's pages and features about all sorts of odds and ends that it hopes will appeal to younger readers. The result is 'Monday Matters' and literally thousands of readers decamping for *The Times* and *Daily Mail*. At the same time the *Telegraph*'s leaders have become politically more central and *The Times* perhaps more hard-line right. Neither is very convincing.

213

This circulation war has shifted the balance of the newspaper industry with the consequences that there is now a gap at the top.

That's the place for the *Independent*. With stately columns of news, law reports, heavy commitment to education, pleasing and restrained use of photographs and graphics and intelligent incisive comment, I see the *Independent* rising above its competitors. They are fighting their battles with the tactics and weapons of the past.

In a fight always choose your own weapons and your own ground. But I don't like this martial metaphor. I'm talking about newspapers.

I didn't know I was so interested in them or that I cared so much about what one looked like.

Yours ever,
Nick

Monday 14 July
This morning I was thoughtfully biting on my thumb nail while waiting for the bath to fill when, with a sensation of the whole world lurching and crumbling to bits, my left front tooth snapped off leaving a hideous jagged stump.

I was near to panic and that curious thought that sometimes accompanies catastrophe rushed through my mind: No! let's play that bit through again, differently. I rang my dentist who at once made me an appointment for 2.00 this afternoon. I asked Charles Moore to find another artist to do the *Spectator* cover and dawdled away the morning, even quite enjoying the experience of not doing very much. Theo made plenty of jokes about 'the whole tooth', and 'taking it as it gums' to keep my spirits high. I didn't get to work until about 4.00, complete with a temporary crown.

While I was doing a somewhat rushed cartoon Etty came to see me. She had a menu from L'Escargot restaurant, where my farewell dinner is to be held. I had to pick what would be served. I chose soup (cold), salmon and then chops because it seemed safest.

Etty sat on my desk smoking a cigarette and I can't quite remember how but we began talking about Morrison and Max and the *Telegraph* generally. She told me Morrison had written an unwise letter to Max and had a difficult interview with him subsequently. She said sorrowfully that Morrison had not done himself any good and was obviously not going to survive too long. She was sad because she is extremely fond of him and also admires him. 'He's a very good man, very sound.' She also spoke with warm affection about Max. She obviously likes and enjoys working for him, and from her account the feeling is mutual.

I tried to convey to her my own feelings about Max and said that should it ever crop up she should say to him that she knows that my

214

leaving the *Telegraph* was not because of him so much as a desire for a change.

I was stimulated to say this by her telling me mournfully that Max had told her my resignation had been the worst blow yet.

She said there is relentless pressure from 'up there'. She gestured upwards.

'You mean from Andrew Knight?'

'Yes.'

'What sort of pressure do you mean – editorial direction?'

'Not exactly.'

She told me she'd been talking to Andrew Knight's secretary in the little office off Andrew's. He had come out and stood looking at them. She shifted her weight into a parody of a casual pose and said, 'You know – little smile . . .' She put on a comical face with lidded eyes and tight smile. 'And do you know what he says? He says, (here she began a soft English drawl instead of speaking in her clear Scottish accent) "And how do you like working for our . . . er . . . impetuous . . . energetic young editor?" Well (she went back to Scottish) I turned round and walked out. I said, "I like it very much indeed," I said, and I walked right out.'

She also told me that the day Bill quit as editor he came to see her and said, 'Don't leave, Etty, and look after Sue, because things are going to get pretty rough here for a while. Max has no idea how hard this is going to be.'

I could just see Bill doing this. The way she told it she made me feel that Bill had felt real compassion for Max as he marched off to the front.

When I took my cartoon in to Max he said, 'We've appointed your successor, by the way.' He opened a large portfolio and I saw that they'd chosen an artist called Gale. I've seen his work around for years and Max said, 'I think he's the best we've seen, I like his line.' The confident way in which he spoke included no invitation for me to comment so I just said, 'Oh yes – I know his work well.'

Max told me they were calling him an illustrator not a cartoonist. 'Of course if he does a cartoon I like, we'll use it. Anyway, he's starting next Monday and I told him to come and make himself known to you. Anything helpful you can tell him perhaps you'll let him know.'

'Yes, of course – pleasure.'

Tuesday 15 July
James Fenton telephoned today to ask where Alexander and I were meeting Nick Thirkell tomorrow and what our plans then were. I had lost and forgotten Nick's address and said I'd go and ask Alexander to call James back.

Alexander asked me whether I'd spoken to Nick since we'd seen him. I said no but I had written to, and spoken to, Andreas. I told him the gist of all that and he said he'd spoken to Stephen and also got the clear impression that the design of the *Independent* was moving our way.

He then telephoned Nick to see whether he'd prepared anything for us. The answer was, 'Yes – it looks a bit *Times*y.'

'Good; that sounds fine,' said Alexander.

I said to him that I had had second thoughts about asking Penny to our meeting. I was afraid that her head of department might find that a bit difficult. Somehow she might seem to be stepping out in front of him. Alexander vaguely agreed, so I went back to my room, phoned James and explained the plan to him and later spoke to Penny. She was as usual sensible and relaxed and easy to talk to, and agreed not to come.

Wednesday 16 July

James, Alexander and I met at Nick Thirkell's office. Nick was nervous; his hands even shook a little as he picked up various papers, and his voice came stumblingly with little coughs.

At last he unfolded the dummy before us. The first impression was of lively elegance. An eagle just to the left of the masthead, symbolising power and independence, looked a bit American and the all-over effect of the page was indeed *Times*y; I spoke these two nit-picking points but went on to praise the work. The masthead was clear and graceful and the other typefaces very attractive.

James and Alexander began to speak and the more we looked at it the better it seemed. Both of them praised it. James wondered if some black rules might not be too dark.

Gradually Nick relaxed and I think felt he had scored.

The *Independent* was telephoned and an arrangement made to meet Andreas at 3.00. James and I rode to Queen Square where he has to see his publisher. At about 12.00 I went to my office and quickly drew a cartoon.

I rang Nick and said, 'I just want to say that Alexander, James and I all think what you've done is brilliant. It is so exactly what we want. You sounded quite nervous when you were talking to us: don't be nervous when you're with the others. Don't be apologetic. We're right behind you.'

'I've been waiting for years to get a chance to design a paper like this,' he said.

'Tell 'em that, too; sounds good and keen.'

But when we were all sitting round a table in the conference room he sounded nervous again. There was Andreas, Matthew, Stephen, Alexander, James, me and Nick. The atmosphere was not exactly

216

unfriendly but I felt tension in the air. Matthew looked tight-lipped and Stephen winked at me. I was not sure what the signal meant, except it was definitely encouraging rather than anything else.

During the meeting Alexander, James and I were jestingly referred to as the 'rebels' and my letter was mentioned once. Andreas said I was plain wrong in much of what I'd said and there was an unusual edge in his voice. I felt slapped down. The letter had been a mistake. I didn't mind too much.

Nervous or not, Nick did well. Hesitantly and with many coughs he expressed our brief very accurately. He made reference to copies of the other quality papers and to the *Independent* dummy. The moment came and he showed his work, laying it out on the table in front of Andreas. Another copy was slid across to Matthew and Steve.

Reaction came slowly. Matthew criticised a small detail. Andreas asked a technical question about the typeface and the computers. He also said it was like *The Times* and then, moments later after comparing the two, he said it wasn't like *The Times*. Nick said, 'I don't think we should just let *The Times* have all the best ideas. If they are good ideas I think we can use them or adapt them.'

In fact his front page was dazzlingly good. It combined classical up and down *Times*-like columns and three stories (one in a long caption) lying horizontal, as in the *Guardian*. There were news-in-brief stories separated by neat thin lines, a detail borrowed from the *Telegraph*. The page was easy to read. The eye ranged comfortably over it from story to story.

One by one, Andreas first, then Stephen and Matthew, they acknowledged the quality of Nick's front page.

It was no contest; the original dummy looked crude and vulgar beside the new one. All three liked the eagle. Again Stephen winked at me. This time I thought he meant, 'Just give us time, we are coming round.'

On the whole I felt the exercise had been successful, but afterwards Stephen said he still felt that there were parts of the original dummy that should survive. This depressed me. I want the whole original dummy – and if necessary the men who designed it – junked.

Matthew too remained somewhat formal and unfriendly. Andreas was nice, but none of them said the obvious thing: 'Right, Nick Thirkell, your dream has come true: design us the *Independent!*'

At least Andreas, by the end of the meeting, had asked Nick to start at once designing some inside pages.

Thursday 17 July
I rang Alexander after breakfast and we had a post-mortem on yesterday's meeting.

We agreed that Andreas had a problem now, with too many designers working separately on the paper. Yesterday Andreas had said that he was riding three horses at once (meaning he had three designers) and that it was going to take all his tact and diplomatic skills to avoid a damaging collision between them. He had also said, 'We are on converging lines.'

All this I reminded Alexander of, and said we must follow up our success with a consolidating manoeuvre. The danger was that Andreas would attempt to merge what he saw as good about the original dummy with what he had been persuaded was good about the second.

'Why can't they just see that Thirkell is the chap?' said Alexander. 'I mean, it's obvious.'

'Yeah. I think it's because instead of just designing a good-looking paper they are trying to incorporate into it a whole lot of nonsense that some market research idiot has raked together. Someone has convinced them that, say, researches have proved people only read leaders which are boxed up in curly lines, so they think that's what must happen. They don't have any feel for the pure harmonious beauty of good layout.'

'You're probably right,' said Alexander. 'I'll call him later and see you at the office this afternoon.'

When I saw Alexander at work he said he had failed to get in touch with Andreas but was writing him a letter instead; 'In spite of the, er, effect of yours,' he said. The letter is saying bluntly that if the *Independent* uses Thirkell's dummy the paper will succeed; if it uses a version of the original dummy it will fail. He wants to head-off any merging of the two approaches. He ended by saying that he, who cannot as a rule make his mind up about a damned thing, feels absolutely certain that he is right about Thirkell. Not only is he certain but he feels very, very strongly about it.

I had to deliver a drawing to the *Independent* after work. Andreas was not around but I saw Matthew. At first he tried to put down Thirkell's design. I told him that he was just plain wrong. He tried to defend their dummy but gradually he began to shift. Not much. He did say Thirkell's work was excellent; and that they were all moving in that direction. He also said that Andreas was visually illiterate. I said, 'Well, he's got me and Alexander; we are not visually illiterate.'

'I'm not visually illiterate either, sweetheart,' he said tartly.

'Then admit that Thirkell should be given the job.'

He began a different tack. There were other designers already employed; they could not be just got rid of.

'You're a fixer,' I said. 'Just fix it. You're the hard man. This decision is too important. I don't want anyone hurt or humiliated, but our careers depend on this decision.'

218

'No more Mr Nice,' he said, and laughed. He urged me to keep calm. Everything would come right.

I then had a similar conversation with Stephen. He said he, more than the others, already belonged to the rebel faction; but he seemed to think the answer lay in some sort of blending of the two styles. He too advised me to be calm and patient. 'When Thirkell arrives with two more pages which are as good as his page one, something will happen.'

Friday 18 July

Alexander and I talked in his office. He told me about a letter he'd written to Andreas. It covered the ground we'd been over before and sounded extremely good. He had put very forcefully how certain he was that Thirkell should be given the job of designing the paper. He had also said that he hoped Andreas wasn't beginning to feel persecuted. He said any idea of merging parts of the original dummy into Thirkell's design was no good. Furthermore his conviction that he was right could not be changed by any amount of research.

'Probably a ghastly mistake to write it,' he said, putting himself down as usual.

I said I was absolutely delighted that he had written and it all sounded terrific to me.

'It's all right for you: you can resign and come back to the *Telegraph* for the same money.'

'More money,' I said.

'Even better.'

'So could you, for that matter.'

'No, I couldn't. I couldn't come back. But for you the design could be a resigning matter.'

'I think you should tell them,' I said, 'that if they don't get the design right I'll leave.'

'Good idea.'

'As a matter of fact, if they don't get it right I think I *will* resign.' He looked at me. 'I mean it, I don't want to work for it if it looks like that shitty dummy.'

'Neither do I,' said Alexander cheerfully.

Saturday 19 July

In my room at the *Telegraph* are all my books and scores of papers and photographs and odds and ends that I must sift through before I leave. At about 2.30 this afternoon I went to Fleet Street to begin this final clear-up. Instead of getting straight on with it I went to see Alexander to hear any reaction he might have had to his letter. His room was empty. As I walked away I glanced into George Evans's office which is right next door to Alexander's. There I saw a wonderful sight. In the space between the door and George's desk a lunch table had been laid with a white table cloth. There were several places where meals had been eaten and several others which remained untouched.

Seated at the table was Ian Watson, who had taken over from Alexander as deputy editor of the *Sunday Telegraph*. He was pouring himself a drink and obviously about to start eating his lunch. As if entering a surrealist picture or finding myself able to take part in a fairy story I went in and said, 'Hello.'

'Hello,' said Ian. 'I'm a bit late.'

'This is the most marvellous sight.'

'It's what's left of the proprietor's Saturday lunch.'

'I've never realised it was held here before.'

'Have a trout,' said Ian.

On the sideboard was a plate with three silvery trout covered in thin slices of cucumber. There were three bowls of salad; one was mixed, one was bean sprouts and one was beans. There should have been three serving maids: one black, one white and one oriental.

I helped myself to a trout and sat with Ian in an extraordinarily relaxed and rather mad mood. We had been there for about ten minutes when Alexander came in. He didn't seem particularly surprised to see me and as he helped himself to food from the side table he said, 'Sorry I'm a bit late.'

Once he arrived we began talking about our efforts to influence Andreas to accept our view of what the *Independent* should look like. We spoke quite freely in front of Ian and once more I saw there were no secrets around here really. All the stuff I'm writing down in this journal is sloshing about somewhere; it's just that this is a narrow vein of it in an inevitably concentrated form.

Perry came and sat with us for a while.

'This is an *Independent* board meeting,' said Alexander. 'Come in.'

'What's he doing here?' said Perry, pointing at Ian.

'He's a visitor.'

We talked about finding a replacement for me on the *Sunday*. I suggested getting no one until they found someone really good. I recommended Peter Brookes as the only man I really respected and even he claims he can't do political cartoons. But he is a very good artist, he has extremely witty ideas for his visual puns and with a bit of help and a lot of money he would be their best bet.

'I see absolutely no reason why you should not continue to do our cartoons,' said Perry.

'They wouldn't let him,' replied Alexander.

'Bullshit,' said Perry grandly. Perry can say 'Bullshit' grandly.

Shortly after this Perry got up to leave. As he went out Alexander said, 'I thought just then you were going to make a great attempt to get Nick back; that magnificent "Bullshit" and then nothing.'

Perry turned and smiled. 'Well, it's useless, isn't it?'

Soon Ian too left. Alexander and I stayed on, as the women from the catering department cleared up. At last all that was left was a whisky bottle and a jug of water. Alexander drank and I smoked cigarettes. Our talk was excited and strangely intense. I cannot find the word but Alexander usually puts a smiling distance between him and emotion. He rarely criticises anyone very much. Now he tore into the *Independent*.

He described the sort of editor the *Independent* needed. He mentioned an Italian and a French one. Ruffling his hair and putting a cigarette in the corner of his mouth he said, 'You know the sort of man, open collar, young, busy, writes a book a minute, energetic, something to say.' He referred to the Italian editor. 'Writes a daily leader, absolutely first class, terrific, puts it on the front page and it goes on till page 23!'

He said Andreas was like one of those characters that used to be played by Alec Guinness, the little guy who by some unexpected sequence of events becomes powerful in the factory or the business or decides to become a criminal, but is not really cut out for it at all.

He went on to give his thoughts on Stephen and Matthew. My spirits were sinking; a vision of the *Independent* as a boring little newspaper, with boringly predictable and decent views just like Roy Hattersley had forecast, rose up in front of me . . . but at the same time an irresistible and delightful mood of irresponsibility swept over me. I thought I could see everything with a clarity I'd never had before.

About the design, Alexander said things were clearly going our way but Wednesday was a turning point. 'At that meeting when we have the second dummy and Thirkell's pages two and three, Andreas must make a statement. He must say that he has come to a decision and whatever adjustments to staff and so on are made necessary the design of the *Independent* is from now on in the hands of Thirkell.'

'And if he doesn't?'

'Then I will resign. It will mean financial ruin, of course,' he was laughing, 'and I'll make a complete arse of myself.'

'I'll make a pact with you. If you resign I'll resign too. I think we'd make bigger arses of ourselves working for a paper that looks like a second-rate *Today* than we would by resigning.'

Alexander continued to drink his whisky. At one point a phone rang on George's desk and Alexander rose, slightly clumsily, to reach out for it. On his way he knocked into an Anglepoise desk lamp and apologised to it very politely.

When he returned to his place he said the most extraordinary thing had happened the previous day. He'd been sitting at his desk when Oliver Pritchett had come in. Oliver, who usually looks preoccupied

221

and amiable, was unusually agitated. He said he'd just seen the most sinister man he'd ever clapped eyes on moving towards Perry's office and was terribly afraid that the man's intention was to murder poor Perry. He was troubled enough by the aspect of this nightmarish intruder to note details of his face and clothes in order to provide the police with a good description: 'He was of South African appearance!' Alexander, on hearing this alarming story, wondered whether under the circumstances they shouldn't call on Perry to see how he was. Oliver agreed that they should and it wasn't long before together they knocked on Perry's door and went in.

Perry was at his desk and greeted them, 'Hello, come in! You'll never guess who has just been to see me.'

'Who?'

'Conrad Black!'

It turned out that Conrad Black, far from wanting to murder Perry, had come to praise him. He told Perry that while held up at Kennedy Airport for some hours recently he had read every Sunday paper on sale. 'And, Perry, I must tell you that the *Sunday Telegraph* was without doubt far and away the best of the entire collection.'

Sunday 20 July

Matthew rang me this afternoon. He said grimly that there had been a second resignation. A Mr Bryant, features editor, late of the *Daily Mail*, had suddenly pushed off. Matthew didn't know where or why but guessed it was to *The Times*. The question therefore was, was there any point in approaching Don Berry? On the whole I thought not. On the other hand, he was a very good man and could only say no, so why not ask him?

Naturally the talk turned to the design. I said, 'Matthew, I'm no longer going to mince words. That first dummy is an absolute catastrophe from beginning to end and in every single detail.' Matthew demurred. I said, 'I want you to think of it like this. Imagine you are proceeding down a road and you come to a division of the way. One turning is your dummy and all that flows from the judgements and decisions that produced it. The other turning is our way. You've got to choose one or the other. There is no middle way.'

In the course of the conversation a thought struck me like a brick. The letter that I had written to Andreas was intended to be about design, layout and look, but in fact strayed over a boundary and trespassed on straightforward editorial decisions. No wonder Andreas had felt narked by it.

I told Matthew I'd just realised this rather embarrassing thing and he seemed merely to agree with me. But he also said several times that Alexander and I had been very influential.

222

I felt still in need of talk when Matthew rang off and luckily James rang. I told him about my conversation with Alexander and very solemnly explained our doubts and anxieties.

When I'd finished there was silence and then a laugh. 'Well!' said James. 'Well, well!'

'Mm.'

'Now look here,' he said in mock seriousness. 'I'm not having this. I mean, if there's going to be all this exciting resigning and such like, well, I want to resign too.'

'You are going to have to. My dear chap, if you think you are going to float off to Manila and have a very nice time, think again. This is a matter of principle!'

'Absolutely, good.'

Monday 21 July

Alexander spoke to me today. He is a little worried about the Wednesday meeting between the rebels and the *Independent*. At that meeting Thirkell's pages 2 and 3 should be examined with *Independent* dummy number 2.

The trouble is that the meeting must be held in the afternoon because Alexander is spending the morning at Prince Andrew's wedding to Sarah Ferguson. But if it's held in the afternoon it may be difficult for me to be there because of my *Telegraph* work. Heigh-ho!

At a party given this evening by Tony Howard I met Trevor Grove. He told me Max was after him to do Morrison's job. I told Trevor he should go instead to be features editor at the *Independent* and I explained that they have suddenly lost the man they had appointed. I gave him my pitch about the *Independent*, and how it should be the toppest of top qualities and he seemed to agree. In the end he said he'd be delighted to be contacted by Andreas and I said I'd fix it.

When I got home I rang Andreas but he was out so I tried Matthew who was engaged for ages. In the end I rang Stephen. But he had never heard of Trevor and told me they were thinking of either Frances Cairncross or Frank Johnson.

Tuesday 22 July

At 8.30 this morning I telephoned Andreas to suggest he got in touch with Trevor Grove. He said he would. He also told me that tomorrow, instead of a meeting like last time between six or seven people, he proposes to visit Nick Thirkell's office either alone or accompanied by Matthew.

This sounds a very promising development. He must be going to discuss terms with him. Is the battle won?

Tonight my farewell dinner was held in a private room at L'Escargot.

I now regret very much that Perry was not invited. The reason was simply that I misunderstood my role in issuing invitations and thought that as the *Daily Telegraph* was doing it they'd follow their own protocol.

The guests were Caroline, Max, Bill, Peter Utley (who arranged it), John Thompson, Morrison, Sue Davy, Colin Welch, Bridget Utley, Simon Heffer, Andrew Hutchinson, John Burgess, Bernard Foyster, Alexander Chancellor, Ed Pearce, Godfrey Barker and Charles Moore.

I had been dreading the occasion, but of course I enjoyed a lot of it very much indeed. It was very nice to see Caroline meeting for the first time people she'd heard me talk about so much, and to see them meeting her. I was particularly struck by the warmth and obvious genuine enthusiasm with which John Burgess and Bernard Foyster greeted her. They have been my nursemaids at the *Telegraph*. When they left at the end of the evening they came and shook hands with her again. John took her hand in both of his and said, 'Look after him, and if you want any advice about how to do it, give us a ring.'

There was a great deal of a sort of summer lightning flashing round the table, although no hint of rain or thunder. I mean that Morrison brooded on his fate somewhere down the table and Alexander and Caroline talked and talked about the *Independent*. Peter made dark criticisms of the old days in an undertone to me and at different times Charles and Bridget gossiped scandalously about some of our colleagues. A lively atmosphere of merry bitchiness and comradeship flickered through the talk and jokes, particularly as the night wore on and people got a little drunker.

I moved around the table to sit next to Alexander at one stage and we had a quick *Independent* board meeting. He said I must not leave too suddenly and he released me from my pact. If we leave we leave for our own reasons separately.

I understand from him that the next day's meeting has been changed to Friday. First of all, Andreas said it should just be him, Nick Thirkell, Alexander, Stephen and Matthew. Stephen said I should be there. The view was expressed that I was too hysterical, excitable and vehement. Stephen said I couldn't be excluded: 'You cannot treat a counter-revolutionary like that!'

In the end it was arranged that I could be there, but James couldn't. I'm not sure whether I want to be or not, but in a way I'd like to be in at the kill. I am also highly amused at the idea of me as this difficult, emotional colleague who raises the temperature all the time. So unlike the calm, good-natured, easy-going and retiring man I actually am.

Max made a charming speech about me and I mumbled a few embarrassed words of thanks. I had not prepared anything and spoke sitting down. I shouldn't think I spoke for longer than five or six seconds – literally. The guests clapped warmly, understanding my hopeless lack of skill at this sort of thing. I could hear Bill intoning in some sort of inane reflex, 'Very good speech!' Later he complimented me on my gift of taciturnity! He is still crazy.

Caroline told me later that Alexander had said that at the moment I was powerful in the newspaper industry because everyone wanted me. But it was important that I used that properly because in the nature of things it would not last.

Caroline responded to Alexander by drawing a distinction between having power and having influence. I have no power. What influence I have will not last, either.

Thursday 24 July

Yesterday went by in a blur. I cannot remember much about it. I do remember that when Penny Jackson rang me from features about my cartoon I told her about the loss of John Bryant the features editor from the *Independent*. She was horrified, and said she had joined the paper and had drawn her confidence in it largely because of his presence.

'What are we going to do?' she wailed. She came to my office to talk about it and went away pretty worried, saying, 'at least it's exciting, I suppose.'

A man came to help me move another load of stuff from my office. He is the *Independent*'s administration manager and his name is Mark Roberts. All that I have left now are a few cartoons, my latest cuttings book and my Vicky books. There is so little there that I can carry it away on my bike on Friday evening.

This morning I telephoned James. I am not certain whether I should go to tomorrow's meeting with Thirkell. Did that tipsy, chance conversation amount to a proper invitation? Is Andreas a bit fed up with my nagging? Has my influence, such as it is, already waned? James told me to ring Andreas and ask him. He said I should not be put down. I am uncertain what I will do. It might well be that my absence will make it easier for them to do what I want them to do.

I mentioned my meeting Trevor and my attempts to get him to the *Independent*. James had met Trevor the day after I had, and has also seen him at the *Independent* office but had not had a proper talk with him.

I said, 'When I suggested to Stephen that they get Trevor he told me he was considering giving the job to Frank Johnson.'

'If they did that I would resign,' said James.

'Would you really?' I asked.

'Yes, I would. Certainly.' He was speaking so flatly and calmly that I believed him. I often underestimate the strength of James's feelings about politics.

He mentioned that he too had not received an invitation to the

225

Thirkell meeting. I didn't tell him that it had been said that I could be there, but that if I was James couldn't be: it would have been mischievous, and would simply have aggravated his feelings of exasperation.

I realised the person I should ring was Trevor and find out what had happened. He was out so I spoke to Valerie, his wife. She told me he was very keen to go to the *Independent*, that he had seen Andreas but that a couple of other people were being interviewed.

I tried to get hold of Alexander at home and at the *Independent*. Instead I got Ed Steen. He told me the features editor front-runner was Ian Jack, one of the first Wapping refuseniks. I have heard him highly spoken of and I cheered up a bit.

'What about Trevor Grove?' I asked.

'Yes, he's been seen too.'

By the time I finished all these conversations I began to agree with Andreas and the others. I'm getting in too deep and trying to affect too many decisions. It is an absurd *folie de grandeur* and I am going to stop it . . .

Wednesday 30 July

I am writing this in France. I left London last Monday with Theo and his friend Luke to spend the whole of August at our house in the Lot-et-Garonne. Caroline and Alexander have stayed in London and are joining us at the end of the week.

Last night I telephoned her to see how things are going generally and she told me there was an urgent message to ring Nick Thirkell. After our last meeting he had been asked along to the *Independent* to meet Mr Mullins, the art director and co-designer with Mr Hawkey of the first dummy. Caroline told me that the meeting had gone badly. Mullins declared Nick's design 'too staid and too like *The Times*', then boxed himself into a corner by issuing an ultimatum – either Nick went or he did.

I was calling Caroline from an unlit telephone box in a little village square. It was 11.30 local time and very hot, the village was silent and the streets deserted. Suddenly some local boys on mopeds came clattering through the night. They paused noisily outside the shuttered café-bar laughing and shouting, then revved up and rode away. I waited, then asked Caroline to ring Nick and get him to dial the number of my phone box.

I sat for a while listening to Luke and Theo chatting sleepily in the car, parked a few yards away. Three of four minutes later the telephone buzzed and, like magic, there was Nick.

Caroline's résumé of the situation was accurate. All through the disastrous meeting Mullins, according to Nick, had made mistake after

226

mistake. He had been upset and had been very unkind about Nick's work. Andreas had continually made sympathetic noises and obviously tried to prevent a breach. Eventually Andreas had turned to Nick and asked for his reaction to all that had been said. Nick replied by saying he saw no way left for him to develop a productive working relationship with Mullins in the light of the vast difference between their respective design ideas and approaches to the job. He said, 'If you are planning on us working together, I think it's time I put on my coat.'

Nick and I talked for some time. I emphasised my support for him and assured him I spoke for Alexander and James too, but I soon realised he didn't need that reassurance. He reckoned that Andreas's problem was that he wanted to be liked and he just couldn't bear the idea of giving Mullins the push.

'He's not giving him the push,' I said, irritated by this formulation. 'He's offering him a new boss. If Mullins doesn't like it he can go, but no one is pushing him.'

'Yeah, I know that's right, but the worrying thing is that if Andreas can be so indecisive over the matter of Mullins what's going to happen when there is a really difficult decision to be made?'

'That is the real worry.'

'I wonder if he really *is* an editor.'

'That question has always been the most important one. My hope is that he *is* an editor, but not the powerful, influential, even dictatorial sort who shapes a paper and makes it an expression of his own idiosyncratic views and tastes, but the sort who is more like an impresario. He may be a man who can spot and attract talented people, weld them into a team and allow them to blossom under him.' Even while I said it I knew it sounded pretty unlikely. The man I was describing would never have produced that terrible dummy, for a start.

I said, 'If Andreas is hoping to avoid trouble by appeasing Mullins he is in danger of running into even worse trouble. Alexander and I would almost certainly leave the *Independent* if it's going to look the way Mullins wants it.'

After a bit, having listened to more details of Nick's meeting, I said, 'I believe that Andreas is actually convinced we are right. It's just that he can't quite see how to deal with Mullins. What's most likely to happen in the end is that Mullins will go and you'll get the job. We should see this as just another step in the process.' Nick agreed. So the question is, what might we do to help Andreas take this step, and what should we avoid in order to make it most easy for him?

We agreed there was nothing I could do. If I rang Andreas or either Matthew or Stephen it would almost certainly make things worse. Nick said he thought he'd like to speak to Andreas alone and try to convince him that he (Nick) was the best bet. I thought this was a good idea. I suggested that Nick's enthusiasm for the job was perhaps his greatest asset. When someone is in Andreas's position, embattled and uncertain, what is more attractive and helpful than someone expressing confident enthusiasm?

I had started this conversation feeling very troubled and depressed about the *Independent*. I finished it feeling slightly better.

The idea of going back to the *Telegraph* is pretty appalling, even if it's still possible now that they have taken on George Gale. The idea of going to *The Times* is dreadful. I would have to be paid an awful lot of money to dull the sheer unpleasantness of that. I feel let down by everyone. The *Telegraph* was shot under me, *The Times* has a horrible sort of brutality about it, the *Independent* is heading towards disaster as ad men and researchers shape its future. Perhaps old Gibbard might jack it in and I could find a slot on the *Guardian* . . .

I feel my professional life has reached a turning point. For twenty years I have felt I more or less knew and controlled my future. I look ahead now and see nothing. It is a frightening experience.

'If you do see Andreas don't tell him that Alexander and I might go if he makes the wrong choice.'

'I wouldn't dream of it,' said Nick. 'Anyway, it's nothing to do with me.'

'Our resignation would be the end, not a negotiating or bargaining point.'

'Yes, I know.'

For the time being at least all my excitement and optimism about the future has simply drained away. I feel exhausted and very depressed. If this holiday does not refresh me things are going to get pretty grim.

I wrote the above this afternoon. It was so hot we had come back from the lake to laze about in the cool house. It is now nearly ten o'clock at night and I have just come back from talking to Caroline on the phone. She told me the following dismal story.

Some time today Nick was informed by Andreas that he was going to continue with his original design team, but he asked whether Nick would come in as an adviser. The reason seems to be, as much as anything else, that Andreas is committed to producing a new complete dummy within a certain number of days and that he cannot do it without Mullins. Or, rather, he cannot find a replacement for Mullins (ie an art director) in the time. The next thing that happened was that Nick got a second telephone call from Andreas who made an astonishing suggestion. He asked whether Nick would work secretly on a design for the paper while the original team worked on in ignorance of their employer's apparent complete lack of confidence in them. Nick didn't say yes or no to this absurd plan, but he told Caroline he did not like the idea. She said to him, 'I hope you said no; it would hopelessly weaken your position.'

At one point a little later in the day Matthew rang Nick to say, don't worry, things were not as bad as they looked.

Finally, Andreas rang yet again to ask Nick to come to a meeting *tête-à-tête* tomorrow lunchtime. What on earth Andreas thinks he is up to absolutely beats me.

I feel very inclined to ring Max and say, 'Darling, forgive me, take me back.' Except that the idea of going on with the boring old *Telegraph* is deadly. Caroline said, do nothing, let them sort it out. I'll ring Nick tomorrow evening and find out what happened.

When I got back from this phone call I told Theo all about it. He said, 'It sounds to me as if that Andrey guy, whatever he's called, wants Nick Thingy and knows he's the best man but just doesn't know how to go about it.'

I said, 'I think you're right.'

He pointed to something at my feet and said, 'Well, just remember . . .' I looked down and saw a copy of *All's Well That Ends Well.*

Thursday, 31 July
I called Nick. Andreas has got himself into the most ridiculous mess. He has said to Mullins that he wants him to stay on but to produce a paper along the lines of Nick's design. The latest Nick has heard was that Mullins is digging his heels in and saying he wants to do the paper his way. Nick has been led to understand that should Mullins refuse to budge, he's out and Nick takes over. I thought that was impossible because if Mullins quits Andreas couldn't find a new art director in time. Nick said not so. They have found one.

'But,' I said, 'surely this means that Andreas is proposing to work with a man he now clearly has no confidence in at all?'

'That's right,' said Nick. 'I also told Matthew confidentially my view of Mullins.'

'What did he say?'

'He was loyal to Mullins and said he liked a lot of his work.'

Nick is to be told some time tomorrow what has been decided. I will call him in the afternoon to find out.

AUGUST

August, *Independent* dummy issue

Friday 1 August

Today was hot. The boys lazed around the house as I did a few chores. I washed up the breakfast things and prepared Alexander's room for his arrival tomorrow. At about 11.00, in the blazing heat, we went to the lake. In the mornings the lake tends to be fairly empty. One or two English families spread themselves out on the little beach; the French come after lunch.

From time to time the boys emerged from the cool water and I rubbed oil on their backs. I was afraid they would get burnt. By 12.30 my own back and face were beginning to smart.

I met some friends, the Baineses, and talked compulsively to them. I explained all about the *Independent* and the stupid mess over the design. The Bainseses have a holiday house nearby and we met years ago at the lakeside when our children played together. It was an odd meeting because it was only after we'd been talking together for some time that Jeremy Baines and I slowly realised that we'd been art students together twenty-odd years before at the Slade.

They listened to my babbling story with polite interest. I listened to my own voice with something like alarm. I sounded off, unusually intense and passionate, as if I were putting more emotion into this professional difficulty than it would hold.

'It all sounds very exciting,' said Judy.

'I hope it all goes well. Good luck; we look forward to the next instalment,' said Jeremy.

A few yards away their son Ben, now a towering young man with a pretty bare-breasted girlfriend, smoked cigarettes. His hair is cut in a curious style, very short all round below the ear line and very long on top. It makes him look permanently amazed, like a jack-in-the-box.

I heard myself saying, '. . . so if Andreas fucks up I'll have to go crawling back to the *Telegraph* or to *The Times*.'

The sun frizzled my mind. The lake sweltered and shone. What the hell was I talking about. We went home at about 2.00. I couldn't take any more sun.

The heat became so unbearable that we simply lay inside for most of the afternoon. I tried to read. The boys played with an ancient Scalectrix set. They had to keep repairing the cars and cleaning the metal track with emery paper.

I am reading *The Shooting Party*, Chekhov's only novel. Its melodramatic and violent story suits my mood perfectly.

At 4.30 English time I drove to the village to telephone Nick. He gave me the boring news that he hadn't heard from the *Independent*.

'Shit,' I said.

'I'm sorry, I didn't catch that,' said Nick.

232

Sweat poured down my back. The door of the telephone box kept swinging shut and the heat made me feel faint.

'I said, "Shit!" '

'Oh.'

I suggested he rings Andreas and if he learnt anything to call me back. I gave him the telephone box number.

I sat outside in some shade, wishing I'd brought Chekhov with me, or a sketchbook; not that there was much to draw except a dusty street and the stone wall opposite. Soon the telephone buzzed.

'Hello. It's me.' As if it would be anyone else putting a call through to this deserted street. Actually, that's not fair. Twice I've seen people waiting for calls outside this very box. 'Andreas is in a meeting so I couldn't speak to him. I left my home number so he may call me tonight. If I hear anything I'll call Caroline.'

'She's left; she's in Paris now.'

'Well, I'll leave it over the weekend and call you Monday or Tuesday.'

Before I went home I rang James and asked him to call me at my phone box. When he did I complained to him about the balls-up over the designers. He was very nice and said he'd ring Nick but I could tell from his voice he was also thinking about his phone bill.

I think I am a little crazy.

Saturday 2 August

Caroline and Alexander arrived this morning. They caught the Paris–Bordeaux sleeper last night and we picked them up in Ste-Foy as they got off the local train.

Later in the day I was driving somewhere in the tremendous heat when I had a fantasy. In it I rang Nick Thirkell and he said, 'It's all OK. I got the job. We're going to be OK.'

So I said, 'I'll buy you a bottle of champagne when I get home – and help you drink it.'

I savoured the scene and felt a small pang of regret as it faded.

Monday 4 August

It was cooler today after a tremendous thunderstorm last night. The day remained overcast and at five o'clock I took Luke and Theo to play tennis.

By the court I met Raphael Sommer, the cellist, who is here organising and playing in a music festival. His glum and rather surly teenage son was sitting nearby and we chatted about how difficult it is to keep teenagers amused and contented. Every now and then David Sommer said, 'I just wanna go home.'

Raphael and I agreed to meet later and perhaps bring our teenagers together.

233

I hadn't planned to, but when he left and the boys were playing tennis I went to the phone box and rang Nick Thirkell. I got straight through to him.

'Well, they said to me, thank you very much for all you've done; you've been an enormous help; we now see how to proceed, and we're going ahead with Mullins.'

I just felt nothing. I didn't swear. I had no fight left in me. Nick said, 'You should talk to Alexander; he isn't very happy.'

I asked Nick to ring the *Independent*, find Alexander and ask him to call in my phone box. A police van drew up outside and a gendarme got out and stood near the crossroads. He stared at nothing and I looked at him. After five minutes the phone buzzed and I heard Alexander sounding fed up and flat.

He told me how he'd come back from the States to find this miserable decision taken. He'd seen a new front page that Mullins had designed, more in line with the Thirkell approach.

'It's not as bad as his first dummy. It's a sort of halfway stage, neither one thing nor another. He's kept the eagle but moved it so that it's between The and Independent. It now reads The (eagle) Independent. He's lost that asymmetry that was so pleasing in Thirkell's layout.'

'Oh, fuck them.'

Alexander was extremely pessimistic about changing anything now. He said, 'I have lost my momentum. I have a job to do. I am going to Washington. I've got to set it all up. I want to get on with it.'

'Yeah, I bet.'

'I came back from the States and Andreas and Matthew looked complacent, pleased with themselves. Matthew said, "What are you worried about? You've won." ' Alexander snorted. 'I said to him that for a start it wasn't a battle, that there's no question of winning, it's a question of getting something right. And anyway, I was a bit miffed. We had gone away, you to France, me to the States, with certain assurances. We were led to believe things were going a certain way and no sooner were our backs turned than everything changed.'

Outside, the grey day was looking duller and duller. The gendarme was looking so bored that it occurred to me he might have fainted from ennui but somehow stayed upright.

Alexander said, 'Matthew talks in these senseless statistics. He says, "I agree with 98 per cent of what Nick says," or, "Mullins's new layout is 60 per cent there".'

I said to Alexander that I would fly home if he felt that would do any good. He thought I should. He said that Stephen kept saying he entirely agreed with us but that he would not do anything about it. He would not state his opposition to Mullins and remained apparently unmoved by the desperate need to get the design right.

234

Suddenly Alexander said, 'Stephen has just walked in; have a word with him.'

Stephen sounded concerned, friendly and reassuring. 'Nice to hear you. How are you?'

'I'm very, very unhappy.'

I gave him my spiel. I said it had been demonstrated beyond question that Thirkell was a superior designer to Mullins. It was obvious from the way that Andreas and Matthew had spoken to Thirkell that they had lost confidence in Mullins. Andreas had gone out of his way to say to me that he himself had a weak spot when it came to newspaper design. Yet, in spite of how much depended on it, in spite of clear opposition from Alexander and me, in spite of recognising Thirkell's qualities, they had decided to stay with Mullins. It was an idiotic, inexplicable and almost certainly catastrophic error. Mullins and Andreas and Matthew had had a go and produced the original dummy. It was worrying enough that things had gone *that* far wrong. That so little had been learnt from that dismal lesson was frightening.

Stephen murmured 'You're right' and 'Quite so' and 'Absolutely' from time to time.

Desperate and depressed, I tried to back off from my violent attack on Matthew and Andreas. 'I'm sorry,' I said, 'I suppose I'm sounding all hysterical and wild again. It's partly that I feel so far away, stuck in this little village surrounded by *vacanciers*.'

'You don't sound hysterical at all. You are making absolute sense.' His mood seemed to snap into a different gear. 'Right, I've got a plan,' he said. 'This evening I'll speak to Andreas and Alexander will speak to Matthew. We'll have another go.'

We fixed for Alexander to ring my phone box at ten o'clock local time and tell me what happened and to find out whether the *Independent* would fly me home to carry on the discussion.

Driving the boys back after their game, I met Caroline and Alexander in Raphael Sommer's car with his son David. The two boys were going to play tennis and Raphael was on his way to the church to rehearse with his orchestra for a concert later in the week. After dropping David and Alexander at the courts and Luke and Theo at home, Caroline and I sat in the church listening to Haydn and Bach. The music calmed me. The orchestra is made up of postgraduate students from the Royal Northern College of Music in Manchester. They are all very young and looked very contented. Caroline said as we left how lucky they were to be driven across France to a pretty little village to stay for a week and play; no wonder they looked happy.

Before ten o'clock I was back in my phone box waiting for Alexander to ring. A young French family were making an interminable call to the woman's parents. The man stood outside playing with his little daughters and a silly looking dog. At exactly ten they left, apologising for keeping me waiting, and the phone buzzed.

I felt cold. I am used by now to sweltering on this phone but tonight I was shivering. A few yards away members of the orchestra were sitting outside the café drinking and laughing. Alexander and I were not so cheerful.

Andreas has agreed to fly me home. The point of this interruption of my holiday isn't absolutely clear. Later, talking about it with Caroline, I came to the conclusion I was making one last bid to get rid of the influence of Mullins and replace him with Nick T. There was no other reason to go. I can certainly get by without a lecture from Matthew about how I have 'won' and how Mullins is really very good.

Alexander described a conversation he'd had with Stephen.

ALEXANDER: Why don't you express your doubts about Mullins to Andreas and Matthew? You say you agree with us but you don't *do* anything. You are in a better position than any of us to change their minds.

STEPHEN: Well, I'm going to give you an answer that you will not find satisfactory. I do agree with you – but I don't think it's quite as important as you seem to. Neither do Andreas and Matthew.

Alexander sounded exasperated with this reply. I was more than just exasperated. I was appalled.

While we were talking Caroline cycled up through the village. She had decided to call her sister on a family matter. I said to Alexander I'd try to get a flight tomorrow or the next day. While Caroline spoke to Louise I rode the bike up and down trying to get warm. A van arrived and picked up the musicians. I cursed Andreas and Matthew.

There is something I've been meaning to mention in this journal. Months ago Andreas asked me to look out for cartoonists, illustrators and comic strip artists who might be employed by the *Independent*. I at once thought of Colin Wheeler, an artist whose work I have liked and admired for years.

I got Colin to redraw a comic strip he'd devised but not yet found a home for, thinking that it might be very good for the *Independent*. I said I thought the strip was promising and that Colin might also draw a front-page daily pocket cartoon.

Stephen said, 'You can make the choice. If he's good enough for you, that's OK. We want you to find artists for us.'

This brought me up with quite a start. It's one thing to bring along a suggestion. It's quite another to make a decision.

I found I couldn't do anything about Colin. I put his strip away with all my things in my new room and more or less forgot about him. I said to myself, I'll make up my mind what to do after the holiday when I am refreshed and rested and more confident.

The point is, Andreas is having to make that sort of decision all the time and it's not easy. I shouldn't really curse him.

Wednesday 6 August
I am sitting in a bar at Bordeaux airport. I have a flight to London in an hour or so and a return flight on Friday morning.

Caroline and the boys dropped me a short while ago and have driven on to the beach for a swim in the Atlantic breakers. I half wish I was going with them and I'm half excited at the idea of dashing away to London to try to sort something out. Caroline and I often say to each other over decisions of this sort, 'It's worth having a go.' It's not so much that I think I'll achieve anything at all, but more that I'd feel regret if I don't try.

They're calling my flight.

As we crossed over Cherbourg clouds covered the coastline and the sea. The captain had said the weather was poor in London and had warned us it might rain.

Over London I could pick out the *Telegraph* building, Regent's Park and then our house and Hampstead Heath. While we taxied to the bay the captain apologised for the bumpy landing.

I took the tube to Old Street, changing once at King's Cross. The squalor was something awful.

It was the oddest feeling to walk into the *Independent* and see Alexander and Stephen at their desks. Half of me was still in France.

I was shown Mullins's new-look front page. It was much worse than Alexander had described. The layout was curiously cut in half about two-thirds of the way down and an advert for whisky was exactly balanced at the bottom right by a weather chart and a map at the bottom left. I felt the whole effect was second-rate and very dull. There was a coloured picture across three columns.

When Andreas joined us in Stephen's office he was accompanied by Matthew who hardly opened his mouth and soon left saying he had to see someone else.

We made small-talk for a while and then Andreas said that he'd been thinking about the Mullins–Thirkell problem a great deal. Every now and then while he pondered, he said, an image of my fierce and anxious face would rise before him. He laughed and pretended to have been afraid. Then he became serious and said that his final decision was that Mullins should be the designer of the paper but that he sincerely hoped that Thirkell would continue to act as adviser and consultant on a part-time basis. He said that there was not the faintest possibility of Mullins

237

being got rid of and that fact must be the basis of anything that was said.

I asked how it was that Mullins, who I understand to have been taken on as an art director to Hawkey, a newspaper designer, had suddenly been promoted to full designer. I said to Andreas, 'As far as I can tell, the only person who has raised the question of Mullins leaving is Mullins. All you, or anyone else, has suggested is that he now works to, and with, a different designer. If he doesn't want to, that's his business.'

Andreas also seemed genuinely puzzled by this change in Mullins's rank and admitted that it was just something Mullins had assumed. Alexander made the point that he felt Mullins has challenged Andreas's authority by refusing to work with Thirkell.

'I mean, you are the editor and it's customary for editors in your position to try out as many designers as they want until they get the right thing.'

I could almost see this shot going home. I don't think Andreas liked the idea of anyone weakening his editorial role. Stephen said, 'There is something else that must be said about Mullins, and that is his contract with the *Observer* does not in fact run out until the end of September. If we use him we will only have a part-time designer all through the critical weeks that run up to our launch. Thirkell, of course, can give us his full attention.'

I tried a different tack.

'It seems quite clear that all of us believe Thirkell to be a superior designer.' I looked at Andreas and said, 'You have demonstrated your confidence in him in several ways. First of all, you liked and were won over by his work but, much more important than that, you have been extremely anxious to keep him on board, even if only as an adviser or consultant. I believe that we should have the best, however difficult it is to secure him.'

Andreas replied that he felt committed to Mullins because of promises made. But that line of argument had already been demolished. He then gave his real reason for being afraid of turning to Thirkell.

'My worry is that I will lose my entire design team just as we start producing daily dummies. His arrival will provoke a walk-out. We'd almost certainly lose Mullins.'

I replied that Mullins might or might not decide to go, but in the end that must not force Andreas into a bad decision. I also felt that should Mullins need to be replaced, that would be possible. I said I did not understand this side of the problem but simply assumed it was all solvable. My approach began and ended with my conviction that the look of the paper was critical.

Soon Alexander and Stephen joined in; the mood remained relaxed and friendly. There were several times when we all laughed at some aside or sudden interjection, and neither Andreas nor any of the rest of us ever turned the discussion into a battle or confrontation. Nevertheless I had a sense right from the start that, while I couldn't see how to budge Andreas from his dependence on Mullins, the meeting was going my way. This was less because Alexander and I marshalled our arguments more forcefully than Andreas, but more because we had something to believe in.

There came a time when we had more or less covered all sides of the question and Andreas said, 'Right, let's go round the room. Stephen, what do you think we should do?'

'I think Mullins should press on with his work on the next dummy,' said Stephen, 'but that Thirkell should be asked to produce a complete design for the whole paper. If when we have that design we agree that it's what we want, he should be given the job.'

Andreas listened and nodded in apparent agreement. 'Nick?'

'I think Nick Thirkell should be given the job of designing the paper. So far everything he has done has been approved of, admired and liked. He has shown his ability and readiness to take and understand a brief. Mullins should be given the opportunity to work with him. I'm not saying that Thirkell is a genius; I am saying he is very good and by far the best designer you've had working on the *Independent*. I think you should go for the best.'

'Alexander?'

'I agree with Nick, but I also know you're not going to do that. Even though that's what I want, it's unrealistic to suggest it. Therefore I say, with Stephen, you should ask Thirkell to design the whole paper while Mullins is going on with whatever he is doing. I'm quite confident that Thirkell will produce work so much better than anyone else that in the end his design will be the one used.'

Andreas immediately accepted this plan. He said he would ring Thirkell and ask him to do a complete dummy in secret. The clear understanding was that, should Thirkell's work be generally approved of, he would be appointed designer.

Suddenly it was over. Thirkell was on board again. I was taken completely by surprise by the speed of this development. We all stood up.

'It's my insurance,' said Andreas. 'That's what I'm going to call it. I am insured now. I like that!' He looked cheerful.

Alexander and Stephen both wandered out of the room and I sat down with Andreas for a few minutes alone. Still not quite believing what had happened, I said, 'Well, what's next? What are you going to do now?'

'I'm going to ring Thirkell.'

'And tell him . . . ?'

'To design a whole paper.'

'When?'

'Not now, I've got someone coming. Oh, not tomorrow either, I'm in Manchester. Er . . . Friday . . . I'll ring him on Friday.'

I thought to myself, I must get Nick telephoned sooner than that, before anyone changes their mind. But for the moment I let it pass.

Ten minutes later when Stephen joined Alexander and me in the pub he was smiling and jovial. He said, 'It couldn't have gone better. Marvellous.'

I told him that I thought Nick should be rung before Friday and he said that could be arranged. 'Don't worry,' he said. 'It's all going to happen. It's fixed.'

'Things have been known to change.'

'Don't worry. Andreas has said he'd do it. That means he'll do it.'

Alexander gave me a lift home and I said to him that I wanted to ring Thirkell myself. I felt it was a good idea to keep him informed, and let him know what was happening. I didn't want him getting fed up and pushing off to another project. Alexander saw no objection.

When I finally rang Nick it must have been about 8.30 or 9.00. I told him everything and he listened solemnly and said, 'Good! Great!' when I finished. He said he would express proper surprise, even amazement, when he heard officially, and not let on that we'd talked.

The only thing I said to him, apart from an account of the meeting, was to mention Andreas's anxiety about losing his design team. 'I think you should find a way of reassuring him that, whatever happens, you can actually produce the paper.'

'Yes, of course.'

'If you really, realistically think you can,' I added rather quickly and with perhaps a note of alarm.

'Of course I can. That's not a worry,' he said.

Thursday 7 August

This morning I did a bit of shopping. I bought tea, Rotring refills and a drawing pad for Alexander (my Alexander), and some Oil of Ulay for Caroline.

At about 11.00 I went to the *Independent*. Again the squalor of the London underground made me shudder. Stephen was in his office and told me at once that Thirkell had been rung and had accepted.

'Who told him? I thought Andreas was away.'

'Matthew rang him.'

'What is Matthew's reaction to this plan? After all, he had presumably been in favour of the Mullins option.'

'He is bored by the subject of the design. He can't see what to do and

240

therefore doesn't really care very much. What Matthew likes is a problem that can be solved; then he picks it up and worries it, like a terrier. He goes on and on until the solution is found. The question of the design isn't that sort of problem. It's all to do with taste and so on.'

'So he was quite happy to ring Thirkell?'

'Perfectly. We're going to meet him at 3.00 on Monday at his office to brief him.'

'Who is?'

'Me, Andreas and Matthew.'

Alexander had asked me to join him and Simon Courtauld, the editor of *Country Life*, for lunch and at about 1.00 we set off for the Blackfriars branch of El Vino. We wondered whether to walk but decided it would take too long. As Alexander was hailing a taxi I saw a bus pull up with Blackfriars Bridge on it.

'Hey, there's a bus,' I said.

'Really,' said Alexander, feigning fascinated surprise. We got on it. 'This is really exciting,' he said.

We talked for a while and as we came round St Paul's Alexander said, 'This is wonderful – *and* it seems to be taking us in the right direction.' At Ludgate Circus he had a moment of real alarm. 'We should turn left here!' he cried, starting to his feet.

'We *are* turning left here,' I said.

'Oh, so we are. Terrific.'

It is extremely difficult to re-create the way in which his only half-assumed amazement that a bus could be used in this way was so comical. But it was. He is very funny but he doesn't make wisecracks. It is his view of the world that makes me laugh. He is continually surprised by the way people behave and has an ironical and pessimistic way of describing it. He is rueful and apparently always expects everything to go wrong. He is also very honest which means he is indiscreet because he just tells the truth. He cannot be bothered to watch what he says.

We sat at a table with Trevor Grove, Peter Hillmore and Oliver Pritchett. Trevor told me he'd got fed up with the *Independent*'s dithering and had more or less accepted a job from Max. He is going to take over from Morrison. He asked about the *Telegraph*. We agreed he'd get on just fine with Don. He seems to know Max well and I think he'll do well there.

I said I was sorry the *Independent* had let him slip through their fingers.

'All decisions there seem to be taken interminably slowly by general group discussions,' he said. 'It's all incredibly long-winded and indecisive.'

Simon Courtauld joined us and soon he, Alexander and I got up to go downstairs to the restaurant.

241

'By the way,' said Trevor, 'my friend Tony Mullins is pretty fed up with you.'

I sat down again. 'Go on,' I said.

'Well – you brought this other bloke in, didn't you?'

'I'm only the cartoonist,' I said.

'All right, he's pretty fed up with the *Independent*, then.'

'Why?'

'Well, they keep mucking about. He doesn't know where he is.'

'As far as I know they are trying out various designs. I don't see why he should be fed up with me about that.'

Trevor looked at me as if to say, all right, you don't have to bullshit me.

'I thought his latest design was rather good,' he said.

I thought, 'Oh-oh!'

'I also liked the original lower-case masthead, in – what was it called – Gibraltar?'

I began to think it was lucky Trevor wasn't the features editor. With Trevor behind him, Mullins would have been in an impregnable position.

'Well, I'm sorry if he's fed up. But I think he's silly. There's bound to be some experimenting and trying-out as they develop a design and layout.'

Trevor smiled.

Downstairs Alexander was giving Simon a blow-by-blow account of the last two days at the *Independent*. We'd been sworn to secrecy by Stephen and obviously it would be a bit embarrassing if Mullins got to know what's going on.

Alexander read my mind. 'I tell Simon everything,' he explained.

'Oh, well, that's OK then,' I said. I thought it is a matter of time, probably about two or three hours at the most, before Mullins knows everything, too.

While we were talking – by now I was being quite as indiscreet as Alexander – Peter Paterson joined us.

'Ah – the rebels seen together in public,' he said.

'What do you mean?' said Alexander.

'Well, I gather that you two sit at one end of the room with your plans for the *Independent*, and the editor with one or two hangers-on sits at the other end with his.'

'What nonsense.'

'I hear you cannot even agree on a typeface for the masthead.'

'Pooh!'

'And that you openly scheme and manoeuvre to get your way.'

'Oh, come on.'

242

'And that everyone is divided and uncertain and doesn't know what's going to happen next.'

'This is just the sort of meaningless, unfounded tittle-tattle that always surrounds a venture of this sort,' I said.

'I thought the whole thing about the *Independent* was that it was a unique phenomenon, and that there's never been a venture like it before,' Peter said.

'All right, this is just the sort of meangingless, unfounded tittle-tattle that always surrounds a unique phenomenon of this kind.'

Peter was extremely well-informed. He was on the whole right about everything to do with disagreements at the *Independent*.

'You've got it wrong,' said Alexander.

'I'm afraid that's not a good enough denial. I won't accept that,' said Peter.

'I am in a position categorically to deny everything you've suggested,' I said. 'Furthermore, a spirit of unparalleled unity and cooperation exists at the *Independent*.'

'Pathetic,' said Peter. 'Just not good enough.'

'You've been misinformed,' Alexander said.

'You're a lying sod,' I said.

'Better,' said Peter, 'but still quite unconvincing.'

When I had been a bit surprised by how much Peter knew, Alexander said, 'Oh, that's probably my fault. I've been shooting my mouth off all over the place.' He's no more indiscreet than any of us. He just admits it, that's all.

When I got home I rang Nick to see what he thought about it all. He said he'd had a phone call from Matthew and it had all gone just as I had said it would.

'I expressed amazement when I heard you were in London,' he said.

'Good! I'm going back to France tomorrow.'

'Have a good time.'

'I'll try.'

'We'll have a bloody good-looking paper,' said Nick.

Wednesday 13 August

The last few days since I returned from my quick dash to London have been ordinary holiday days. We had some sun and one spectacular downpour. The latter was so violent water cascaded through the roof and even seeped through the walls. We got soaked. For days afterwards people asked each other about the damage caused by the rain. Like everyone else I spent the next day or two trying to repair the roof and prepare for the next storm. But it hasn't come. We've had hot sunshine.

At breakfast this morning someone knocked on the kitchen door. I expected it was a meter reader or a neighbour's child. We were sitting

243

on a terrace at the back of the house but when I went through to the kitchen I saw at once it was the lady from the Post Office with a telegram.

I took the blue folded paper back to the terrace and we all looked at it. Theo wanted to open it and I gave it to him. I was in no hurry. I felt certain the telegram was from someone at the *Independent* and I felt anxious. This could be the final decisive information – but which way did things go . . . ?

Theo began tearing it open and I took it from him and unfolded it. The spelling was odd but the message was clear.

NULLINS HAS RESIGNED.
THIRKLE FULLY ON BOARD.
REGARDS. STEPHEN AND JAMES

A wave of something like exultation rushed through me. I raised my fist like a footballer who has just scored, and began wondering what had happened.

The telegram had been sent on Tuesday evening. The meeting with Nick Thirkell had been on Monday afternoon at 3.30. It has not taken Mullins long to jack it in. I put off telephoning Stephen until about 6.00 pm local time. I don't know why. I was curious to know what had happened but a lethargy had come over me. If it was all over, what difference did it make how it had happened? I rang in the end because I thought I really must respond to such an important telegram.

I got through to Bibi, Stephen's secretary. (I like her name very much. It sounds extremely friendly. I always think of it as two Bs and B is a very nice letter.) She rang me back in my phone box. Stephen came on the line, pleased and excited.

'Isn't it marvellous? It all turned out all right.'

'Tell me the sequence; what actually happened?'

'Well, yesterday Andreas got a letter from Mullins saying that as the *Independent* was no longer going to be the exciting-looking, new modern, mould-breaking paper it was originally intended to be, he felt there was no place for him on it.'

"What had precipitated it? Why write it that day?'

'I think he knows we wanted a more classical newspaper, that Thirkell's influence was very strong and he just didn't like it.'

'Do you think he knew about your new arrangement with Thirkell and the meeting the day before?'

'No, absolutely not. Not a chance.'

I was sure Stephen was wrong about this. I told him that Trevor Grove had told me Mullins was angry with me '. . . because you brought that other bloke in.' Mullins was well informed.

Stephen simply did not believe he could possibly have had a clue

244

about what was going on. He said the meeting with Thirkell had contained a shock: Nick had at once accepted the job, but also named his price – £1500 per page. This was so expensive that he had been asked to produce only ten pages. However, the next day Mullins resigned and as then the *Independent* would only be paying one designer, not two, the price became acceptable.

Nick came to the *Independent* with one of his partners and for the next six weeks will work full-time on the paper.

Alexander came on the line, sounding very contented. He teased me slightly.

'Listening to Stephen it sounds as though you are not as pleased and happy as you should be.'

'You know me – never satisfied.'

'You should be.'

'I am really. Honestly. I am absolutely delighted and very relieved.'

He said, 'I heard what Stephen was saying about Mullins not knowing what was going on with Nick Thirkell. I'm not so sure he's right about that.'

'Nor am I. How has Andreas taken this turn of events?'

'He appears to be absolutely thrilled to bits. I had to go to lunch yesterday, here at the *Independent*, and Andreas was all smiles and seemed quite excited about something. At one point he said to me, "Isn't it extraordinary that that insurance was called in within twenty-four hours?" ' Alexander gave his spluttering laugh. 'I didn't have the faintest idea what he was talking about. I didn't dare ask for fear of making an utter fool of myself. At that time I didn't know about Mullins's letter and I'd forgotten Andreas had called Thirkell his "insurance". Anyway, he's over the moon, as they say.'

He asked when I was coming back and I said on 30 August.

'I'll have gone by then.' He is leaving for Italy in a week or so but will be passing through London sometime in September on his way to Washington. 'Perhaps we'll meet then and have a drink or something.'

'Yes, let's. Well, goodbye. I've really enjoyed all this and I'm glad it's turned out the way it has.'

'Yes, the battle is won.'

'It's not a battle,' I said, mimicking him. 'It's merely a discussion about getting the design right.'

Splutter! Splutter!

'I know. I know it's not a battle; but I keep thinking it is – and that we won.'

'So do I,' I said.

'See you in September then.'

'OK.'

'Bye.'

'Bye.'

After this I more or less stopped thinking about the *Independent* for the rest of the holidays. Now and then I tried to imagine what working for it would be like, but the future was unusually blank for me. Time stood still. Caroline and I mucked about in the garden. We drove with the boys to the Pays Basque for a few days and hired canoes and spent the day paddling down the Dordogne.

Saturday 30 August

We arrive back home at about 3.30 or 4.00 this afternoon and unpacked the car and said hello to Hiroko, our lodger, and to Moppet the cat, and a couple of hours later made a cup of tea and sat down to look at the letters.

The traditional groaning at the bills and the reading of jolly postcards identical to the ones we sent had hardly begun when the telephone rang. It was Alexander Chancellor, surprisingly still in London. I was a little alarmed to hear him say, 'Could we possibly meet; perhaps for lunch tomorrow?'

It wasn't the invitation, it was the tone of voice that worried me. He said, 'Look, I won't talk now, you must be very busy, just back from your holiday and all that sort of thing.'

'Hang on,' I said. 'Just give me some idea of what's the matter. I'll be awake all night wondering, otherwise.'

The story he told me was incredible.

What has happened is that when Thirkell was taken on as designer and a fee worked out, he announced that in a week's time he was starting a fortnight's holiday. Andreas was disconcerted, but Thirkell and his two partners, Carroll and Dempsey, said don't worry, they would produce an entire dummy in a week. This hopelessly unrealistic proposal was accepted by Andreas, and everyone waited in considerable excitement for the *Independent*, as it were, to be born. When the week was up Thirkell, Carroll and Dempsey arrive with their dummy newspaper and presented it at a meeting with Andreas, Stephen, Matthew and Alexander plus two new characters called Crosier and Lloyd. These last are *Independent* staff men who as far as I can tell are called production editors, and are technicians-cum-designers or layout men, super-subs who actually put the paper together at night.

Thirkell had hardly begun to speak when, as he told me later, 'like wolves' Crosier and Lloyd began a merciless attack on the design. They launched themselves even at the front page which had so pleased everyone the first time it was seen.

No one defended Thirkell, who ploughed on past pages two and three and revealed the features, the centre spread, the City and arts pages.

Alexander was appalled. All except the first three pages were more or less identical to Mullins's original design, but if anything worse. The dummy was a disaster. It was an unharmonious rag-bag and there was no support for it from anywhere. Crosier and Lloyd found a few good things to say about the sub-Mullins bits but sustained their bitter attack.

Thirkell's optimism and excitement was destroyed and as the atmosphere became unbearably tense Andreas suddenly exploded. He said the work was a disgrace and that it amounted to nothing less than a fraud. He said one or all of Thirkell's team must undertake then and there to be in the office working on the design every day until the launch, or he would not pay them a penny. Matthew (as Stephen told me later) interjected, 'This is a rip off . . .', 'disgraceful effort . . .' and similar blustering expressions of fury. Thirkell's men left the meeting to discuss the situation and returned immediately to say they'd never been treated in such a shameful way before and were quitting at once.

The débâcle was over.

Alexander said he felt bad about not having done something to stop Lloyd particularly from being so nasty but the fact was he could not bring himself to support Thirkell's awful work.

In the next couple of days he had tried with some success to bring about some sort of peace and reconciliation between Thirkell and Andreas. They spoke to each other and it looked as if something could be worked out, but Thirkell more or less wrecked any chance of salvaging anything by disappearing to the Isle of Wight for his holiday. All that had been agreed was that when he returned on 8 September he would look in as some sort of design consultant. Meanwhile Crosier had been producing page after page in a style reminiscent of Thirkell's front page but nothing like as good.

The only other news Alexander had was that a TV man called Morrison had been appointed features editor and someone else with a lot of nerve had been fired for putting a Mercedes on his expenses. Bruce Bernard was given a three-week trial period as picture editor but left after two weeks for reasons that were not clear to Alexander.

So the *Independent* starts producing daily dummies the day after tomorrow without a design or a designer and without a picture editor.

'Christ,' I said, 'I can hardly believe it.'

I sank at once into a dull and depressed state, muttering about going back to the *Telegraph* and moaning. Alexander rallied me by telling me not to be stupid. What he actually said was that I shouldn't talk nonsense and that I'd look a complete bloody fool if I left now.

We began to look for something that could be done. All we came up with was that Thirkell must be got back. I said I'd ring Thirkell and find out what he was thinking and where he stood, and that I'd also ring Stephen to find out what I could from him about Andreas's feelings and plans.

Alexander had spoken a couple of times to Thirkell in the Isle of Wight but he wouldn't budge. His holiday was obviously terribly important to him, perhaps for some private family reason. Alexander's view of Stephen was that he was incurably wet. Stephen has a way of appearing to be extremely anxious about things but incapable of doing anything to improve them; if not incapable, he is unwilling. Perhaps he sees himself as too junior to Matthew and Andreas to be able to take them on. Perhaps he believes he is more effective gently wringing his hands to draw attention to problems rather than by fighting against decisions he thinks are catastrophic.

Several times Alexander wailed to me, 'I'm supposed to be the Washington correspondent, not a bloody design consultant. I've got a job I'm supposed to be doing.' I feel the same. Apart from all this I've got to start producing daily cartoons in a couple of days. It's always hard starting work after a holiday. This time it's going to be much, much worse.

I telephoned Thirkell in the Isle of Wight. He said he was still very keen to be the *Independent*'s designer and said, after a bit of pressure from me, that to prove how keen he was he would break his holiday and come back early. His account of the terrible meeting identified Lloyd as his chief persecutor. He also said he felt that he'd let me and Alexander down badly and that it has been 'sheer madness' to say that he'd design the whole paper in a week.

Sunday 31 August
At 9.30 I telephoned Alexander. His wife Susie answered and I asked her whether she had any bright ideas about what to do – it was Susie who first thought of opposing the Mullins/Hawkey dummy with an actual design of our own, and I have always half hoped she would come up with a bold idea of that sort when difficulties appeared overwhelming. I told her this and she laughed and said she had nothing to offer in that way. The whole thing was just an incredible mess. With Alexander it was arranged that I'd ring Andreas and ask whether we could visit him in a couple of hours to discuss the design. Alexander and I agree to meet before that to clarify our arguments and suggestions.

It turned out that Andreas was in the country. By a bit of luck I got his number and rang him there. He was relaxed and friendly and did not appear at all alarmed by the turn of events. He was a bit disappointed but felt everything was proceeding smoothly. I told him that I could get Thirkell back early from the Isle of Wight and that I felt it was terrifically important. By coming back now he would demonstrate his commitment to the *Independent* and by asking him back we would show

248

our confidence and dependence on him. His early return would have the further advantages of giving him more time when time was critically short.

Andreas appeared to agree in principle but he has a peculiar way of withdrawing from a commitment. He tends to ramble off into metaphor. He said it was good news that Thirkell was being so cooperative but he didn't want him back too early. 'We are all geared up to produce our first proper printed copies of the *Independent* on Monday. I don't want Thirkell around because I don't want to introduce grit into the machine.'

He meant it was just not the time to tinker with the design.

My view was that if Thirkell were to be given the job of designing the paper it was vital he should be around during the coming week to learn as much as possible about practical problems of newspaper production. Also, you simply cannot give someone encouragement they need if you think of them as 'grit in the machine'. But I let it pass. Andreas said he'd like to meet us and that it would have to be this evening at 9.00. He said he'd come to my house.

He urged me not to be depressed or to sound so anxious. 'Things are nothing like as bad as you seem to think.' He praised Crosier and Lloyd and was guarded about Thirkell but prepared to accept that the worst aspects of their disastrous dummy were not entirely his fault.

When I reported all this back to Alexander he said this evening was out because he was having dinner with Bron Waugh but he said he'd come round to my house right now to talk and plan some more. We finished up sitting in the garden with Caroline, having first coffee, then bread and cheese and cold meat and a very good bottle of wine. We spent all the two hours or so he was there talking about the *Independent*. Much of the time we were laughing at the awfulness of what was going on, and gossiping as we always do about how absurd people are. I enjoy indulging in this malicious and critical joking, and everyone I know does it about everyone else all the time. It is curiously undestructive. You can think someone is an utter fathead and still be pleased to see them and enjoy working with them.

One of the little things Alexander told me was that Crosier had redesigned the eagle that Thirkell put by the masthead. It is now a horrible spiky, flying bird carrying a rolled up copy of the *Independent*. When he saw it Alexander thought it was so awful he had burst out laughing. And when Alexander bursts out laughing it is quite explosive.

Before he left to take his daughter out to lunch we made a list of things I must say to Andreas tonight about Thirkell and how he must be deployed. It was all to do with practical tying-down sort of things, like where will he sit, what will Crosier be told about his arrival, who will he be briefed by, how long will he stay, etc. I wrote down some of

249

these things but I lost the bit of paper and eventually faced Andreas without it and had to rely to my memory.

When Andreas turned up, at about 9.30 this evening, I was struck by how exhausted he seemed and how he was making an effort to be calm and measured in his remarks. Perhaps he could be more accurately described as being under great stress. A strange, wild mood lurked just below the surface of his outward behaviour. I went through what I could remember of my list and all his answers and reassurances were just what I hoped they would be, but all were without conviction. I felt he was making the noises he knew I wanted to hear, but he was not committed to deal with the obvious consequences of his declared intentions. I did not feel sure of how far he would back a Thirkell decision against opposition from, say, Crosier or Lloyd. As I pressed him I ran at once into Andreas's madder side. His eyes glittered and his voice hardened and rose a tone or two as I yapped at his heels. I provoked him into a strange muddled statement about Mullins and Lloyd.

He said he was glad Mullins had gone because he felt let down by him. Mullins had behaved very badly. I was uncertain why he would speak like that but he soon made it clear.

'If someone joins me they get my complete and unswerving loyalty. I will stick by them come what may. Right or wrong I will always stand by them. I did to Mullins. He repaid me by walking out.' I felt this was a bit unfair on poor old Mullins who had been a bit mucked about, after all. But the real problem about what Andreas was saying was in the first bit. If he gives all his new colleagues absolute loyalty and support, what happens when his colleagues disagree? Presumably he passionately supports both sides.

He went on to make it clear that one of the people he now gives devoted backing to is Nigel Lloyd, the production editor. Praise was poured on the guy. He was an absolutely first-class man, honest, hard-working, dependable and thoroughly decent through and through. Andreas mentioned a tragedy that had recently struck Nigel Lloyd's family. The way this was introduced into the conversation tied up my feelings in what I thought was an unfair way. I have the deepest sympathy for Lloyd for the loss he suffered but that does not affect my opposition to his professional judgement. Immediately after telling me this personal and distressing detail Andreas also said that Lloyd had come to him no fewer than five times to say that unless the *Independent* went back to the old Mullins design there would be a disaster. In Lloyd's view the traditional design of the paper that I favour will simply not work.

Andreas emphasised yet again that he has a blind spot when it comes to layout and design. This is unnerving, because if he cannot tell a good design from a bloody awful one how can he confidently and effectively support Thirkell if and when he produces good work that Crosier or Lloyd don't like? I tried to put this to Andreas but it was difficult; he signalled quite clearly that he did not want to be pushed.

While we talked he ate what was left of the salami, ham, pâté and cheese that we'd got in this morning. He didn't drink much because he was driving but I was quite surprised by how he steadily cleared the plates.

At one point I dared to suggest that too much democracy in a small organisation (as opposed to a whole country) was dodgy because it could lead to decision by committee, with consequent loss of clarity. He said flatly that he had his own way of doing things and he found it worked very well. He also mentioned his own quick temper, describing it as 'a problem': rare and only certain things provoked it, but it was devastating when it came. He said one of Thirkell's comrades had set it off during the terrible meeting.

'It was something he did that was aggressive, a tilt of the head, a way of lifting his chin. I thought to myself, "The only thing to do is to pound him" – so I did.'

Although he'd just said his temper was a problem, the last remarks were made proudly, almost boastfully.

Underlying what was being said, Andreas had a theme. It was that everything was all right; I needn't be depressed; nothing was as bad as I appeared to think it was; we were on course. I think this is utter bullshit, but I can't quite work out whether what's needed is panic or calm.

I am cast down. My confidence in the *Independent* is as low as it's ever been. Everything I have tried to achieve over the look and design of the paper has failed. I am certain that it will appear looking less good than any of the existing quality papers including the *Telegraph*. My dream was that a super, clean, elegant paper would appear on the news-stands, a paper that would make readers feel at home and in good hands. Fat chance now. . . .

Among the subjects that cropped up during the couple of hours Andreas was with us was the departure from the *Telegraph* of Morrison Halcrow. I'd heard that he'd finally got the bullet. I must find out what happened. I mentioned Tony Howard. Alexander had lunch with Tony a few days ago and suggested he might write a political column for the *Independent*. Tony, to my surprise, has not pooh-poohed the idea. Andreas, however, would not discuss it with me. He merely said, 'Oh, yes, Alexander said something about that – I may give Tony a ring in a few days.'

I remembered a time when finding a top columnist was considered vital to the paper. Alexander had told me that his overture to Tony was stimulated by him hearing that in the absence of a columnist Matthew and John Torode would each write a weekly column.

I also realised that Mullins had not been replaced although at one time losing Mullins had been one of Andreas's big anxieties. I asked whether he was to ever be replaced and he was vague again.

'Perhaps. There is a very good No. 2 who is doing all right. McGuinness. I think I over-valued Mullins or the need for an art editor at one time.'

As usual our conversation was friendly and enjoyable, albeit at times alarming. And Andreas was so tired I felt a lot of sympathy for him.

Almost his last words to me were, 'We expect a drawing from you tomorrow.' A chill went through me at the thought.

SEPTEMBER

September, *Independent* dummy issue

Today is my 51st birthday. I feel more middle-aged than ever. Usually I think of myself being about 34, sometimes about 14, but now I feel all of 51.

I wanted to get to the office early because there is so much to do but I didn't get away until after 11.00, and on the way I stopped off to get a new spark plug. The engine sounded a lot better once I had fitted it. In my office a dream-like mood took me over. I wandered in small circles vaguely looking for pens and books. I picked up bits of paper and set them down again. I pushed my huge new drawing-board against the wall and arranged a table near it. The lead from the Anglepoise lamp would not reach the wall socket.

From time to time I drifted round the building, on several occasions going to the wrong floor in my confused state as I tried to find the picture desk or foreign department.

I sat at my desk and tried to read newspapers and that's what I was doing when Caroline turned up for a birthday lunch with Alexander. We had a nice meal together; Alexander was very funny telling stories about his family and work. We didn't really talk much about anything very seriously. I got a headache and felt nervous. Caroline looked extremely pretty and sometimes I thought she was aware of my distracted mood.

Back at my desk I began to try to put a cartoon together. I could only find one layout pad with a few blank pages. I have to leave the office and walk to the nearest tube station to buy a *Standard*. When I went to the picture library to ask for pictures of trade union leaders to draw from, a charming young man told me he didn't know where anything was at the moment but that he'd get me anything I wanted from an agency. 'I'll do it at once,' he said.

'How long would it take to get a picture?'

'Oh, it would be done immediately, at once.'

'I mean literally, how long would I wait before the picture was in my hands?'

'No time at all – an hour.'

My heart sank. For twenty years I have relied on the superb *Telegraph* picture library where I could get a reference picture of almost anything or anyone in seconds.

Another young man was kneeling on the floor of the tiny room. Several photographs were spread out in front of him and he was gazing at them in a stupefied way.

I began to panic.

I think I was feeling so disoriented and isolated partly because I did not yet feel part of the *Independent*. I was still a visitor, or at best an absolute new boy. All round me in the long newsroom down one floor, or just outside my office where John Torode has his leader writers, people are sitting in front of what look to me live TV screens. They gaze fixedly at the screens and sometimes look down at the keyboard with puzzled and lost expressions. Their deep involvement with the technological world that they are living in and working in deepens my sense of being an outsider. Sometimes several people group themselves round one of the hundreds of VDUs and they mutter what are to me incomprehensible words about what has happened on the screen.

The office was working at full blast. The atmosphere gave out a dull tension. I wanted contact with someone. I tried to be practical. I needed to find out what size to draw my cartoon, so I went and found Michael Crosier.

I perched on his desk and said, 'Hello. We've met.'

'We have indeed,' he replied in a guarded sort of way. He was not unfriendly.

In the brief discussion that followed I guess we were both being a bit careful, polite to each other, but distant. I was depressed when he gave me the dimensions of the space given to my cartoon. It was far too small but I didn't say anything about that.

No one had worked out quite how the cartoon would be slotted into the page. The size given to me did not include space for a caption, should I use one. When I pointed this out it created a flutter of anxious clucking from the two young men who were actually working on the centre spread layout. I suggested the solution that Stuart Reid used on the *Sunday Telegraph*: the space I had was constant but the cartoon was drawn more shallow if I wanted to use a caption. This was agreed.

I think they all realised the cartoon space was too small because Crosier himself said, 'None of this is really fixed yet – we're still having problems with this page.' It was not the time to get into a discussion about that. I tried to be as cooperative as I possibly could and went back to my room to try to think.

. I realised with heart-stopping fear how much my work at the *Telegraph* depended on the huge back-up the *Telegraph* provided, both in a practical and personal way. I missed John Burgess and Bernard Foyster; I missed the picture library; I missed being able to pop out for an evening paper or a packet of peppermints; I missed familiar corridors and faces. But oddly enough I also knew that I didn't want to go back to all that. The idea of still being there depressed me. It was the old *Telegraph* of five to ten years ago that I was missing. Conrad Black's *Telegraph* had no appeal.

I did a cartoon. On a scale of one to ten I rated it about 4–5; but getting something done, anything, is better than the famous blank sheet of paper. Doing the first cartoon after the holidays is very like breaking your duck. You may not get off the mark with an elegant and bold boundary, but you have something to show for your efforts.

The next problem was that the machines that process the cartoon on its way to being printed would not take the card I had used to draw it on. It was too wide and too thick. Furthermore there was not a process department to apply tint, the mechanically shaded or dotted areas of the printed cartoon. The art department staff who faced these problems made little or no effort to deal with them. Crosier, who was standing by, was also apparently baffled by the situation. No one was quarrelsome or upset by it. It was almost boring, a kind of irritating interruption of whatever else they were doing. I was bored by it too.

Solutions appeared. Someone found a sheet of Letraset tint that I could apply myself. I enjoyed doing that, as a matter of fact. I have often been irritated by the crudeness and insensitivity of the way tint has been applied to my drawings.

The problem of the size of the card had a charming solution. One machine had created a hurdle and another machine cleared it. Near where we were standing was a large, flickering, brand new, high-tech photocopying machine which took a reduced picture of my drawing of such excellent quality that it could be processed instead of the original. I liked that very much. I liked being able to keep my drawing. I carried it away back to my room, and sat stunned by the day.

None of the accounts I give of events in this journal is true, in the sense that they present only fragments and details recalled by a faulty and biased mind. For instance, throughout this day, although I say I was feeling isolated, many people had cheerfully greeted me, shaken hands, patted me on the shoulder and been more than ready to welcome me completely into the *Independent*. John Torode and his lot, including the obituaries editor, James Ferguson, who all sit just outside my room, simply could not have been nicer. They at once included me in their personal coffee-making system, gave me a wastepaper basket, helpfully answered my enquiries about where things were or who to ring to get things done, and did everything to help. And I really liked them all for it.

Michael Crosier was a bit cool, but probably no cooler than I was being, and anyway he was concentrating completely on bringing out the paper. Matthew, Andreas and Stephen were similarly occupied. In a way the most familiar, real and comforting event was when my lightweight, high-tech, push-button telephone gave an electronic tinkle and I heard Caroline's voice asking, 'Hello. How is it?'

I looked around my office. It was a terrible mess. My brand new white drawing-board was smudged with ink and dirty fingerprints. The nearby table was covered in empty plastic cups and littered with pens, pencils, pencil sharpenings and bits of india rubber. On the floor were piled my books from the *Telegraph* and all my old cartoons.

I realised I had time to start tidying up, but I had no heart for it. I wanted to go home.

Tuesday 2 September
I cannot recall much about today. It was very like yesterday except that it was one day on. A copy of the *Independent* was lying in my office. It was real. It had headlines and stories and features and advertisements and photographs. Elegant it wasn't. Classy, not at all. It was dull. The best that could be said for it was that it was not heading in the old Mullins/Hawkey direction. It was exactly what Stephen has said it would be, that is, a quality English newspaper that looked as if it had been put together in Manila. It looks like a cheap, Eastern copy of something.

There was one incident that alarmed me. Sometime in the afternoon Andreas came into my room. He had a mildly preoccupied air, almost distracted. He asked if I was OK and said he hoped I would not feel too cut off. He urged me to come to any conferences or discussions that were being held and feel free generally to join in. He then asked whether I had read a story in today's *Independent* about someone who owned the original drawing of the only cartoon of mine 'Sir William Deedes', as they incorrectly dubbed his lordship, had ever turned down at the *Daily Telegraph*.

I said I hadn't read it and he asked me to.

'Is it true?' he asked. 'Is this story accurate?'

I laughed. 'No, it isn't,' I said. 'I had several cartoons turned down for various reasons by Bill.'

'Right!' said Andreas with unexpected intensity. 'I'll have a word with the young man who wrote it. I will not have that sort of slackness. Did he check the story with you?'

'No.'

'You were in the building?'

'Yes. But Andreas, it isn't important. Surely you can't take it so seriously.'

His voice rose. 'I take it extremely seriously. It is inaccurate and I will not tolerate the *Independent* being inaccurate.'

'But –'

'It matters very much indeed.' He left the room. I was left thinking, what is the editor doing bothering about a small exaggeration in a light-hearted piece in yesterday's paper when there is dummy No. 2 to be got out?

Charles Moore rang. 'You've been avoiding me, haven't you?'

'Yes.'

'Well, I've tracked you down.'

'Oh God!'

He wants me to do a cover next week for the *Spectator*. I begged him to let me know the subject in plenty of time.

I asked Melanie, Andreas's secretary, to order me some art and drawing materials. She got them delivered with marvellous speed and efficiency.

I tried several times to get a chance to talk to Penny Jackson about design and layout, but she was always too busy.

Matthew asked me to attend a meeting on the layout of the centre spread. Michael Crosier was there and one or two layout people. The problem turned on an advert which had been sold and which took up space needed for leaders. None of the people there approached the problem with, as it were, a designer's eye. They simply looked for space where it might crop up. Once they found it they considered the problem solved.

I suggested shifting the leaders, the leading article and the cartoon over to the other page. In other words, switching the leader page and op-ed page round. First of all this idea was simply rejected. When I asked why, Crosier sucked his pencil and muttered, 'It would be possible.' Then it was decided it was far too big a job to be attempted now and the notion was forgotten. I mentioned it to Andreas later and suggested to Matthew that Thirkell might work on it. My motive was pure enough but one side-effect of this solution would be that my cartoon suddenly would have more space too.

I did my cartoon and got it photocopied just like yesterday. I also found time to put my books in the shelves and begin to sort out my clutter.

Wednesday 3 September

Today's *Independent* is an advance on Tuesday's but it is an advance within the dull confines of the abilities of the people doing it. We lack a designer's touch and an all-over art editor's organising eye. I notice I wrote 'we' lack, but I still feel disorientated and alone at the office.

The day passed like the last two days, in a preoccupied daze. I tried talking to one or two colleagues about the design of the paper. Sebastian Faulks came into my room and we agreed about the lack of elegance and style and class in the present look. I was trying to nudge him into a position where, should Andreas or Matthew solicit his opinion on the dummies, he would not just say they were very good.

Each time I see Andreas, Matthew or Stephen they are so obviously relieved that there is a paper coming out at all that details about layout for the moment hardly seem relevant to them. Andreas even has a phrase for this state of affairs. It is, 'We are where we should be'. This is nonsense. If it means anything at all I suppose it might mean, 'Things could be worse', or possibly, 'Well, we are on our way'. What I don't like about it is its vague air of satisfaction. I want much more panic and alarm around – even desperation.

Stephen dropped in. He was his usual slow, thoughtful, careful self. We talked about the need to sharpen up the design all round and he said Thirkell would do that. He also wisely suggested that Thirkell should be provided with some of this week's dummies before he comes in on Monday.

When I mentioned the rather boring front page Stephen depressed me by saying that the problem was that no one was editing it. Andreas should have been but had too much to do and was leaving it to others. Somewhere a choice of stories was made, somewhere someone put them together on to the page. But nowhere was there a decisive editor shaping the whole thing.

The last thing he said was that as far as he knew Crosier didn't know Thirkell was coming in next Monday. Or if he did he did not know in what capacity. I said I thought it was important that he should be told and that he should be preparing to work closely with Thirkell on the centre spread, all the feature pages and the front, not necessarily in that order. Stephen took a note and said he'd speak to Andreas. He said, 'I'll try to get him to discuss it with Crosier, but the funny thing about Andreas is that he is incredibly brave about some things and a terrible coward about others. He will face some problems with unflinching staunchness, but try to get him to say something quite straightforward and simple to, say, Crosier and he waffles about all over the place.'

I wish I could crash the barrier that exists between me and the *Independent*. I know I am not a joiner. I think of myself as somewhat isolated. It gives me a sense of freedom – not freedom to run away, but to think. I have always been aware of this tendency. Even at school and when I used to work in the theatre I always kept myself separate from the institutions I was spending my time in. Perhaps during the last few years at the *Telegraph* I did feel I belonged there, but it took nearly twenty years and the feeling seems to have survived the change of ownership.

If only I felt more confident of Andreas's editing. If only I felt more sure of Matthew's judgement. If only Stephen was more abrasive. If only Alexander or James were in the office. If only, if only. . .

Thursday 4 September
Again the paper looks better than yesterday, except for the weirdest-looking books page in the history of journalism. In many of the reviews the book under discussion was not identified. Very strange.

Andreas came to ask me what I thought and of course I had to say it's good and, yes, it's better than I feared and, yes, I agree it's on the

259

right track. But as soon as I raised a criticism or a doubt he swamped me with a testy, 'Yes, yes, we know that's not quite right yet, but we are getting there, aren't we?'

My attempts to alarm him merely irritated him. We were not talking the same language. He seemed unable to see the difference between a well laid-out page and a dull page. He said that although he could be faulted in many ways his sense of timing was impeccable.

'We are exactly where we should be.'

Perhaps he's afraid of peaking too soon.

Today some, but not all the newspapers I asked to be delivered were on my desk. In the afternoon a boy brought me a *Standard*. I am pleased about these developments.

Penny Jackson told me about what it's been like working on features layouts: fairly chaotic. She was pleased to hear a designer was arriving and said she and her head of department would like to talk to him about layout. She understands the technical difficulties involved in making certain changes and she should be able to help Thirkell quite a bit.

I forgot to say yesterday that after my chat with Stephen I rang Thirkell. I told him that the appearance of the paper was heavily influenced by his work and that he should expect cooperation when he arrived. I said, 'It's OK – better than I feared, much better. But it's dull.'

'I knew it would be,' he replied, without disguising a note of satisfaction, then added words to the effect that he was glad because now they'd see how essential a designer was. I was irritated by this aside. In a way it was understandable, but there was nevertheless a meanness about it. He is still smarting at the memory of the reaction to his dummy, but he ought to take up his share of responsibility for that disaster.

Friday 5 September

My newspapers were not delivered to my desk today. Luckily I had not really expected them to be, and had bought copies on my way in. Once again the *Independent* was looking better. Still a long way to go, still quite undistinguished, but it is by no means a disgrace.

I arrived early to attend a meeting of heads of departments on this week's five issues. Nearly all the time was taken up with a discussion of the technical matters of production and difficulties with the new machines; everyone was finding them extremely hard to manage. By far the most striking memory of the meeting was how quarrelsome Nigel Lloyd was. He crossed swords with almost everyone in the room except Andreas, who always agreed with him. At one time Stephen, usually so mild, spoke to him quite sharply saying, 'I have not finished,' when Lloyd tried to interrupt him. Once when Stephen raised a problem

Lloyd said nastily, 'Sounds to me as if you are raising pre-emptive excuses for cock-ups you are going to make in the future.'

I looked at him with dislike and surprise. He caught my eye and winked. I stared at him for a moment then looked away. He is a very difficult man indeed. I'm surprised Andreas claims to like and admire him so much.

I was worried by how little the content of the paper was discussed. They went through various errors in a desultory fashion but there was no overall plan made, no statement about editorial intentions.

I feel more every day the editorial vacuum at the centre of this paper. It's depressing rather than frightening.

When I had done my cartoon I took it off to photocopy and found to my dismay that the machine had gone, and it's replacement was too small to take the size I'd drawn the cartoon. The big machine was now in the computer room, but that could not be entered without a special security card. I eventually got someone to let me in but it took ages and is another problem to overcome each day.

I took the photocopy to the layout people and they said they didn't want a cartoon today because on Saturday's paper there was a profile and a large caricature on the leader page where the cartoon normally appears. I had specifically asked Andreas about this after this morning's meeting because weeks ago he'd said he'd probably not want a cartoon for the Saturday paper. Today he'd said quite brusquely that of course I should do a cartoon. I went to see him, more surprised that he didn't know whether he wanted a cartoon or not than annoyed at wasting a day's work. He was apologetic and smiled and shrugged. It seems incredible that he is so ignorant about what's going in the paper.

I collected a set of this week's *Independent*s and drove off to the *Spectator*.

I met Stephen Robinson in Charles's office and told the two of them about my anxieties and doubts about the *Independent* and showed them the copies I had with me. While they both had minor criticisms to make they were both obviously surprised by how good it was. Charles said, 'If this appeared on the streets tomorrow it would not be a disgrace.'

Saturday 6 September
Nick Thirkell came round for coffee this morning at about 10.00 and stayed until almost 1.00.

His first reaction to the dummies was that they were a lot better than he had expected. I could see as much in his face as he looked at them. I think he was pleased and reassured to see how closely they clung to his original work. We went through each issue and discussed each one's weaknesses and good points. He has a way of not listening. Several times while I was talking to him he continued to flick through the paper as if lost in his own thoughts.

261

He was keen to show me the dummy that had been presented at the disastrous meeting. Alexander had said it was bad, but it was much worse than that. It was atrocious. I could not hide what I thought about it and I could see that he was cast down. Several times he insisted that there were good things in it to be retrieved. I said that in that case he should retrieve them; but I was shocked. I cannot understand how he could have the nerve to present such a load of garbage.

He would not be pressed into saying how he thought he should proceed next week, or where on the paper a start should be made. When I asked him bluntly what he would propose he replied, 'Well, I'm not going to go in on Monday and be told to sit somewhere and to go through the papers and start saying what I think should happen. I'm not going in there like their tame designer.'

'What do you mean?'

'I shall go away and work in my office.'

'Why?'

'Because otherwise it looks like I'm just knuckling under. Andreas's last words after that meeting were, I'm not paying you a penny unless one of you is in the office 9.00 to 6.00 every day until launch.'

I made a speech to him about wiping out the hot words spoken at that meeting and said that somehow or other he had to make a good working relationship with his colleagues on the *Independent*. I said that if he didn't I couldn't see how any good could come from his presence. I fell over backwards to make him approach the job without the injured pride that he clearly feels at the moment. In this I do not think I was very successful. It's perfectly possible, even quite likely, that long before next week is out he will have withdrawn again, this time for good.

This display of petulant ill-feeling and the memory of his dummy meant that by the end of our session I did not feel all that cheerful. But I urged him to ring Andreas and to try to see him before Monday if possible, because Andreas would be tied up in meetings all that day.

Several times he said, 'We can do it.' But I've heard him say that before and it did nothing to put my fears to rest.

Sunday 7 September

Andreas rang this afternoon for Thirkell's phone number. When Thirkell had telephoned last night to request a meeting Andreas had said no. Now he's had second thoughts.

Monday 8 September

I telephoned Thirkell at 8.15 to ask him how yesterday's meeting had gone. He sounded lugubrious and nervous, but said it had been helpful and he'd see what the day would bring. He even said he might ask Crosier out to lunch.

I dropped off two drawings to Charles Moore on the way to work. I'm so disheartened about the *Independent* that I told him he must hurry up and get the Aussies who own the *Spectator* to buy the *Telegraph* and install him as editor.

'And bring you back with a vastly inflated salary,' he said.

'That's it.'

When I got to work I learnt from an exasperated Matthew that Thirkell had been in and then gone away saying he would not work in the *Independent* office. Feeling utterly fed up with Thirkell and the whole bloody paper, I went to see Crosier. His attitude was clear: he was triumphant. Thirkell had played into his hands. He said, 'I don't know where he is or what he's doing, but he cannot go on mucking us about like this. He'll come back some time with his suggestions. But as far as I'm concerned, that's what they are – suggestions.'

Stephen's view was that by walking out of the building Thirkell has made an idiotic blunder.

I rang Alexander in Italy and spoke to Susie. She was busy bottling tomatoes and Alexander was out. She said he'd ring me at home later. When he did we had a moan to each other. He was very angry with Thirkell and listened to my description of last week's dummies in a depressed silence.

'We've been taken for a ride, haven't we?' he said.

'Yeah. Or rather – we've gone for a ride.'

What we meant was we both felt let down. All the talk, all the assurance, all the high hopes and ambitious plans were nonsense. The actual paper in the end promises to be a bland, dull bore.

Tuesday 9 September
Caroline left for work early this morning and I felt restless in the quiet house. The boys were still asleep; it was 8.15 and I'd already had some tea and skimmed through the *Telegraph*. On an impulse, almost for something to do, I rang Nick Thirkell. I intended to be reasonably calm but knew I was feeling angry with him. As I questioned him about what he was doing and why he was refusing to work at the *Independent* building he sounded more nervous than ever. He said he'd been up since 3.30 working on the centre spread. I told him he was crazy to work at 3.30 in the morning, that he must get things done right, not done quickly. Then I really laid it on him. I said I'd worked very hard to get him this job and that I had stuck my neck out for him. Now I was demanding something from him in return. I wanted him to agree to work at the *Independent*. There were many people there who were expecting a designer to help them, and needed to be able to talk to one. Furthermore, in order to solve the layout problems we all had he needed to discover what they were from the journalists on the spot. It was simply making

everything slower and more difficult if he insisted on these fleeting visits. I didn't give a sod for his feelings any longer. I think he said he would come in to City Road. I remember saying, 'Goodbye – see you later.'

He never did come in. Later in the day I passed Andreas on the stairs and he called out to me accusingly, 'I'm a bit fed up with Thirkell. I haven't seen or heard from him since yesterday morning.'

The day had been pretty frustrating for me, and for my cartoonist colleague Colin Wheeler. Both of us sat in my room solemnly drawing cartoons until about 4.15 when we went downstairs to show them to Andreas. He was in a meeting, as usual, and Melanie told us that there was no paper being produced today after all. It had been cancelled at 9.00 this morning. 'Didn't anyone tell you?' she asked.

I was not pleased. I then waited until after 6.00 to see Andreas. I had to see him to talk about Colin, my own problems, and to discuss, if possible, Thirkell. Earlier in the day I'd asked John Torode why more people weren't panicking about how boring the paper was. John has given up panicking and has sunk into a passive gloom. He says all his suggestions for brightening up the paper 'in the end just run into the sand'.

When I made one or two suggestions to Andreas this evening he managed to kill the ideas stone dead at once. Any notion of taking on, say, a humorous or light contributor was a non-starter. We are so far over the budget at the moment that it cannot happen. Instead he says we can find humorous writers among the existing staff. That's where our political columnist is also coming from. It's all quite hopeless.

Andreas looked at my glum face and said, 'We're like someone learning to drive. We've got to learn to drive this thing. I'm teaching my son to drive at the moment so the metaphor comes to mind. Now, when you are learning to drive you are tense and nervous and you do things wrong – but you gradually get the hang of it.'

My heart sank to my boots. Learning to drive? At *this* stage? Oh, Jesus.

Wednesday 10 September
This morning Caroline said that I was getting my view of the *Independent* out of proportion. She has listened to me railing on to Alexander and to her about how awful everything was and how depressing and doomed, and she said that for a start things were *not* that bad and anyway my attitude was infectious and I would simply destroy what confidence there was around the place if I whipped up alarm and despondency.

What she is saying is wise, but in my heart, although I know the paper will improve and Andreas and the rest of us will 'drive' it better than we are doing now, I don't think I'll ever enjoy the *Independent*. It's too sane, in a way. There is not enough eccentricity and oddity and originality. The high-tech system smooths out the idiosyncratic touches that would add colour and fun to the thing.

I telephoned Pryha, Nick Thirkell's wife, to try to find out from her how to get Nick into the *Independent* office, but she had not discussed it with him. She was friendly and interested but couldn't help – apart from saying that she'd talk to him and try to make him believe that he would be welcomed and supported if only he'd be there.

By chance I met Michael Heath just off St Martin's Lane where I was buying sandwiches to take to work. One of the things I miss in City Road is a good snack bar or sandwich shop. Michael said he'd like to come to the *Independent* for a couple of days a week to illustrate features. He doesn't want 'the grind' of a daily pocket cartoon. I said I'd try to fix it.

Colin and I sat in my office drawing cartoons and talking in a desultory way. Stephen came in once and said Andreas was running out of patience with Thirkell. He also mentioned one or two changes of layout that I approved of, in fact more than approved of – my spirits lifted a little. They were editing decisions of the kind I had feared were not being taken.

I tried to speak to Crosier in a helpful way about laying plans for what happens when sooner or later I fail to produce a cartoon. I said, 'Supposing I begin to feel I'm not going to get a cartoon, or events have out-dated the one I've done, or I get ill – what is the latest I can let you know, to give you time to fill the slot?'

'Well,' he murmured, thinking deeply, 'not later than, say, midday – we'd have to know by then.'

This reply floored me. I looked at him incredulously and I thought with yearning of Don Berry.

I said, 'If I came to you at midday and said I can't think of a cartoon, I'm going home, you would say, "What are you fucking well talking about – you've got five hours to think of one." '

His smile changed to a sheepish grin but he did not like my tone. 'Well,' he said, looking me straight in the eye, 'I've got plenty of good cartoonists who could *always* run something up for that spot.'

'Oh really,' I thought.

I called on Charles Moore on my way home at about 4.45. To my surprise he said Nick Thirkell had just left on his way to the *Independent*. Charles has been discussing some work with him. I was delighted to hear he was at least dropping in on the City Road.

Later I telephoned Stephen to hear how things had gone and he reported they had seemed OK; Nick had met and talked with Andreas and Crosier. At about 9.45 Nick rang me at home and gave a more detailed account of his visit. Three important things emerged.

265

(1) Crosier opposed 80 per cent of what Nick suggested; (2) Andreas was reasonably encouraging about the suggestions, which left Nick feeling optimistic; (3) it has been arranged that Nick works at the office all day three days a week (Monday, Wednesday and Friday) until the launch.

Nick said he'd found an ally in the art room, a man called McGuinness, whom Andreas had praised to me as Mullins's excellent No. 2.

Thursday 11 September
The paper is looking tackier and tackier. Today it was full of great white spaces. The pages had been sent off at edition time whether they were ready or not – and they weren't.

Michael Heath dropped in to see Andreas as I had arranged yesterday. They came up to my room and Andreas explained that Michael would have a small retainer and come in to draw illustrations as required. After Andreas left Michael, Colin Wheeler and I sat around and talked. I had a cartoon half drawn and didn't mind the interruption. The three of us discussed cartooning and for the first time in weeks I felt I actually *was* someone.

Later, after they had gone, Nick Thirkell suddenly appeared. I had heard he was in the building. He brought with him a design for the centre spread. It was about 5.30 and I'd finished my work and could therefore give him my full attention. He was his usual nervous self – stumbling over words and leaving sentences half finished. He lit a cigarette (he rolls his own) and said, 'Well, this is crunch time.' It turned out that what he meant was that Andreas seemed to like the spread but Crosier, who also liked it, was opposing its adoption on the grounds that it was no better than the layout they already had and that it was difficult to make the switch to it.

Nick said that he needed an absolutely clear statement from Andreas saying that he (Nick) was the one and only designer; that this bit of design must now be used; that the rest of the paper must at once be designed in a similar style; and that Crosier must understand that he must abide by these decisions.

I tried to get from Nick what had actually happened at the meeting. Firstly of all he said the meeting wasn't over yet. It has been interrupted by Andreas having to go to another meeting but it was due to start again at 6.00. The more I listened to Nick the more I got the impression that actually Nick was home and dry. It seemed to me Andreas was giving him all the support he needed but was trying at the same time to save Crosier's face. I told Nick I would hang about and even come to the meeting if he felt I was needed, but that he must simply be firm and confident and he'd get his way.

I also told him his design was terrific. The more I looked at it the more I liked it.

At six o'clock he went off and I rang Alexander in Italy to tell him what was going on.

He had received a couple of dummies from last week and said, 'They're not bad.' He stretched out the word 'bad' into a long sort of groan. He listened to the latest news and said he thought things could be worse. His attitude was that Nick should just get on with the job and all would be well. We agreed that there was too much *amour propre* sloshing about – at least from Crosier and Thirkell. I promised to ring him again tonight if there were any dramatic events to report, otherwise I'd ring tomorrow.

I hung around outside the glass-walled room where Nick, Crosier and Andreas were talking. I could see Nick's suspicious and tense expression. Crosier was trying to look languid and relaxed. Andreas had his back to me and was doing most of the talking. I wondered whether to go in but was afraid of making things worse by quarrelling with Crosier or becoming too aggressive with Andreas.

When the meeting broke up I had a brief word with Andreas and Nick. Andreas had accepted the new design for the centre spread but insisted on one or two minor but irritating changes. Crosier, I gathered, had accepted Nick's presence and position as designer. Nick had been ordered to proceed with more designs of other pages, but slowly. Andreas reached as usual for a metaphor. 'We cannot go too fast – I am afraid of overheating the machine. If Nick is going to change too much too soon there will be' – I braced myself – 'too much grit in the machine.'

Saturday 13 September
Alexander is back from Italy and I went and had a drink with him at 6.30 this evening to fill him in on the last two weeks. I'm afraid I painted a pretty depressing picture.

He'd come back from holiday with a stomach bug and was feeling pretty rotten anyway. But it was very good to see him and to talk freely about things.

I complained about two main flaws in the paper: the design, and the absence of humour. It's all so stodgy. He said there is not much we can do about the latter and we've shot our bolt about the former. So we drank some wine, had a good laugh and gossiped.

Once he's in Washington I am going to miss him very much.

Monday 15 September
At ten this morning there was a meeting of the staff of the *Independent* which was addressed by two officials from the market research company that has been investigating the reactions to last week's dummies. Some

274 readers from the Greater London area filled out questionnaires and allowed themselves to be interviewed.

The results were encouraging rather than terrifying and showed us to be more popular with AB readers than C1 readers. Both groups criticised the paper for being humourless. The market researcher summed up by saying, 'You've got the approach right; they want a classical, quality paper but it must have more vitality, life, zing, sparkle.' He also said that to project his findings across the nation was silly from such a tiny sample, and that if he did he would promote dangerous complacency because in his opinion the paper was right on course. Everything he said was lively, intelligent, even interesting in a funny kind of way, but useless. It told me nothing. I either had my previous beliefs supported or thought his findings mischievous nonsense.

There were a lot of questions after the presentation, so some people took it seriously. Nigel Lloyd took the opportunity to have a crack at the eagle: 'Any response to the masthead and the little birdie?'

I took a number of cartoon and art books to the office today to help me draw. I feel I must build up some sort of decent reference library. There was no dummy produced so I left the paper early and went shopping for some drawing materials.

Tuesday 16 September
I was on the phone before 8.00 this morning to Nick arranging when he'd come to the paper today for a meeting on the design of the centre spread, so that Stephen and I could protect him from Matthew and Crosier's criticism. Nick told me that at Friday's meeting Crosier at one stage sat on Nick's layout. He didn't mean Crosier criticised it, he meant he put his fat bum down on it and at the same time put his foot on another of Nick's designs on the floor nearby. Today's meeting should be a laugh.

Actually, when it came to it the meeting was an anti-climax. I arrived five minutes late and found Nick, Stephen and Crosier sitting in front of a photocopy of the new layout talking in a desultory kind of way about it. The design had taken care of the problems that the previous effort had presented. It was perfectly good although the letters were less well presented than before.

After a bit Stephen said to Crosier that he thought it should go ahead to be 'formatted', whatever that means, and Crosier just said OK and that was that.

I asked how I could change the shape of my cartoon occasionally from shallow across five columns to deep across three. This is necessary in order to be able to do certain drawings. Nick was very unsympathetic to the idea. He said it would throw the whole design out of wack. I was quite shocked by his blank refusal to think of it as a problem that I wanted help with. Crosier was in like Flynn. He said there were all sort of ways that I could have deep three-column drawing. 'I'm with you on this,' he said smiling at me.

Nick left as soon as the meeting was over and took with him instructions for the next bit of design to which he should address himself. Crosier also left.

I went down to Fleet Street to meet Peter Utley and his secretary Sarah in the Kings and Keys. As I came round St Paul's and headed down Ludgate Hill I had a pang as I realised how much I love this bit of London, and how much I dislike City Road.

It was very nice to see Peter and Sarah. He is going to *The Times* in the New Year. He said that working out his time at the *Telegraph* is hell. Everyone is being very nice to him but he feels awkward and embarrassed and wants to be away, to get it over with.

He told some good stories. The strangest was about a letter he'd got from Andrew Knight asking whether he could continue to write for the *Telegraph* after he'd joined *The Times*. The idea seemed to be that he would write an equal number of pieces for both papers each week! I've never heard of such a suggestion. Peter thought it quite barmy.

The *Telegraph* sounds pretty hellish, morale low, circulation settling down to a loss of 5000 readers a month, general political dithering and uncertainty everywhere.

'The only person really loving every minute of it is Bill Deedes,' said Peter with a wicked laugh. 'He writes lots of chatty pieces and comes to conferences. he waits until Max gives an opinion of something and then agrees with it.' Peter sketched in a devastating picture of Bill shamelessly contradicting himself from leader to leader and moment to moment. Bill has developed a little preamble to statements about the *Telegraph* along the lines of '. . . as someone largely responsible for the paper's misfortunes I feel duty bound to . . .' Peter's contempt is only half amused.

Peter never consulted Bill about leaving the *Telegraph* and eventually, once it became known, Bill came to him and said, 'I've not offered any advice because it seemed impertinent to offer advice to someone as experienced and wise as you.'

'In other words,' said Peter, ' "I'm not going to do a damn thing to help you." '

I asked after Max.

'The last time I saw Max, yesterday or the day before, he said to me, "Ah, you're just back from holiday – so am I. All the way down to London on the train I literally wept because going back to this job is so awful." ' Peter said, 'I don't suppose he actually, literally wept – do you?'

'I dunno – perhaps he did.'

'Perhaps.'

Sarah made a little speech to me, prompted by Peter, and then gave me a 1920s Parker Duofold fountain pen that she'd bought with money collected from my ex-colleagues on the *Telegraph*. Then she kissed my cheek and curtseyed!

Thursday 18 September

Today Nick's centre spread design was used and it looked terrific. For the first time I began to think that, just maybe, the paper might look passable by the launch date. There were mistakes in the way the centre fold printed, gaps left here and there – but they were obvious errors, not poor design.

I rang Nick and congratulated him.

I was looking forward to seeing tomorrow's paper but this afternoon there was a power cut. All the computers shut down. Many stories were lost and the night's paper was eventually abandoned. So there will be no paper tomorrow.

Sunday 21 September

I showed Thursday's *Independent* to my brother-in-law Charles Medawar and his wife Caroline when they dropped in for a drink this afternoon. Charles said he was quite impressed and that it was much better looking than he'd expected. Caroline liked it too.

'I'll buy it when I can't get the *Guardian*,' she said. 'I sometimes can't buy the *Guardian* and then I never know what to get.'

Alexander telephoned from Washington this evening to ask how things were going. He sounded cheerful. It was 1.30 in the afternoon there and a fine hot day. He was going to meet Charles Moore and Christopher Hitchens for a drink and dinner later. I asked what Charles was doing there.

'Oh, he's so grand. He's driving around Virginia in a limousine this afternoon and has a full day of meetings tomorrow – then he's flying home.'

I found myself giving Alexander a fairly upbeat account of the situation at the *Independent*. I said the paper was looking better and that Andreas seemed to be aware that it needed generally livening up. There had been talk about finding a comic writer to create a light-hearted spot somewhere. I told Alexander that I had said to Andreas and Matthew that the headlines could be better written and the photographs better chosen and that all writers could be encouraged to liven things up; Matthew had agreed and felt everyone ought to take more risks.

Wednesday 24 September

Monday, Tuesday and Wednesday have just slipped by. The paper is being produced but it is full of blank spaces and errors caused by technical problems. Penny told me that last week's power cut had given several computers serious nervous breakdowns, and she was afraid too much is being asked of the system. Otherwise the general look of the paper is not bad, though there are still poor parts to it. The feature pages need designing, for a start – they don't differ enough from the news pages. There are too many vulgar, tarted up graphics and fifth-rate illustrations.

I haven't seen Nick T for days so I rang him this morning to see whether he was still working on the design. He said he was but that Andreas was insisting on going so slowly that nothing was in fact happening. Whether Andreas is nursing Crosier's feelings or simply failing to see how much needs to be done or is fed up personally with Nick I don't know. But how he can order Nick to slow down at this stage of the *Independent*'s destiny beats me. Nick recently asked Andreas what he should do in the next few days. Andreas said, 'Nothing at the moment.' Nick then suggested writing a report on what he considered needed to be done and fast. Andreas leapt at the idea.

'Yes – good – excellent. Write a report!'

I had lunch with Tony Howard yesterday. He told me that *Independent* couldn't survive. He prophesied that Robert Maxwell would take over the paper by March and that Andreas would be fired. He had all sorts of mandarin arguments to back up this melancholy scenario.

I said I had a hunch that the *Independent* would not only survive, but prosper.

The *Observer* is doing a profile on Andreas this Sunday and we talked about him for a bit. I told Tony about Andreas's sudden likes and dislikes for people, for instance his outburst about Mullins. I also told Tony how Andreas habitually introduces a certain emotional element into discussions and I mentioned his passionate statement of loyalty and affection for Lloyd, and his going out of his way to express distress for the tragedy Lloyd has suffered.

Tony said the *Observer* was doing some sort of deal with the *Independent* to share computer outlets. He grinned. 'That's why we've been so nice to them. It's not just because we like them.'

I've been sharing my office with Colin Wheeler lately and like having him around. We discuss cartoon ideas and help each other and also share out the work that the home, features and foreign pages come and ask for. We've both done quite a few extra drawings for the paper. Stephen told me that I mustn't ask to be paid for them because there's no money.

I'm having to get to work horribly early these days – all the pages go away much earlier than I grew used to at the *Telegraph*. But I mustn't lose my free mornings.

There was a large meeting today addressed by Andreas on the finances of the *Independent*. I was chatting to Colin and missed the start. By the time I arrived the meeting was well under way and Andreas was speaking financial gobbledygook to the attentive staff. Stephen was hanging around at the back of the crowd.

'What's he saying?' I asked.

'Just that we've got a bit more dough than we thought.'

'Do I have to listen?'

'Not at all.'

'I'm off, then.'

'Sensible feller.'

I met Matthew later and he asked how I liked my cartoon on the front page, which is where it appeared today.

'OK,' I said. 'Perhaps it was a bit small.' (The drawing done for a shallow five columns appeared across four on the front.) Matthew looked ever so slightly pained.

'I thought it looked fine,' he said.

'So did I. But it made a bit of a problem on the centre fold.'

'Didn't you like the photos?' Two photos had been crammed into the cartoon's space, one slightly deeper than the other.

'I didn't like there being two crammed together and I didn't like them being different depths.'

'That was done on purpose.'

'Well, it was no good.'

'You can't say it was no good. You could say you didn't like it. Both others did.'

'I *can* say it's no good – and I *do* say it's no good. I believe there can be a successful presentation of pictures and an unsuccessful presentation. This way, with its idiotic step, gives me a headache and it's no bloody good.'

Matthew was nettled. He looked furious and repeated that I was merely giving an opinion. For some reason or other he said that that layout of pictures hadn't been used before. I contradicted him and mentioned two examples in one particular edition where it had been done previously, and added that it was no good then either.

Later I tried to mollify him by saying I liked to be on the front page and that I hoped we'd do it again. He went away to talk to someone else.

Crosier called out to me. 'When you marked the back of your drawing S/S the other day it came back from the photo department across nine columns.'

I could see he was getting at me but I couldn't understand how. 'What are you talking about?'

'It came back same size.'

'I didn't mark any drawing S/S.'

Seeing I was not going to be embarrassed he turned away. 'Oh,' he murmured, 'it must have been someone else.'

Alexander called from Washington. I had no news for him.

Thursday 25 September

This journal is heading with a dying fall towards its conclusion. The launch of the first quality daily paper this century, or whatever it is, is not approaching with fanfares and tension and high excitement. On the contrary, I get the impression at City Road of a kind of ordinariness. There is a degree of anxiety, of course, because of technical difficulties and the ever-present deadlines, but the staff goes about producing each dummy with no verve.

Last Tuesday Caroline and I went to see a preview of Jonathan Miller's *Mikado* at the ENO. It was marvellous. The set alone rocked the audience nearly out of their seats. As the curtain went up a palpable wave of delight broke over the theatre and there was a burst of applause. You could feel the confidence of the performance and their pleasure in the production. Everyone in the place was having fun. Eric Idle was superb.

In the days before they first performed in front of an audience the company must have been excited. Jonathan must have wondered whether the British would take to such an outrageous joke; the designer must have longed for his work at last to be made public; the opera singers and Idle must have been tense and nervous at the idea of the risks they were going to take; and it all boiled up to a great evening in the theatre.

At the *Independent* there is no parallel with this first night thrill. All is calm, matter of fact, uninspired. Crosier steps smiling through the open-plan offices, his shirt gleams and the creases in his trousers are like weapons. Other journalists, frowning intelligently, solve the problems the day brings. Matthew struts about with his odd little short strides. Andreas has a furrowed brow and a determination not to decide or do anything in a hurry. Penny purses her lips and gazes at her VDU. All is quiet, no one rushes. The silent computers accept their mysterious instructions, and a dummy paper emerges.

If the paper had been properly designed I'd feel a bit like Jonathan's set designer longing for a reaction to all I've worked to achieve. If the paper had one or two elements that were the equivalent of Eric Idle appearing in an opera at the Coliseum I'd be on tenterhooks to see how the public would respond. If there were a clear editorial line on anything

273

at all or an issue or constellation of views that I knew Andreas was going to take up and develop, then I'd feel the drama of going in to support my paper. Instead there is sensible, careful progress, well within the speed limit, towards a sensible, careful launch.

At least, that's how it seems to me. I suppose it's possible that somewhere someone is excited about it all. Andreas, Matthew and Stephen must be a bit tensed up – although in Andreas's case he's pretty tired. I wonder how Jonathan Fenby and John Morrison and Tom Sutcliffe and the other heads of department are feeling. Perhaps, like the case of *The Mikado*, they are in a terrific and pleasurable state of anticipation of a successful launch. But I doubt it.

Perhaps it will happen during the coming week – the last one before the big day.

Sunday 28 September
Driven mad by the nasty little eagle on the front of the *Independent*, I tried to draw one myself. I borrowed some bird books from Bill Oddie who lives next door and copied buzzards and kites and eagles and even falcons and hawks, but I couldn't get it right.

I showed one effort to Caroline. It looked like an angry parrot, and she agreed.

Monday 29 September
I did two lino-cuts of eagles early this morning but they were no good and I went into work in a bad temper. At 11.00 there was a big meeting arranged. It was called a forward planning meeting. Everyone was there and forward planning took place. It was done by heads of departments reading out lists of things that are going to happen soon which they are planning to write and commission articles about. Once, something like a conversation or argument started when John Torode said the *Independent* must publish an article on the Tories' defence policy. He said it may say clearly that there is a gap between their aims and the amount of money available. Matthew agreed but began saying this matter was too complicated for one piece to cover adequately and proposed a series of articles. I thought, he is not thinking like a newspaper man, he wants to impress a whole lot of international experts working at the Institute of Strategic Studies. I was glad to hear Sarah Hogg and Andreas and others not exactly shoot him down but not go along with his ideas. Some sort of reasonable compromise was worked out.

The meeting was laid back and quite friendly and workmanlike – but as usual I missed the fun that such meetings can have. No one fooled about, there were very few jokes. Stephen was very good, so was Sarah Hogg. We are a pleasant bunch of people but we need a Peter

Utley, a Colin Welch, an Alexander Chancellor, a Charles Moore, a Tony Howard, some articulate witty proselytising journalist who could stir things up and be outrageous. Oh, the drab common sense. Nevertheless, it was clear that this was a serious and experienced bunch of newspapermen and there's no doubt that they can produce a good paper.

In the afternoon there was a second editorial meeting at the end of which I had hoped for a session on Nick Thirkell's report, but this was put off until 6.30. I asked Andreas whether I could get Thirkell to come too but he said no. I expressed some anxiety to Stephen about Thirkell's exclusion but he said, 'Don't worry.'

The meeting didn't begin until after 7.00. Present were Andreas, Stephen, Crosier, McGuinness (the art editor) and me. Crosier opposed all Thirkell's perfectly sensible proposals. He had even brought along new designs for the features pages. But, bit by bit, he gave ground. It was agreed that the masthead should be centred, the headlines and by-lines centred and other small but significant decisions were taken.

Once I was stung by Crosier's referring to 'his' designs into saying that Thirkell, not he, was responsible for the look of the paper. He snorted and folded his arms and looked away. Another time, when he said something about the design, I referred him to Thirkell's report and said, 'Well, that's funny because the *designer* holds quite a different opinion.' And he paid me back. When Andreas asked me if I would have a go at doing a logo for a feature page Crosier murmured smoothly, 'With respect, if Nick *is* going to try to do that drawing, we must let one of my artists do one as well.' As if he was saying, 'You will do that drawing over my dead body.'

The whole meeting was unpleasant and pretty useless. Stephen was very good and McGuinness was helpful and nice. Andreas was quite drained. I don't know how he keeps going. His stamina and will power are immense, but his judgement is faulty. When I criticised the eagle he said, 'I ordered that drawing. I told the artist I wanted a "yukky" eagle.'

'What's a "yukky" eagle?' I said.

His reply was incomprehensible and as far as I remember had something to do with not wanting anything too arty and delicate.

I left the meeting angry, frustrated and depressed. Stephen felt the same. He telephoned me at about 9.30 to express his misgivings about the way things are going. He chided me gently, saying that lately I had withdrawn from the design battlelines. He said I mustn't give up. He urged me to speak frankly to Andreas who, so he said, still finds my views on the design helpful. I am finding it increasingly hard to keep up the pressure.

Stephen is an interesting man. At this late hour his cool unhurried approach is paying off. At one time I tried to whip him into activity; now, slowly and steadily, it is he who is applying the pressure to improve the design. He is not exhausted or over-excited. He is sympathetic to Andreas's predicament and understands the editor's unwillingness to face violent confrontations over the design. He undertook to speak frankly to Andreas. 'I'll call him in the morning, when he is fresh – that's the best time to try to influence him,' he said. It is as if Stephen paced himself well and is emerging as one of the coolest people around.

Tuesday 30 September
At 8.00 I telephoned Andreas. During the night I had worked myself up into a frightful rage about the way Nick's designs were being received, and I have decided to bloody well tell Andreas that this opposition was buggering-up the look of the paper. Andreas was in the bath having already been out jogging. Ten minutes later he rang back. I tried – God, how I tried – not to sound too wild but I finished up furious. I said Crosier should not take it on himself to 'improve' or tinker within Thirkell's designs. Andreas tried to say that certain progress has been made after last night's meeting.

'Yes, but every bit resisted by Crosier,' I said angrily.

Andreas gently told me that he had already decided to call Thirkell and get him onto the features page problem.

Now I pray that touchy, defensive, nervous Nick T can take advantage of these last few days to find a way of improving the *Independent* before the launch. And that Andreas will support his designs.

When I showed my cartoon to Andreas this afternoon to get it passed, he looked at it for a while and then said, 'I've said it before, and perhaps you are tired of hearing it – but I think you are doing your best work ever for us.'

'No, I'm not tired of hearing it,' I said. 'Thanks very much.'

He looked up from the drawing and smiled. He has a particular smiling expression that is something like a challenge when he is going to say something a bit risky. 'You are working very well – even though I know you are very angry about other things.' His smile widened. 'Perhaps we ought to keep you angry,' he said.

'There's no need to do that,' I replied. I took this exchange to be his way of saying that he did not hold it against me that I had rung him so early in the morning and blasted away so vehemently.

On my way home I called on Charles at the *Spectator*. Some days ago he and I discussed finding someone to write a comic column for the *Independent*. He'd subsequently telephoned to say he'd found a possible writer.

He asked me to lend him a couple of volumes of pieces by Michael

Frayn from the *Guardian*, which I did. I understood his writer wanted to study Frayn's work.

Charles was being immensely secretive about who this writer is. 'No, no, I cannot tell you.'

'But, Charles, I've told you all kinds of secrets.'

'I know you have – but you'll understand when you find out who this is. They will write under a pseudonym. They work for someone else, you see . . .'

Charles has promised to send me this mysterious person's first efforts some time today. They had not arrived at the *Independent* so I called to pick them up. I thought they were quite promising but as presented unsuccessful. I was struck by, but carefully didn't mention, a certain disagreeable arrogance about the style and content. The reason I was careful not to say anything about it was that it suddenly crossed my mind that Charles himself might be the author, or even his wife Caroline. He remained silent on the matter of who the pieces came from but undertook to pass on my remarks and get some more stuff for me to look at. He never revealed the name of the author to me.

We went and had a drink at the pub. I showed a number of *Spectator* hacks who were sitting around drinking a copy of the *Independent*. All agreed it was looking good – but boring.

Charles and Michael Heath and I sat at a table and chatted about newspapers. It is that sort of company and talk that I miss so much at City Road. Perhaps when Heath begins work with us I'll see more of him; which will be nice.

"NOW, LET'S PUT AN END TO ALL THIS VIOLENCE."

September, *Independent* dummy issue

OCTOBER

THE MOUSE THAT ROARED

October, *Independent* dummy issue

Wednesday 1 October

I had barely arrived at my desk when Stephen came to say that the features logo that I had been vaguely working on had been done by someone else. In an irritable way I said, 'OK' and he said, not without justification, that he understood I was not very interested in doing them because I thought they were a rotten idea anyway. I half admitted this and we were chatting about it when Matthew came in. Somehow or other he was drawn into the conversation and I finished up have quite a row with him. What got me angry was his disparagement of Thirkell and his unquestioning support of Crosier. At one point I was standing face to face with Matthew and more or less shouting at him, saying everything that was good about the look of the paper was Thirkell's work, or based on his work, and I could not understand why his suggestions were met with such opposition from Crosier and indeed from Matthew himself.

Matthew first of all asked me not to shout at him and then said that I was just plain wrong. In his view the designer of the *Independent* was Crosier. Thirkell was merely a 'design consultant'. He made it clear that as far as he was concerned he was prepared, if he had to, to listen to Thirkell, but that was about it. His suggestions and designs were of little interest.

In face of this version of how the paper had been designed I felt more depressed than anything else, because I realised how little Thirkell or I could now achieve. A wild sort of frustrated anger kept me boiling away at Matthew's maddeningly superior manner, but I made a huge effort not to lose my temper completely.

I said I was sorry I was shouting at him but I was motivated by the firm belief that Thirkell had a lot to offer still, and Crosier's *amour propre* was standing in the way of design improvements.

Matthew said Crosier saw me as a hostile force doing what I could to make his life more difficult. Some truth in that, I thought. I replied that if that's what he thought he ought to come right out and say so to me, not go in for disguised attacks of the kind I've had to put up with. Matthew began to say that was unfair to Crosier when Stephen quietly butted in to point out Crosier had indeed been pretty offensive at the last meeting. Whereupon Matthew sensibly backed off and said, 'Well, I wasn't there so I can't comment.'

This confrontation ended without peace being made and after Stephen and Matthew left I felt silly for having got so worked up.

Colin, who had been listening, was amazed to hear me behave so violently. 'I've never seen you talk like that before,' he said.

'Did I sound very angry?'

'Frankly – yes, you did.'

'How angry?'

'I thought it might all really explode.'

'Oh, hell!'

Shortly after this Crosier came in to speak to Colin about a drawing he'd done. I took the opportunity to raise the matter of his feeling that I was hostile to him.

I said we should try to talk openly about our disagreements and try to keep the interests of the paper foremost in our minds. I saw no reason why a clash of opinions should turn into a personal quarrel. He was unmoved by this approach and went off into an account of his own merit and achievements in the course of which he, like Matthew, more or less denied Thirkell had donated anything to the paper's design and therefore what I was saying was nonsense. I felt myself churning with such dislike of this preposterous view that I cut the conversation short. I felt by now that I had generally gone far too far in allowing my feelings to be expressed and was kicking myself for losing my cool. I didn't mind about annoying Matthew or Crosier but I had not done Thirkell any good and had also upset Stephen.

I rang Alexander in Washington and had a moan to him. That cheered me up. He said that I shouldn't be upset because actually the *Independent* is looking pretty good and that's what really matters, not who claims the credit for it. He is giving a launch party on Wednesday to which Susie will bring heaps of Tuesday's first issue. I wish I was going to it. Stephen is hoping to pop over on Concorde!

When I bumped into Matthew in the corridor later I said, 'Forgive me, please, for my burst of temper,' and I patted him on the back to show I was feeling contrite. He muttered something which I didn't catch so I don't know whether I've made peace with him or not.

Thursday 2 October

Michael Heath started work here today. I took him round the heads of department and they all welcomed him enthusiastically. He was immediately asked to do drawings for the City and foreign pages and ended up doing about five cartoons then and there which he drew with astonishing speed and apparently no effort.

It was extremely pleasant sharing a room with him and Colin. They make the sort of jokes and asides and remarks that I have felt the absence of around here and I cheered up a lot just from being in their company. Both of them seem to be able to talk and work at the same time. I've never felt before that I was one of a roomful of artists, and as other people came and went with their requests for various cartoons I had a sense of how useful we are to the paper – which for some reason I've never really apprehended when working alone.

Michael showed me a cartoon of his in today's *Private Eye*. It is based on a drawing by Picasso, and his enthusiasm for the original and the use he had put it to delighted me. He likes to come on as a no-nonsense hack who can churn out what's required; but talking about Picasso he reveals the sensitivity and subtlety that lie behind his witty drawing.

Matthew looked pretty stony-faced whenever I saw him around the building. So much so that when I got a chance to speak to Andreas I said to him that I was worried about the effect of my behaviour in expressing my views to both Matthew and Crosier so violently. I asked Andreas to believe that I had been motivated by a desire to see the paper looking good; if the expression of my frustration was making for an atmosphere which was unpleasant and unproductive, then I was sorry and I had resolved to try to be less volatile in the future. He listened calmly, with an attentive and friendly expression. When I had finished he smiled and said, 'No, don't change – your views are listened to.'

I cannot remember his exact words but he didn't seem to be critical of me for being explosive. This I suppose could be part of his general preoccupation with keeping everything going. That is to say, he may be absolutely livid with me but sees it in everyone's interests to avoid pushing things towards confrontation. Anyway, I felt reassured by such a sympathetic response.

I finished my work by about 3.30 and filled in the afternoon reading, thinking about next week's *Spectator* cover and writing up this journal. I couldn't go home because Nick Thirkell had arranged to come in with some designs at 7.30. He asked me to be there and to go over his suggestions from about 6.00. When he arrived he had photocopies of existing pages clipped to his improved versions. He went through them all, first pointing out what he didn't like on a page and then revealing his solutions.

I thought everything he'd done was excellent and if adopted would instantly improve the look of the paper enormously. He had even had a new eagle drawn which I tried to improve by redoing the head, without much success. My only suggestion to him was that he reverse the order in which he showed his work. In other words, to present his pages first, saying why he had done what he had done and then comparing it with the existing design. Otherwise it sounded as if he was going in for a relentless attack on all the work everyone else had done up to now ('this looks weak and spindly, this logo is no good, these lines are fussy and distracting'). By following my advice I hoped he would throw the emphasis on to how good his work was rather than how unsatisfactory he found the existing look. I felt too it was a mistake to appear to criticise the paper too much when lots of people had worked as hard as they could to make it what it was.

Nick at once began switching round all his designs and clipping them together with his work on top. When 7.30 came we went one floor down to the meeting. He left my office a minute before I did in order that we should not appear together as a team – although this little precaution was unnecessary as we then waited until nearly 8.15 before Andreas was free to see us. First of all he was at a leader writers' meeting discussing the *Independent*'s line on nuclear weapons. Then he had a TV interview on record. When we finally got into a room with him I asked how the hell he found the energy to go on. He smiled and shrugged and I felt yet again how tired he was.

The meeting was pretty useless. Andreas was too knackered to be decisive about anything although he was always good natured and polite. Stephen was very effective at seeing why Nick's ideas were good. Matthew left early saying he felt he had nothing to contribute and made some remark to the effect that to him our arguments were of the 'how many angels can dance on a pin-head' kind. I said very little because I judged Andreas was sympathetic to Nick's suggestions and was afraid that if I began pushing him he'd resist more.

In the end Andreas had to go to deal with a crisis in the newsroom and the meeting ended with him saying he wanted to sleep on it all. I repeated to him before he left that it was possible to get bogged down in circular arguments about the merits of one change or another. I felt one could approach Nick's designs another way. It is his great strength as a designer that all his work simplifies and clarifies the presentation of the copy. The effect is to throw one's attention on to the content of the paper. Andreas said he'd bear my words in mind.

Outside Nick and I spoke together briefly. We reckoned things could have gone worse but I did not have much hope that much more would be changed before the launch.

My mood is hard to describe. I feel depressed and irritable. I have little energy or fight left in me. I hardly care whether the *Independent* is a success or not. I can't seem to make it matter one way or the other. I am aware of a vast gap between me and it or, to put it another way, I feel no personal or emotional commitment to the paper – just a fairly bored goodwill and mild exasperation.

I don't feel healthy, either physically or mentally, and I am afraid that this jaded state of mind is producing a false picture in this journal of the build-up to the launch of the *Independent*.

Because I feel so dull about it I slip into the assumption that everyone else does too. But I am almost certainly mistaking a degree of fatigue among my hard-working colleagues and their consequent lack of liveliness for an absence of concern about the paper's success. For all I know everyone else in the whole outfit is on a terrific high and hardly able to wait for the big day.

For instance, I heard from Charles Moore that Stephen had been told by Andreas to take a few days off because he was working too hard.

Perhaps there are lots of others – like Stephen – nobly giving their all – while I moon about barely able to move.

Saturday 4 October
I forgot to mention that on Thursday evening while Nick and I waited to see Andreas and the others we watched an advertisement for the *Independent* on TV. It shows a man being clouted round the head by rolled-up newspapers while sharp voices-over harangue him with their newspapers' opinions. Eventually he is knocked right off the screen and then slowly rises again, this time quietly and thoughtfully reading the *Independent*. The punch line is, 'The *Independent*. It is. Are you?'

I thought it was a ghastly advert which managed to associate the violent hitting of the man with the product being advertised.

I told Stephen I didn't like it. 'Nor do I,' he said, smiling bravely. 'It cost two million pounds.' I suppose he meant the whole campaign, not just that advert.

Riding around London with Caroline on my motor bike this morning I saw a couple of hoardings with big posters for the *Independent*. They featured the same catchphrase I'd seen on TV. I thought they looked quite good but very reserved and down-beat.

Monday 6 October
Well, this is the day. I tried and tried to feel excited, but all I felt was irritable and nervous. Perhaps that is a form of excitement . . .

I went to work early, arriving at about 9.45. One of the secretaries was making coffee. I looked through Friday's *Independent* to see whether any of Nick's latest design ideas had been used, but none had. Pity. I drank some coffee and began skimming through the papers. I sketched out a couple of ideas and thought I'd draw one of them up properly so as to have something done in case I got into difficulties later.

The office was quiet and tidy and I got along OK for a bit. The foreign desk rang to ask me to do a drawing for a piece from Manila by James Fenton. Michael Heath came in. 'Thought I'd better be here today,' he said, and got himself some coffee. He prepared himself somewhere to work and in no time had several requests for illustrations. Later in the day Crosier told him to stop drawing; practically every page had a Heath on it and some had two. As fast as various editors were commissioning work Crosier was having to kill it.

Colin arrived and also began scribbling out ideas.

My drawing slowly began bogging down. 'Do you two have days when you just can't draw?' I asked.

'Yeah,' said Michael.

'Christ, yes,' said Colin.

'Well, I've got one today.'

'Only one thing to do,' Michael said with a sigh.

'Shoot yourself?'

'Drink! I can't half draw when I drink.'

I was drawing Tom King's face over and over again, making the same mistakes each time. I began to swear and mutter. Colin tried to help by suggesting that I left King out of the picture.

'Is he essential?'

'No, he is not fucking essential. It's just driving me crazy not being able to draw him.'

Michael came and looked over my shoulder. 'Dunno what you're on about. You've got him – you just can't see it.'

I managed a passable shot in the end. Yet another journalist came in to ask Michael to do a drawing.

'Not allowed,' he said. 'I could do it, but I've been told I mustn't. Go and sort it out with someone called Crosier.'

Mystified, the young man went away.

Michael suddenly went off into an outrageously camp monologue. 'Oh, yes – *I* can do your drawings but Crosier says no. Can't think what's got into her. She's all upset today. Carrying on. Flapping about. I don't know why I bother. I don't have to do this, you know. You come in here – all bossy – "Do a drawing . . ."' He went on and on. It was very funny.

I'd almost finished my drawing when Andreas came in. He was relaxed and cheerful. He looked at my cartoon and said he liked it. There are ten or so characters in the drawing. 'I like a drawing you have to read,' he said, and smiled as his eyes ranged over the picture. 'Very good – that's fine. Was it Low,' he asked, 'who used to do cartoons with lots of people in them?'

'He sometimes did,' I said.

'Mm, thought it was,' he said.

People do say the strangest things about cartoons.

The foreign desk rang to ask if I had done the illustration for them yet. I looked at my watch and was horrified to see it was 3.30. The day had just vanished away. I promised I'd do the drawing in half an hour. I got it all done and handed in, and realised I'd finished this important day's work. I still felt completely flat except I suppose for a mild feeling of relief that I had broken my duck, as it were.

I called on Stephen in his little office and asked him how it was going. His mood was rather like mine, I think, for very different reasons no doubt. He was relaxed – even laid back – apparently quite unexcited by the drama of this day.

He said, 'Everything seems OK.'

I asked whether I'd burnt my boats with Matthew by quarrelling with him the other day.

'Oh God, no. I had lunch with him immediately after that scene. He mentioned it but didn't make a great thing of it. All he said was something about you getting very intense about design, and I said, "Of course he does – he cares very much about it." '

'Good,' I said.

'Matthew loves to stride about looking terribly tough – if he seems a bit icy it's probably not even aimed particularly at you. You know Matthew – it's just how he is.'

Stephen's greatest strength may be his ability to make people feel good. I didn't believe what he was saying. I know quite well that Matthew is cutting me but Stephen managed to remove the irritation I feel at Matthew's behaviour.

He asked if I was coming to the celebration champagne party in the office at midnight.

I said, 'I thought I might look in.'

'Of course you must – bring Caroline. Bring . . .' I think he was trying to remember the names of my children but his voice tailed away.

Still feeling I wanted something more from this day, I went to Andreas's office. I said to him that I had not shown him my cartoon before handing it in, because I'd taken his earlier reaction to it as it being passed. He had been talking to Matthew when I came in and broke off and smiled cheerfully. 'Of course, of course,' he said.

'Well, good luck,' I said.

He made some response. It was about how pleased and optimistic he felt with everything and he added something about how and why he had not used any of Nick's latest ideas.

Biting back an expression of my disappointment, feeling it the wrong time to start squabbling, I said, 'It looks great – the whole paper looks great.'

As I turned to go, saying I'd see him later at the party, I looked at Matthew to include him in what I intended to be a friendly moment. He avoided meeting my eyes and looked straight ahead with a curious tight smile on his face.

I went home.

Caroline was out between 8.00 and 10.00 and by 11.15 we were both very sleepy. She said, 'If this wasn't an occasion – a once-in-a-lifetime thing – I'd say "Let's go to bed".'

There was something odd about driving through the streets to work at that time, and from outside the *Independent* looked deserted. However, on the first floor large groups of journalists and staff were gathering. There was a kind of excitement in the air. Caroline and I hung about not quite knowing what group to join or where to go when suddenly there was a move towards the second floor.

In a sweeping rush we were hustled up the stairs and into the large open space just outside my office. Food was laid out and in the crowd here and there people already had champagne. The voices rose to the familiar party roar. Caroline was having a lively conversation with Audrey Slaughter the women's page editor. Colleagues greeted each other and grinning faces loomed past out of the throng.

I pushed my way to the drinks table and brought Audrey and Caroline glasses of champagne. The party was under way.

Caroline quickly felt in the party mood. I watched her becoming more and more animated. I let her feel all the buzz, sipped my champagne and wished I wasn't such a wet blanket. I watched a journalist from the City pages crawling on hands and knees across several desk tops. His eyes were fixed on a plate of sausage rolls. He reached out and took a handful of them and with a look of immense concentration he crawled backwards the way he'd come carrying his booty.

The bar was no longer pouring champagne – if anyone held out an empty glass they were handed a bottle. At least, that's what happened to me.

Caroline was getting brighter and brighter. 'I want to see Andreas,' she said. Then the first copies of the paper arrived. They blossomed in the crowd as they were reached for and opened.

We pushed back through the crush to the relative quiet of the front of the building. I took two *Independent*s from a heap on the floor. Andreas, smiling and laughing, was signing copies and kissing secretaries. The mood of the evening was turning euphoric. Matthew was standing nearby. Caroline tried to catch his eye to say hello but he avoided her too.

'It's a bit thick that I should be cut as well,' she said. Alison, Matthew's wife, said hello and smiled.

I gave my two copies of the paper to Andreas to sign. On the first one he wrote:

> To Nick! Thanks for supporting us
> Andreas

I was distinctly disappointed by this inscription. It sounded as if he feels I am to the *Independent* what a supporter is to a football club. I thought I was a player.

On the second he wrote:

> To Nick – thanks for joining the great adventure
> Andreas

This too seemed wrong to me. Once again I felt excluded. To be thanked is to be kept at a distance. You don't thank a close colleague –

287

you thank strangers and underlings. However, I expressed none of this and carried off my papers as if I were highly delighted.

Caroline said he was probably writing the same thing on everyone's paper and anyway he was on such a high that he could not be expected to write sensitive, haiku-like inscriptions. She was probably right.

We found ourselves near some foreign room staff, one of who was complaining about two ghastly mistakes in the paper. I hoped he meant the horrible illustrated index top right on the front page and the appallingly twee decoration round the heading on the health feature page. But actually he meant the use of the word 'terrorist' in a headline to describe a man on trial who has not yet been found guilty; and the words 'in Cure d'Ars' after Patrick Marnham's by-line.

' "In Cure d'Ars," ' he shouted. 'Patrick Marnham up the Cure's Arse – bloody hell.'

Andreas passed by, heading into the centre of the party. He was muttering, 'It's time for a toast – I'm going to propose a toast.' We were swept along with the group that surrounded him. Someone began tapping a bottle to signal for quiet. The insistent ringing taps provoked loud shushing noises, and soon Andreas stood amid the party debris with all eyes on him. He spoke very briefly, thanking everyone who had worked so hard to produce the paper, and then raised his glass and said, 'To the *Independent*.' There was an enthusiastic roar as everyone drank, and a burst of applause. Then the entire crowd broke into song with 'For He's a Jolly Good Fellow', and cheered. Andreas stood and looked around him as if noting individual singers with special pleasure and amusement. He nodded and smiled and looked completely happy.

The party flowed on around this touching moment.

I caught sight of Stephen. He was talking to someone in the library, and was visible through the glass wall. I wanted to talk to him and the library looked so quiet and empty.

He was saying something to a man I'd last seen at the *Independent*'s first office in London Wall. They were quietly congratulating each other on the paper's birth.

It was pleasant to be in a quiet corner. I fetched a bottle of champagne and we talked. Now and then people drifted by, pausing to talk to us for a while. Stephen was in the same state he'd been in earlier. Not elated, not high – if anything he was rather subdued.

I commented on his quiet mood and he shrugged and said, 'I don't know what's wrong.' He smiled. 'Tired, maybe.'

'I bet you are.'

We talked about the first issue. I couldn't help listing some of my complaints. He took them well and urged me to be patient. 'We can get these things right. We've got time.'

Someone asked Stephen to sign a copy of the paper. He took it and said, 'I'm not very good at this – I never know what to write.'

'Write your name,' said the man who'd made the request. They were obviously friends.

'Write "with love" as well,' I suggested.

'No, that wouldn't be quite right,' he said. After a bit he wrote something and several people asked him to sign their copies as well. When he'd finished I asked him to sign mine.

He didn't ask what he should write this time but straightway scrawled:

> To Nick:
> Who more than anyone is responsible for this design
> Stephen

He wrote the same words on my other copy. I thought it was very nice of him and felt pleased and touched.

Caroline meanwhile had dashed off to talk to Andreas and come back with her newspaper inscribed 'To Caroline – love, Andreas.' I asked her what she had said to him.

'I congratulated him on a really heroic achievement, and that I thought what he had done was terrific and that I hoped whatever happened in the future he felt wonderful tonight – and he said, "I *do*".'

At about 1.30 we decided to go home. I said goodnight to Andreas and told him I too thought what he had done was magnificent. We shook hands.

It had been nagging at me that I hadn't spoken to Matthew, not so much because I give a damn about his silly behaviour but tonight it seemed wrong not at least to speak to each other. I'd even said a chilly hello to Crosier earlier on. Matthew was leaning against a wall surrounded by people. I went up to him.

'Matthew!'

He had to look at me. On his face was the same peculiar tight smile that had been there this afternoon.

'Hi,' he said.

'I want you to sign my papers. The others have and I want you to as well.'

For a fraction of a second he hesitated, then he said, 'OK. Got a pen?'

He managed somehow to express the hope that I hadn't got a pen in which case the deal would be off. I handed him my big red Parker Duofold. He turned away to rest the paper on the wall and wrote:

> You were the longest pull – but worth it every day
> Thanks for joining – love Matthew

He handed me back the paper and I gave him my second one. While he began writing again I read the first inscription. I took it as a peace offering, as if he was as fed up with the awkwardness between us as I was. He returned the second paper on which he had written:

Nick – I love you and I don't even mind Thirkell
Matthew

This was a more complicated message; it seemed to combine quite strong affection with a degree of vexation, even reprimand. Certainly, he was expressing a condemnation of Thirkell that he must know would irk me. On the other hand it was late, and he had drunk a certain amount and the party was in noisy full blast all round us. It was most likely a sort of risky joke, or jokey challenge. Anyway, I said thanks and laughed.

We exchanged a few more words that I can't remember – something about the paper looking good. I do remember him saying, 'This paper is not just going to be good – it's a paper we can be proud of.' Come to think of it, he must have been drunk because he said this very solemnly as if it were a very important statement.

I said, 'Good-oh,' or something like that, and Caroline and I left. Linda gave me a kiss on both cheeks when I said goodnight to her. She looked very happy.

Outside in the street Caroline said, 'God! I've drunk more champagne this evening than. . . . What an occasion – what a wonderful party. You did the right thing. Whatever happens, when you joined them, you did the right thing . . .'

Epilogue

The *Independent* was a huge success. For Andreas, Matthew and Stephen, the launch was a triumph. The risks they took paid off and from Day One, faint hearts and mockers fell silent: the *Independent* was here to stay. It is better looking now than at any time since it began, and during its first three years the paper has won lavish praise, and been very influential, above all in the area of design and in the presentation of its outstanding photographs.

The *Daily Telegraph* has also prospered. The disasters so often predicted, and so much feared, never happened. Under Max Hastings's editorship the paper has become enormously profitable once again.

Even after 7 October 1986 it took me some time to settle down and stop taking such an apocalyptic, not to say self-centred, view of the details of the look of the new paper. With hindsight, I can see that during the squabbles and disagreements in the weeks before the launch, I got many things out of proportion. I found it particularly difficult to understand quite how vast an operation the three founders were directing and perhaps therefore failed to appreciate what complex problems of production they and other colleagues were having to face, while I was so preoccupied merely with the appearance of the paper.

It follows that the account I have given is no more than a description of how things appeared from where I was at any given time. In the sense that nothing in the journal is invented or deliberately distorted this version is true, but of course it is not the whole truth. Inevitably it expresses all my prejudices, however objective I might have imagined I was being at the time; that is the nature of a journal. It is in the end about the informal side of newspaper men and women at work, the friendships, allegiances, disagreements, quarrels and reconciliations that underlie the formal structures, the public front of any large organisation.

I have two views about newspapers. One is that a free press is essential for a healthy society, and I can feel quite emotional about

291

7 October 1986, first edition of the *Independent*

being a part of ours. I enjoy the variety of our newspapers and the amazingly different slants they can put on the same events. It is in that difference of course that the value of our press lies.

This variety of views is also central to my other attitude to newspapers, which is summed up in a remark made to me by Richard Bennett twenty years ago when he was letters editor of the *Sunday Telegraph*. We were discussing a book he had written and I asked him why he worked in newspapers instead of a university perhaps, or a publishing house.

'Because,' he replied, 'newspapers are the highest-paid fantasy world I know.'

Index

attitude to *Independent*, 7, 32, 55,
    109–10, 228
joins *Independent*, 186, 194–6
on design of *Independent*, 200–6,
    209, 210–11, 215–23, 227,
    237–43, 245–9
Chernobyl, 120, 121, 122
Clapp, Suzannah, 15, 18, 19
Clark, Vic, 84, 94
Clover, Charles, 143–4
Compton Burnett, Sarah, 62, 64,
    134, 189–90
Cook, Peter, 130, 131
Courtauld, Simon, 241–2
Cox, Paul, 148–9
Critchley, Julian, 136, 137–8
Crosier, Michael, 265–7, 272–3,
    282, 284–5, 289
    and Whittam Smith, 249, 259,
    271
    on design of *Independent*, 246–7,
    255, 256, 258
    opposition to Thirkell, 250, 251,
    262–3, 268–9, 275, 276, 280–81

Daily Mail, 33, 38, 81
Daily Telegraph,
    atmosphere, xiii–xiv, 47, 61, 63,
    76
    changes, 69, 71, 79, 84, 88, 96,
    116, 122, 163, 167
    decline of, 2–3, 16, 30, 31–2, 39,
    40, 53, 57, 80, 132
    format, 81, 88, 90, 92–3, 96
    new technology, 15
    readership, 15, 74, 75, 92, 137,
    138
Daily Whittam (early name for
    Independent), 32, 33, 34, 37
Daubeny, Peter, 19
Davie, Michael, 183
Davy, Sue, 26–7, 67, 84, 100, 131,
    156, 207, 208, 224
    and Max Hastings, 56, 71–2, 88,
    126
    as secretary to Bill Deedes, 8, 46,
    60, 63, 68

dismissal, 133–5, 141, 145, 150,
    185
trying to join *Independent*, 158,
    183–4, 194
Day Lewis, Sean, 146
Deedes, Jeremy, 209
Deedes, W. F. (Bill), 17, 20, 26–7,
    134–5, 152, 182, 224, 269
    and Max Hastings, 43, 118–20
    and *Private Eye*, 59
    as editor of *Telegraph*, 30, 36, 103,
    149, 207
    crisis at *Telegraph*, 3, 5, 39–41, 48,
    100–101
    dinner at Downing Street, 161,
    162, 164
    leader writer for *Telegraph*, 131,
    145, 185
    leaving, 60–61, 62–4, 66–7, 106
    life peerage, 168
    personality, 7, 38, 46–7, 122,
    126–7, 179, 180, 190, 215
    profiled in *Observer*, 58
Dickens, Charles, 64
Dudley, Nigel, 8, 10, 36, 59, 76–7,
    137, 179
Dudman, John, 149
Duke of Windsor, 130

Eastwood, 40, 162
El Vino, Blackfriars, 74–5, 241
    Fleet Street, 72–3, 187
English, David, 107
Establishment Club, 19
Evans, George, 39, 168, 219–20
Evans, Harold, 76

Faulks, Sebastian, 139, 258
Fawkes, Wally, 16, 110
Fenby, Jonathan, 274
Fenton, James, 21, 67, 73, 113, 161,
    198, 211–12, 223, 225–6, 233,
    284
    and Whittam Smith, 121
    joining *Independent*, 18, 61, 68,
    70–71, 80, 95, 110–11, 114–16
    personality, 8–9, 11–12, 14, 19
    talent, 76, 82, 140, 142–3

theories about *Independent*, 22–3,
25–6, 178–9, 202, 215–17, 227
Ferguson, James, 256
ffolkes, Michael, 18, 136
Fildes, Chris, 42–3
Financial Times, 5, 195
Fleet Street, 80
Foot, Michael, 57–8
Foyster, Bernard, 38, 84, 147, 185,
188, 255
and Max Hastings, 128–9
as picture editor on *Telegraph*, 30,
68, 74, 93, 120
at farewell dinner, 190, 207, 224
personality, 142
Fraser, Antonia, 19
Frayn, Michael, 44, 276–7

Gaddafi, 108
Gale, George, 215, 228
Gardyne, Jock Bruce, 13, 59, 60,
100–101, 135, 136–7, 179,
189–90
Garland, Caroline, 71, 172, 182
naming *Independent*, 5, 37
on holiday, 233, 235, 236, 237
on joining *Independent*, 12, 16, 20,
38, 115, 162, 166, 168–9,
174–5, 183, 198–9, 211, 224,
226, 228–9, 264
on joining *The Times*, 132
opinion of journal, 111, 124
socialising, 82, 102, 131, 207, 254,
286–90
Garrick, 118, 120
Garton Ash, Tim, 18, 25, 61, 80–81,
172–3, 178
Gay Hussar, 54
Gedye, Robin, 139–40, 147
Gibbard, 18, 228
Glenholmes, Evelyn, 82
Globe, 75
Glover, Stephen, 17, 31, 32, 181–2,
204, 265, 283–4, 285
design of *Independent*, 36, 48, 91,
201–2, 216–19, 224, 235,
238–40, 244–5, 259, 263, 280

personality, 8, 21–2, 142, 161,
248, 260, 275–6, 286, 288–9
planning *Independent*, 2–6, 26, 91,
198–9
recruiting, 16, 19–20, 23–5, 33–5,
37, 44–5, 67–8, 77–9, 100, 140,
158–60, 176, 184, 196
Gower, 128
Green, Maurice, xiv, 33, 60, 136
Green, Mike, 108, 148, 186
Gross, John, 11
Gross, Miriam, 18, 19, 44–5, 196
Grove, Trevor, 102, 223, 225–6,
241–2, 244
Guardian, 15, 18, 58, 126, 133

Halcrow, Morrison, 102, 134, 136,
161, 175–6, 224
at *Telegraph*, 14, 40–42, 48, 56, 63,
94, 98, 118–19
dismissed, 189–92, 214, 223, 241,
251
job offers, 58
personality, 182–3, 214
Hampton, Virginia, 208
Hartwell, Lord, 1, 5, 16, 25, 83, 88,
92, 107, 131, 135–6, 168, 187
chairman of *Telegraph*, xiii, xiv,
40, 48, 60, 93, 99, 100–101,
207–8
personality, 62–3, 66, 208
popularity, 17, 39
Harvey, Brian, 30, 131
Hastings, Max, 71, 194
and salaries, 78, 79
as editor of *Telegraph*, 43–4, 48,
52–7, 58, 65, 67, 72, 74, 88, 94,
97–9, 100–102, 107, 108,
111–13, 116, 118–20, 126,
128–9, 132, 135–40, 145–9, 157,
162–3, 173, 176–7, 184,
189–92, 269
in conference, 76
losing power, 90, 91–3, 167
personality, 44, 45–6, 68–9, 83,
84, 95–6, 103, 106, 122
politics, 97, 109–10, 114, 161
relationships with staff, 134,

295